SOPHIE
THE FINAL VERDICT

Senan Molony is an award-winning journalist based in Dublin who works as a political correspondent for the *Irish Independent*. As crime correspondent with *The Star*, he was the first national specialist to arrive on the scene of the Sophie Toscan du Plantier murder in 1996, where he was met by local journalist Ian Bailey, the newspaper's 'stringer', who later became the prime suspect in the case.

Molony was at the forefront of crime journalism in Ireland for many years, from covering the murder of journalist Veronica Guerin to giving evidence against the Gilligan gang in the Special Criminal Court. He has reported variously for the *Evening Herald*, *Irish Daily Mail* and *Irish Independent* on tribunals, trials and murder investigations in Ireland and Britain.

A 'Scoop of the Year' winner at the inaugural National Newspapers of Ireland Awards, he is author of bestselling book *The Phoenix Park Murders* about the infamous political assassinations of 1882. Senan has also written books about the *Titanic*, *Lusitania* and other ships, and devised and presented a number of television documentaries in Ireland, England and the United States.

A student of James Joyce and author of a book about *Ulysses*, he has long earned a living writing about politics at Leinster House.

SOPHIE
THE FINAL VERDICT

SENAN MOLONY

HACHETTE
BOOKS
IRELAND

First published in 2024 by Hachette Books Ireland

Copyright © Senan Molony

The author and publisher have endeavoured to contact all copyright holders. If
any content used in this book has been reproduced without permission, we
encourage owners of copyright not acknowledged to contact us at info@hbgi.ie

Map: GerardCrowley.com

A CIP catalogue record for this title is available from the British Library.

ISBN 978 1 39974 263 4

Typeset in Berling LT Std by Palimpsest Book Production Ltd,
Falkirk, Stirlingshire

Printed and bound in Great Britain by Clays Ltd, Elcograf S.p.A.

Hachette Books Ireland policy is to use papers that are
natural, renewable and recyclable products and made from
wood grown in sustainable forests. The logging and
manufacturing processes are expected to conform to
the environmental regulations of the country of origin.

Hachette Books Ireland
8 Castlecourt Centre
Castleknock
Dublin 15, Ireland

A division of Hachette UK Ltd
Carmelite House, 50 Victoria Embankment,
EC4Y 0DZ

www.hachettebooksireland.ie

CONTENTS

In memory of Sophie
For her circle
And for the people of the Mizen

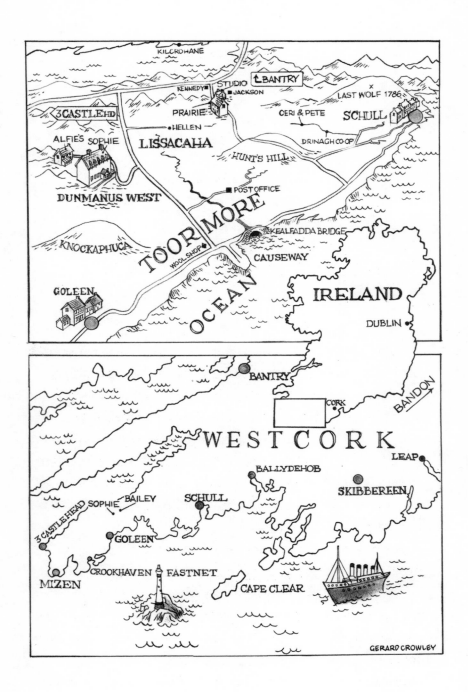

PROLOGUE

Two days before Christmas 1996, a nation was stopped in its tracks. A report on the RTÉ main evening news told of a suspicious death, a foreign woman found in a pool of blood at the bottom of a boreen. The state pathologist was due to arrive at the remote location. There would be a postmortem. Little was known about the victim, the report said, but 'darkness accentuated the isolation of the area'. Then the sucker punch: 'A murder inquiry seems likely from tomorrow.'

There was no specific mention that the woman had been alone, or that the boreen where the body was found was the driveway of her holiday home. The general description of the area was Toormore, six miles from Schull, itself very much an out-of-the-way town in West Cork, just a little knuckle on the finger of the Mizen Peninsula.

The following day was Christmas Eve, so further details

were drowned out by a public preparing for the holiday, concerned though people must have been. Especially about a guest from far away who had evidently, at this special time, found no room at the inn of Irish hospitality. But soon enough, long before the Christmas decorations came down, the gruesome details emerged. About the crushed skull of the petite female. The vast number of pounding blows. The suggestion that she had fled her bed in terror.

The victim was a visiting Frenchwoman, quickly named as Sophie Toscan du Plantier. She had been savagely murdered on the night of Sunday, 22 December leading into Monday the 23rd. I was sent to the place after Christmas, the first national crime correspondent on the scene. Our 'stringer', or local reporter, was a man by the name of Eoin Bailey, hired by *The Star* to guide a photographer and I through the strange terrain.

We were met outside Schull by a suave and self-assured figure, a giant in himself and, it would soon seem to me, in this genre of journalism. Superbly well-informed, like a raddled Raymond Chandler, he rattled off facts and gee-whiz features of the crime, as if airily recounting salient points of the Black Dahlia murder. I could only imagine how close he was to some Deep Throat source. Clearly, he was completely trusted by at least one garda of senior rank.

Eoin Bailey was, of course, Ian Bailey. Abandoning Gloucester after a bitter divorce, the Manchester native had washed ashore in West Cork in 1991, changing his name in a bid to become more Irish than the Irish themselves.

When, seven weeks after Sophie's body was found, Ian Bailey was first arrested for her brutal killing, the scales fell abruptly from my eyes. Until then, I'd been utterly beguiled by his performance, even as my instincts had been perplexed and my rational reconstruction of events confused. I never dreamed I had been working hand-in-glove with a man who would soon admit to being the prime suspect. Now, to realise that the killer insights he'd given me were from the suspected killer *himself*, I felt as if I'd been struck by lightning. Everything that had been eluding me in those first few weeks made perfect sense.

I knew then with blazing clarity that there was no garda source. He had not been furnished with intimate and astounding details of the crime by anyone, outside of himself. I felt sick to the pit of my stomach.

I have been nauseated many times since that moment of awakening, as further facts emerged to validate my suspicions. I managed to secure the first interview with Bailey post-arrest. I was fully awake to him by then, hearing and seeing with new eyes his twisting ways at work.

I stayed in touch with him over the many years that followed – not just as a journalist, but with a growing duty to Sophie and her family, and to something bent utterly out of shape by Bailey: the truth itself.

This story has haunted me and my career for almost thirty years. It's a story I could not fully tell before, in an Ireland whose defamation laws effectively shield many criminals: simple, subversive and sociopathic alike.

The system places the onus of proof on a libel defendant. How can a newspaper give proof where no prosecution took place? In the event, Bailey sued several newspapers – and was badly burned, stuck with a bill that he could not pay but which badly dented the media publishers. He studied law and became a serial litigant, effectively patrolling any intrusion of veracity into his widening web of lies.

Yet there comes a day of reckoning. As this fascinating and endlessly shocking murder case moves inexorably into Irish history, Sophie Toscan du Plantier should finally be vindicated – and honoured – with the truth of what occurred.

That time is now.

CHAPTER 1

A Journalist's Journey Begins

The call to go to West Cork came through from Dave O'Connell, news editor at *The Star*, and bang went the idea of more time off over the holidays, even though Christmas had passed. The whole country was about to be in the grip of the grotesque, unexplained murder of the visiting Parisienne, and, as a crime correspondent, trouble was my business. 'Martin will be around to your house to pick you up,' said Dave. 'Oh, and I'd bring an overnight bag,' he added languidly. This was going from bad to worse. I mentally shredded appointments – mainly drinking, let's be honest. I was thirty-three years old, and now the brother, home from England, would have to amuse himself. The missus was already out at work; I'd ring her later to let her know. Away for a day or two.

Martin Maher was one of the newspaper's photographers. Journalists and snappers go about in news teams, and Martin would be driving and claiming back all that glorious mileage. West Cork, no less. It was a payday for him, I thought, as I mournfully packed my bag – toothbrush, inhaler, pyjamas and stubborn electrical leads that squirmed like snakes – but for me, nothing but four to five hours of bouncing around, the roads being bad, and having to listen to Martin grouse about Jim Dunne on the picture desk, his boss and special-ised subject. He was, in general, terrified of Dunner. Anyway, Happy Christmas.

I took a last slug of coffee heading out the door, my bag slung over my shoulder, notebook in the pocket. 'Do you need a pee?' I asked Martin, who had come from the Dublin suburb of Marino to Castleknock – it was going to be a long drive. He shook his head and I climbed into his red Peugeot 205 van with a heavy heart, as he shoved some equipment aside to make way. I threw my bag in the back and settled down for the long, uncomfortable journey ahead.

Martin jammed the van into gear, then screeched away. Snappers were always rough with their vehicles, I'd noticed, but tender with their cameras. What did I know about this job? he asked. Not much. Dave had rung with the bare facts. I had been trying not to pay too much attention to the 'woman murdered down in Cork' over the past few days, as that was work and I was on a much-needed break. Dave had said to get to Schull, that we'd meet our stringer on top of a steep slope outside the town. 'Some bloke by the name of' – I checked a scrap of paper torn from my pad – 'Eoin Bailey.' Martin grunted, clearly having never heard of him. Some chancer, probably.

I felt a stab of worry. What steep slope exactly? What if

we went to the wrong one? And where was Schull anyway? Martin chucked me the *Road Atlas of Ireland* as he negotiated the twists and turns for heading south. I turned to the page indicated by a numbered box at the back, on the outline of Ireland. 'Okay, get to Cork first, obviously, then it's the N71 you want. Bandon, Clonakilty, Skib . . . Ballydehob. Christ, Martin, it's a very long way. They call it Schull' – I tapped my head – 'but it's more like the arsehole of Ireland. Will there be enough light?'

This question was already playing on his mind. 'Ah, Jesus,' he said. It was December and already past 10 a.m. leaving Dublin, so we wouldn't arrive 'til late afternoon. Martin gave another little surge on the accelerator. He's already fretting over Dunner, I thought.

Along the way, we pulled in to refuel and buy a paper for the latest on the story. Never one to miss a prank, I approached Martin's tank carrying the petrol nozzle, not diesel, causing him to have a conniption. It was all in the game, and it was a great game then, when newspapers sold. Murders sold them, big events; and this was a woman. We would not be going anywhere if some bowsie had kicked his father down the stairs in dreary Drimoleague.

1996 had been a bloody year. Nineteen women were murdered, starting with Marilyn Rynn, who got off a bus in Blanchardstown after a Christmas party and promptly vanished. Her body, hidden in undergrowth, wasn't found until January. There had been a cold snap and it miraculously preserved the DNA sample that nailed her killer. David Lawler, who looked like a 'Jesus freak', was the first offender ever trapped in Ireland by his own genetic identity.

That atrocity was followed by the murder of Joyce Quinn, a Kildare shopkeeper, who stopped to give a lift to a young neighbour, Kenneth O'Reilly, who turned out to be sexually obsessed with her. He killed Joyce in a flurry of stabbings when she stopped to drop him off. Soon, the blood-drenched litany had the Women's Aid agency cataloguing 'femicide' for the first time in Ireland.

In June, the journalist Veronica Guerin, whom I knew personally, was blasted to death at close range as she sat in her car. My new next-door neighbour, Charlie Bowden, was involved in that callous murder, carried out by the Gilligan drugs gang. I soon moved house. So did Charlie, turning state's evidence when caught in an Aladdin's cave of imported drugs. He entered Ireland's first witness-protection programme. I twice gave evidence as to what I knew in the Special Criminal Court. Ironically enough, the man who sold Bowden the house and my former next-door neighbour, Garda Paul Moran, was now in the Emergency Response Unit. He stood in front of Bowden in the dock, wearing a Kevlar vest, his hand ready by the butt of a Glock pistol. Three men from the one semi-detached building: the not-quite-defendant turned tell-all, his armed defender, and a reporter-cum-witness: Muggins.

The Star did murders well. A relatively recent creation, the paper was eating heartily into the circulation of British tabloids in Ireland. It forced the creation of Irish editions for some of those titles, with Dublin newsrooms. *The Star* had won a niche by responding early to killings, collating facts and photos, and the others were now catching up. *The Sun* and *Daily Mirror* had joined the fray, most notably with the body-in-the-boot murder. The details were truly ghastly. A sickening smell forced the opening of an abandoned car's boot at Athlone railway station. Revealed were the remains of missing nurse Philomena Gillane. Suspicion fell on the husband, Pat Gillane, who appeared broken-hearted at the funeral, with red eyes, accepting the condolences of friends and neighbours. I subsequently sat down in his kitchen for a one-on-one with Pat, not the first time I had interviewed a murderer with both of us knowing he was the killer. Pat knew it for sure and I relied on my journalistic sixth sense. As the questions became more pointed, he started worrying a steak knife on the table. 'What's all this, Pat? Are you going to murder someone else?' He was subsequently jailed for life and lost an appeal. All in all, I thought I was by now pretty experienced; I had seen my first byline in a national news-paper, *The Irish Press*, back in 1983. I knew my onions.

'At last,' said Martin, 'this is Schull now', rousing me from some late-afternoon reverie.

I shifted in my seat, bones aching after long confinement. It looked a pretty enough place and we had made good time; there was still plenty of light. All we had to do was find this steep slope on the other side of town. Our prom-ised stringer ought to be there already, the paper having hired him for the day. Soon we were indeed ascending, and as we did so, a Shakespearean figure stood gaunt against the sky. I remember turning to my colleague, grimly hunched at the wheel, and gesturing ahead. 'I know West Cork is bohemian, Martin, but *this* is ridiculous.'

We slowed at the summit and it fell to me to call from an open window: 'Eoin Bailey?'

The single-word reply, delivered in a crisp English accent so at odds with his name, was itself Shakespearean. 'He,' the man answered grandly.

He crouched down to look in at us – two little elves of industry – and we immediately had a problem: Bailey was just too big. Martin's marvellous van had only two seats. There was nothing for it but to open the Peugeot's hatch-back and for me to crawl onto the ribbed steel inside, my discomfort about to get a whole lot worse. Our guest came first. The passenger seat was rattled back and lank-haired Eoin managed to somehow inveigle himself into the available space, a curl of his black Crombie coat covering the gearstick, which Martin brushed away.

'So, you can take us from here?' asked Martin of his guest, as I ferreted through my bag for my notebook.

Bailey indicated assent, flicking a finger in an onward direction, and we were off again.

'Right then – hello, Eoin, nice to meet you and all that,' I said from my ridiculous position, lying behind him, almost flat on my back. 'Can you please tell me everything you know about this murder, starting with the victim?'

CHAPTER 2

Movement towards Murder

In weak winter sun, short days before, Sophie Toscan du Plantier had flown into Ireland on Aer Lingus flight EI-0512 from Charles de Gaulle airport. Another passenger on the flight, Mary O'Flaherty, recalled the frustration of a delay on the tarmac in Paris. She was in 4E, the middle seat, with a woman seated to her right, at window seat 4F, who 'seemed to be travelling on her own'. There was no conversation, not even about the need to get airborne. While stopped at Dublin for refuelling, most of the passengers onward-bound for Cork stood up to stretch, but the 'quiet and reserved' lady in 4F remained seated.

Shane Minogue, an engineer from Clonakilty, was on that flight. The woman he had noticed in the departure lounge in Paris was now also in the baggage hall in Cork when they arrived at their final destination. Touchdown was at 2.25 p.m. Shane too noted that the woman was travelling alone.

Verna Hyde, car-rental agent with Avis, looked up at her next customer. 'The woman gave me her gold credit card. The name was Sophie Bouniol.' A full credit voucher was produced, obtained through a travel agent, carrying the alternative name of Toscan du Plantier. 'As far as I can recall, I asked for her driving licence and wrote particulars on the rental agreement. The same with her telephone number in France,' said Verna. 'I completed the rest of it and she signed.' The car was new, a silver Ford Fiesta, registration 96 C 14459, and mileage 12,733. It was due to be returned in less than a week, on St Stephen's Day at 9.15 a.m.

Verna Hyde recalled a small woman who was alone and spoke good English, with a French accent. Of slim build, she had 'browny, auburn hair' and wore a brown coat with a woolly, furry effect. The woman 'seemed a bit distracted and was not taking any notice of what I was doing. She was pleasant at the same time'. Verna estimated her as 'early forties'. It was a fair guess: Sophie was thirty-nine. 'When I asked for a contact number, she gave it and said Dunmanus. She knew her way around. When I asked if she knew where the car park was, she said yes. She was very familiar with Cork airport and her surroundings. I didn't take any notice of what baggage she had, although I know she had a trolley.'

In mid-afternoon, Sophie drove her rental Fiesta into the little petrol station at Camier's shop in Ballydehob. A bustling town on the main road linking Cork city and Schull and all points beyond, it was a good place to stop. On the forecourt were bags of kindling, coal and briquettes – useful to start a fire at her holiday home, still twenty kilometres away. One of the attendants put the items in her car and directed her inside to pay.

Kitty Kingston, manageress, recalled the unaccompanied woman as 'thin, small, blonde', with shoulder-length hair, and remembered she drove a silver Ford Fiesta. Nothing further was bought, but the purchases in pursuit of a homely open-hearth put the customer over the qualifying amount for the seasonal Grand Raffle.

As she handed back the lady's change, Kitty said, 'I asked her name – to put in a book for a turkey draw for Christmas.' The visitor looked pleased, then frowned. 'She asked me what day the turkey draw would be taking place.' Full of chat, closing the till, Kitty cheerily supplied the date – and heard, after a pause, a drowsily accented answer.

'Whatever day I told her the draw was on, she said she thought she would not be around.' So, the woman did not sign the entry sheet, already scrawled on by others. 'I had a short conversation. She spoke English. She told me it was a stick-shift car. She appeared to have trouble pulling up, and I'd been looking at the car jerking. She said she was going west for Christmas, and it occurred to me that it was unusual to be on your own.'

Sophie pleasantly said goodbye and left. A glitter outside the shop window flashed, stopped, shone again, as the silver car lurched forward a little, then drove smoothly away. Kitty Kingston would remember her gentle face in days to come. In the meantime, the plump turkey was destined to be won by someone else.

*

Eventually the silver car scrunched up the driveway to an imposing two-storey cottage, though more resembling a farmhouse, at Dunmanus West, Toormore, West Cork. Sophie hopped in and out of the Fiesta, in more stop-start manoeuvres, to first open the six-bar entrance gate some seventy metres from the house and then to close it behind her vehicle. It was dark as she did so. Above her loomed the building, mantled by hills, facing out to sea. The secluded setting, yet stunning views, had persuaded her to purchase.

The house was warm and cosy in the modest and narrow interior that belied its imposing frontage. There was no need to set a fire; it already glowed in the grate. Sophie's house-keeper, Josie Hellen, had seen to everything, dotting windowsills with sprigs of holly for a seasonal touch. She'd remembered to check the bath, which she found spick and span. This was reassuring, because in April a year or two before, Sophie had complained to Josie that the bath was dirty when she arrived, much to Josie's chagrin. 'Excuse me,' she'd insisted, 'I cleaned the bath.' Josie had run upstairs and 'straightaway saw that it had been used. I had cleaned it on the Thursday, and this was Friday, so it was used on Thursday night.' The house had then been checked to find where the bath bandit had entered – and an open window was discovered at the back porch. Locks were quickly acquired and fixed, to stop it from ever happening again. Who could have possibly done it, and why? They suspected the next-door neighbour, Alfie Lyons, aged sixty-six, who had no running water at the time and with whom Sophie had minor differences. He was being prosecuted over cannabis possession and supply. Sophie wanted Josie to keep any newspaper story that might appear about him. Alfie would eventually be fined IR£170 by the District Court.

On this Friday, however, with no bath issues, Sophie settled into her restful retreat just after 4.30 p.m. Next, she made a telephone call to Josie Hellen, thanking the house-keeper for all her preparations. Sophie had already told Josie prior to arrival that she would be alone on this trip, hoping to 'rest and organise her work'. The conversation, in which Josie welcomed Sophie back again, was short and mutually respectful. Sophie rang off. A girlfriend then rang from Paris to check that she had arrived safely. Agnès Thomas was a friend from Unifrance, the French cinema monolith, where Sophie had worked. Yes, the trip had been fine, and she was happy to be back in Ireland, Sophie said. She mentioned she was going to go to sleep in the little bedroom, over the kitchen, because it was warmest. It was then 11.15 p.m. 'I was her best friend, we were very close,' said Agnès, who knew the property from a previous visit. 'We talked to each other all the time, because she was preoccupied with her husband, her family life, the baby that she wanted to have.'

*

Four kilometres east of Sophie's house was the home of another Ford Fiesta, this one white and nine years older than Sophie's rental. It belonged to a Welsh artist named Jules Thomas, who lived at a homestead known as The Prairie, in the nearby townland of Lissacaha. The Irish name *Lios an Chatha* translates as the 'ring-fort of the battle'. At the time of the potato famine in the mid-nineteenth century, a landlord named Somerville planted a wood that became known as 'The Prairie', a jocular indication of the local propensity to call black white, and vice versa.

Living there, too, was Jules' man-about-the-house, an Englishman named Ian Bailey, his identity restyled as *Eoin* Bailey to suit insertion into the Irish countryside. Dark and very tall, he'd been a fixture for about five years; or, as he put it that December, 'sixty-four moons'. A dabbling poet and committed drinker, in time he would become known simply as 'Bailey', his moniker for decades to follow. Technically, Bailey didn't reside at The Prairie. He rented a building known as the studio from Beryl Thomas, Jules' mother, two hundred metres away on the same road. This habitation was cold, damp and in a state of disrepair, which meant that Bailey spent most of his time in the warm and comfortable house nearby. Also living at The Prairie were Jules' three daughters, none of whom belonged to Bailey biologically. Saffron, known as Saffy, was twenty-two, her sister Virginia, called Ginny, was nineteen and their half-sister, Fenella, was fourteen. They did not like Ian Bailey, a disruptive force who had invaded their home and lives.

On the Friday when Sophie was travelling to her holiday home, Bailey professed to be at home all day, gardening and writing. That is, until around 10 p.m. that night, when the white 1987 Fiesta containing Jules and Bailey came rolling down the hill on the R591 from Lissacaha. When they were travelling together, Jules mostly drove – which was not to say that thirty-nine-year-old Bailey did not comment adversely on her abilities, as other occasional passengers could testify. The car turned left, onto the R592 that led into Schull and what would become a weekend of pre-Christmas celebrations. The couple went to The Courtyard bar, leaving the premises after midnight to head for the hills, this time with Ian Bailey in the driving seat. The Welshwoman and the Englishman had a strange co-dependency, an artist and opportunist flung together by fate. To the outside eye it was just another workable West Cork hook-up.

Meanwhile, an innocent traveller had finally settled gratefully into her Irish retreat as the chaotic couple rattled off home.

CHAPTER 3

Sophie in Her Solitude

On Saturday morning, 21 December, Sophie awoke in the warmer back bedroom of her holiday home. Her normal sleeping place was a 'pedestal bed' at the front of the house, facing the coast. She had often marvelled to others about the searing flash of the Fastnet lighthouse, far out to sea, which beamed into her bedroom at night. She found it reassuring, a security light of Victorian grandeur, with its warning optic perched fifty metres above the rock, its slender pillar pounded mercilessly by the waves. Always without effect.

The cottage was in a mountain cleft, a hidden cocoon of only three houses. Behind her own was that of Alfie Lyons and his partner Shirley Foster, and a good deal farther away was the home of the Richardsons, an English couple who were almost always absent. The only others in the immediate vicinity were croup-swishing cattle and a string of horses, with some sheep dotted about. This was why she always kept the six-bar gate at the end of the drive closed, to stop them from entering. There was another gate, behind the house, leading into the lane to Alfie and Shirley's place, which required a knack to open, a diagonal lift. On the land between them stood a storehouse that Sophie initially thought she had acquired when buying the house – only to later discover that wasn't the case.

Her cottage had been paid for by her husband, the French movie mogul Daniel Toscan du Plantier. He had visited Dunmanus West only once, years before, content to leave it as a bolthole for his wife. Meanwhile, the outhouse ownership issue had been resolved in Alfie Lyons's favour, and although it rankled a little, he was not an unreasonable man. In any case, they had been perfectly pleasant in greeting each other since, as is necessary when sharing a driveway. Sophie would have seen lights on in the Lyons house the evening before, as she arrived in dropping darkness to her own.

Finbarr Hellen, housekeeper Josie's husband, had ninety acres of what he described as 'mountain and roughage' close at hand. With a farmer's precision, he could say that 'Alfred' Lyons had five or six acres, Sophie ten and the Richardsons three. There were dry stone walls, thick hedges of briar, and fences strung with barbed wire to delineate the complicated borders of all these empires and enclaves, with Finbarr likely the only one who understood it all. He knew that Sophie's house had been originally owned by a Michael McCarthy, who willed it to Patrick McCarthy of Skibbereen, who sold it to Dan Ryan, who transferred it to a teacher from Limerick, Donal O'Connor, who had then sold it through an estate agent to the French couple in 1992 – though only Sophie's name now appeared on the deeds. Finbarr continued to use some of her pasture for grazing, 'and she did not object'. Sophie had wanted to know however if he was ever going to station a bull nearby, 'as she wanted to walk the land owned by herself and that's all she was interested in', keeping safe, he said.

It was Finbarr who put in the six-bar gates at Sophie's request, at both the bottom of the drive and as a link to the Lyons' lane. 'Alfie used to have a few goats around, and the goats ate Sophie's shrubs,' he said. Next Alfie started wiring off the boundary between his land and Finbarr's. There had been words because the latter 'told him not to put the barbed wire on top as it would destroy my horses'. They did not talk for a couple of months. Next Alfie was 'careless' with the gate at the bottom and a sign had to be put up: 'Please close gate.'

Alfie and Sophie had little to do with each other, Finbarr thought. At noon that Saturday, Finbarr was out with his son John, aged fifteen, tending cattle. He spotted a silver car parked outside Sophie's place. 'I had a notion to go to the house and talk to her, but I didn't,' he regretted.

It was afternoon of the 21st by the time the silver Fiesta purred into life, followed by choreography with the gate. Sophie's car turned left up the track to the road, which had a median of tufted grass. She turned right and met the winter sun and welcome sight of the sea. It was a matter of fifteen minutes before the last crest was mounted and she slid down into Schull. Within moments, she had parked and was entering The Courtyard bar on Main Street, intent on a late lunch. Owner Denis Quinlan spotted her sitting at the fireside, possibly the last tourist of 1996. 'She stood out because of her dress sense.' She was on her own and might have been having coffee. He was unsure because it was busy. The barman, Ernie Cantillon, had a better picture: he remembered serving the stylish French lady an open crab sandwich.

After lunch, about 2.30 p.m., Sophie shopped at Brosnan's Spar supermarket, yards from The Courtyard, a steel basket over her arm as she passed through the aisles. A detailed receipt emerged later. She bought matches, the *Irish Independent*, Persil detergent, a cookery magazine, some parsley, a tray of yoghurts, bottles of Ballygowan spring water, a large bag of penne, lardons of bacon, a single courgette, chicory, onions, mushrooms, leek and potato soup, carrots, mixed vegetables, salami slices, cooked turkey, a bottle of Monini premium extra virgin olive oil, and a tube of Fox's Classic biscuits. The bill came to IR£22.18, all smilingly bleeped through by Marguerite O'Leary on the checkout at eleven minutes to three. Marguerite recalled the lady was wearing a tan coat. She paid with a gold credit card and the pair jointly bundled the goods into Spar plastic bags.

Fifth-year student Oliver Brooke was also working in Brosnan's that day. He was asked by Sophie whether they stocked the newspaper *Le Monde*. He checked, then said it would have to be ordered from Cork, but would be available the next weekday morning. 'She said she would not be in again until Monday afternoon. I informed her we would keep the copy. I asked her name, and she said Sophie. I asked how it was spelled, and she told me. She did not leave her surname or address; it wasn't necessary. I asked her if she wanted it for the rest of the week. She said only Monday, but would inform us if she wanted more. She had good English, but spoke with a French accent.' Oliver then saw the lady leave alone and head towards the bank.

Local resident Ceri Williams, originally from Wales, was also shopping in Schull that day. Distracted by children, Ceri 'physically bumped' into the woman as Sophie came out of Brosnan's supermarket. 'I said "sorry" and she said "*pardon*", and that was it. We walked on. I noted she was a very chic dresser and carried herself well.' The lady was wearing a pale scarf, similar in colour to her hair. She was slim, not particularly tall, wearing trousers and a dark knitwear jacket.

'She stood out – and as I worked previously in France, I took her to be French. She walked very confidently and appeared attractive in general, and these things caught my eye.' She didn't mention any coat.

Ceri was sure that Sophie was also spotted by Ian Bailey – whom Ceri saw on the opposite side of the road while she was still outside Brosnan's. She recalled that he began walking in the same direction as Sophie.

Next Sophie stowed her shopping in the rented Fiesta, then made a bank withdrawal from an ATM in the sum of IR£200, the transaction traced to exactly 3.25 p.m.

At 4.15 p.m. that day, Sally Bolger went to feed her two ponies near Sophie's house. She and her husband had just gone urban from a previous address in Dunmanus East, and Alfie Lyons had allowed their ponies to graze temporarily in one of his fields. Sally noticed a silver Ford Fiesta at the house in front of Alfie's. It was becoming dusk, but the lights were not yet on in the house.

It appears that Sophie put away her shopping, the items distributed to their usual places. But then she got back into the hire car, drove down to the main road to a spot called Kealfadda, and turned right. There was a sighting of her by a fruit and veg trader named Jimmy Camier, who had an open-air trade in Goleen, a colourful little village five kilometres from the Kealfadda turn. No one knows why she went there – perhaps she simply fancied some idle sightseeing before the fading of the light. Jimmy had been 'thinking of closing up' when he had a last visitor, a polite foreign lady, who purchased some vegetables. Little was said, with some pointing, and then the pair smiled goodbye. Jimmy remembered her radiant face, the retreat to a small silver car.

*

Once again that Saturday evening, the pre-Christmas revellers in Schull included Jules Thomas and Ian Bailey. It was after 7 p.m. when they arrived at The Courtyard bar, where they had been the night before, and where Sophie had eaten a crab sandwich hours earlier. As the drinking began, Jules' daughter Ginny was separately meeting friends elsewhere in town. At some stage after 11.30 p.m., Ginny and Jules made their way home together, but without Bailey. In Jules' words, 'My daughter Ginny Thomas and myself did not want a late night, so we left him there and drove home to Lissacaha.'

Mark Murphy, a Schull local, went to The Courtyard at 11 p.m. At that stage, Jules Thomas was still there. 'At closing time I asked if anyone wanted to come back to my

23

house for a drink,' he said. The only acceptances were from Ian Bailey and fisherman Robert Shelly. 'We brought our own drink,' said Mark, who purchased four cans of Heineken. 'I think Ian Bailey bought cans as well. He also had a naggin of whiskey. We got to my house at about 12.30 a.m.' An hour later, Mark went to bed and left Bailey and Shelly talking to his mother, Patricia. She subsequently told Mark that, at 2 a.m., Bailey left to walk or hitch the almost seven kilometres home, 'but came back after a short while and asked to stay the night'. He was allowed to sleep on a couch downstairs.

Patricia's partner, Tony Doran, had gone to bed at midnight and was annoyed to be 'wakened by noise down-stairs, people talking', but did not go down to remonstrate. 'I went to sleep eventually.' Patricia came to their bed as late as 6 a.m., he said. Tony rose late the following morning and was downstairs by 11.30 a.m. 'It was then I saw Ian Bailey. He was coming out of the front room. I don't particu-larly like the guy and I went into the kitchen to make myself breakfast, and he followed me and stood there watching. I said to him, "If you want to make yourself a cup of tea, go ahead." He started to make a cup, and while doing so started talking, saying he should be in Bantry plucking turkeys for twelve midday. It was now already near that time. I think the reason he said it was because he thought I would offer to drive him. He mentioned it a few times. The last time, I said to him, "You are going to be very late, aren't you?"' An irritated Doran then left and drove away on his own. Later that Sunday, he said to Patricia, 'Of all the people to bring into the house, it had to be

Bailey.' He explained: 'I have seen Bailey in pubs, shouting and screaming his poetry down the back of your neck, and he disrupts pubs. I know about his drink problem and a few people close to Jules told me about her being assaulted – and getting an eye injury. The same people told me that it had happened to her before.'

Mark Murphy, who had organised the impromptu after-party, came to Bailey's rescue with a lift: 'On the following morning, midday to 1 p.m., I got up. I drove Ian Bailey back to The Prairie. It could have been 2 to 2.30 p.m. on Sunday, 22 December when I dropped Ian Bailey off at his house.'

The precision with times was helpful, because Bailey's movements in the hours thereafter would become subject to intense scrutiny in the dark days to come.

CHAPTER 4

Her Last Day Alive

Strawberry-blonde Sophie had always possessed a fiery streak. A flouncing child with defiant eyes, she never quite lost her strongly self-willed nature in adulthood, though she mixed it with selflessness.

'Sophie was open to everyone, very close to poor people, and kindness itself,' said Eric Gentil, her occasional chauffeur. 'She once brought a homeless young man into her apartment so that he could have a meal – without considering possible consequences. She did not perceive the danger that could present itself. She believed the world around her was of the same nature as herself – wise, understanding and natural.'

Sophie Andrée Jacqueline was born on 28 July 1957 in baby-booming Paris, a city reasserting itself after the Second World War. Her father, Georges, was a genial dentist and a man of infinite patience. Marguerite, her mother, was more forthright – and would become a tough deputy mayor of the second arrondissement, a district of the Right Bank. The smallest division of the capital, it nonetheless boasted the Grand Rex, largest cinema in Paris, where Sophie would be treated to a movie after making her First Holy Communion at nearby Notre Dame cathedral, with its flying buttresses and grinning gargoyles. The growing child bossed around her brother Bertrand, two years her junior, and got a name for wolfing Roquefort cheese. 'She was very lively,' remembers her uncle, Jean Pierre. 'But a bad singer. If she opened her mouth to sing, it was a catastrophe.'

The siblings grew up in the urban bustle of rue Tiquetonne, close to Châtelet-Les Halles railway station and the former fruit and vegetable market, and also near the Louvre, a cultural oasis by the Jardin des Tuileries. School was in the city, and Sophie was like the children's book character Madeline, fiercely brave amid the adult throng before joining a crocodile of pupils close to the main gates.

Every August, when Paris emptied, the family retreated to the cool south-central highlands of the Lozère, home of Georges Bouniol's parents, and where entrancing and outspoken Marguerite Gazeau was born. In Lozère, Sophie felt oxygenated, freed from the claustrophobic city. This untamed place, and the wild creatures that inhabited it, spoke to her soul. She painted rocks, hills and sky, the stone farmhouses and spilling streams, wondering at the openness of the idyll that is the least populated department in France. She hardly thought there could be another place like it – until the dentist and civil servant thought their tomboy could do with improving her English, packing her off for the summer at age fourteen to Ireland. Her mother was to fall pregnant with a third child, Stéphane, while the eldest was away.

Sophie found herself staying with the madcap McKiernan family of eight children in Sutton, north of Dublin. They tried to spoil their paying guest with special meals, until she insisted on mucking in with everyone else, downing mince and mash, and fish fingers with foreign red ketchup. The McKiernans had a caravan and set off for the south – where Sophie's eyes were opened to the beauty of the countryside, the glossy cows and the surging sea. She jumped at the chance to come back the next year, this time with Bertrand, and there were intermittent letters for years afterwards. Ireland had achieved mythic status, an ever-present ideal as she entered womanhood.

Sophie did her baccalaureate, then entered Paris 1, its designation after the break-up of the Sorbonne following the 1968 student riots. The fever of that year had passed and college days were relaxed, the lecture theatres just a twenty-minute walk from her home. She threw herself into societies, such as art appreciation – although she was nominally studying law. There was no legal vocation; she and her parents merely thought it a good foundation for an undecided entrant to the wider world. Then she suddenly clapped eyes on another student, the dark and brooding Pierre Jean Baudey.

Headstrong Sophie was suddenly head over heels, and the eyebrow-raising impetuousness led straight to the altar. *C'est la vie*: Georges and Marguerite could only smile through as the newly expecting Sophie married in Orléans at the age of twenty-two. Their first grandchild, Pierre-Louis,

was a wonderful balm to any anxiety they had, arriving in
March 1981.

Then Sophie was done with marriage, just as she was done
with law. She moved into a small apartment with her
one-year-old son, taking small jobs – one she loved at a book-
shop – while the tot was in crèche or with his grandmother.

Life was fraught for a time before the newly divorced
young woman landed a plum PR job with Unifrance. It was
work she adored, even if her strong personality led to fric-
tion with her line manager. All would be smoothed out by
an executive named Daniel Toscan du Plantier, the man
who would become her second husband. It was a slow-
burning relationship. He frequently invited her out, and she
sometimes went. She knew he was married; but he insisted
he was getting divorced.

At the Cannes Film Festival, Daniel invited her to a lavish
dinner hosted at a chateau by *Le Monde*. A card at her place
setting read 'Toscan du Plantier, escort' and she angrily tore
it up, looking daggers at her sheepish companion. A politi-
cian then mistook her for actress Isabelle Huppert – one
of Daniel's former lovers – and finally she had had it, pushing
back her chair and abruptly exiting. Daniel found her
outdoors, and she read him the riot act.

'An assertive character, she argued her point of view with
pugnacity but also diplomacy,' said Gentil, who became their
driver following their wedding in 1991 conducted by
Marguerite, mother of the bride. 'He and Sophie seemed very
in love with each other. They called each other on the phone
all the time in the car. Their warmth and loving intonation
did not indicate any discord. He often gave her flowers. Daniel

was a ladies' man. But Sophie was different. Elegant, with little make-up, she didn't try to please or attract attention.'

She had always been assertively independent, and yet incongruously trusting. A friend, Fatima Zandouche, revealed that Sophie at one point allowed a Paris tramp to sleep at night in her car, parked near her apartment on the rue Rambuteau. Something of the same reckless impulse must have sent her to Ireland at the last minute, in the dying days of December 1996.

Her final words to her mother were not 'Au revoir'. For some reason, Sophie concluded their call with 'Adieu, Maman'.

*

On the morning of Sunday, 22 December, Sophie had some reading to do, since she and her husband had talked of remaking some classic French cinema shorts from earlier in the century. In the afternoon, with work out of the way, she decided on a drive to Three Castles Head at the upper end of the peninsula. A triad of turrets stood within one perimeter, that of ruined Dunlough, the fort of the lake. A thirteenth-century version of an infinity pool was found here, a small freshwater lough threatening at any moment to tumble into the briny Atlantic. The strange conjunction was said to give rise to misty effects, and there were tales of a mythical Lady of the Lake, a water-walking banshee of dire portent who was said to roam the ripples.

Sophie, wearing trusty boots, parked her car and tramped the windswept walk about the foam-flecked lake, the old stones of the tumbled stronghold telling of a fallen time.

Next, Sophie visited a French couple, Tomi and Yvonne Ungerer, who lived in the closest house to Three Castles Head. Tomi was a writer and illustrator from Alsace who had written over 120 books and whose motto was 'expect the unexpected'. Yvonne, who was a former international model, said of Sophie: 'She probably would have known of Tomi from his reputation as a writer in France. She would come here for walks when on holiday.' It turned out they had a mutual friend, a French minister of culture, while Tomi knew of Sophie's husband and his standing in their homeland, where Daniel, head of Unifrance, was a personal friend of President Jacques Chirac.

Yvonne had left to pick up her sons, Pascal and Lukas, who were away at college but coming home for Christmas. It had to be about 1 p.m. when she went, 'because of the bus' with its scheduled stop, she said. 'As I was preparing to leave I saw a silver car, smallish. I am not good with cars.' It was likely Sophie's Fiesta, left in the car park while she wandered. 'It was facing west towards the sea,' unoccupied. 'When we got home,' she said, 'Sophie was here with Tomi. This would have been about 2.30 p.m. He has told me since that she was here for about half an hour . . . in front of the fire, drinking wine. Tomi was very enthused about her presence. It was apparent to me that they had been engaged in a deep, interesting conversation. Tomi does not like trivia or gaps. He likes intelligent conversation.

'I came into the kitchen to prepare a fry for the boys. Sophie came in also, to watch me prepare. She was curious, particularly about the cooking. There was general coming and going. We were speaking in French. I cannot ever recall

31

speaking English to her. She spoke about her parents near Toulouse, her son at school in France, the theatre, and what was going on in Paris. She did not mention her husband, or anything about Ireland. She said she had no special plans for Christmas, but was unsure about her return date to France.

'She spoke about a feeling of foreboding she got from being up at the castles. We spoke of old Irish Celtic stories about the area up there – that is, the Lady of the Lake. We then retired again to the sitting room. We were both, Tomi and I, enthused about her visit . . . I felt it was the beginning of a very good friendship.' Sophie left at 4 p.m. 'It wasn't dark, but getting dark. We exchanged addresses.'

Yvonne asked Sophie what she was doing for the next few days, meaning Christmas. She replied, 'Nothing special.' Yvonne said, 'Don't be alone: give us a call or we'll give you a call.'

Tomi recalled how Sophie had two glasses of red wine as they discussed how Ireland was alive with literature. On the question of her foreboding, he said, 'She may have sounded a bit anxious, but it is difficult to put my finger on it.' She indicated the reason she was in Ireland was to be alone, which was strange, but he could understand.

Tomi found her well-read and vivacious. She refused a third glass of wine, but accepted the gift of half-a-dozen eggs 'for her supper'. Sophie was wearing expensive-looking, black-leather trousers, brown suede hiking boots, a white or cream ribbed polo neck sweater, a beige wool blazer and a navy jacket. The illustrator also noticed a navy woollen cap and wine-coloured gloves. Taking her leave, with smiles all round, Sophie drove away.

The Frenchwoman piloted the Fiesta on a twenty-minute drive to Crookhaven, nine kilometres farther east on the Mizen Peninsula. The village was something of a geographical fetlock on this leg of land, with a large expanse of water to be skirted on the way in and out. But there was all the time in the world as Sophie's rental glided past Chimney Cove and Galley Cove, into Crookhaven with its pier and pubs, lobster pots and bobbing boats.

At O'Sullivan's bar, the inner door opened and admitted Sophie. She would regularly come to this pub when in Ireland because the landlord, Billy O'Sullivan, his wife, Angela, and their twenty-nine-year-old son, Dermot, all spoke fluent French. Sophie was welcomed with Christmas greetings. Dermot served her a pot of tea with slices of lemon. His father took the money for the minor transaction, while Sophie sat by the fire for a while. Another customer, Gerard Kelly, who was with his wife, Aileen, noticed a spitting log suddenly tumble from the grate. He was amazed at Sophie's instant reaction. 'She picked up the burning timber' with deft fingers, throwing it back in, 'and may have burnt her right hand'.

Sophie had a second cup of tea. She was still there at 4.45 p.m., noticed barman Dermot. At some point soon thereafter, the little Fiesta ferried Sophie home in darkness, past coastguard cottages on the other side of the inlet, the winking beacon of the low Crookhaven light, through Shanavalley and Spanish Cove, into Goleen, the last remaining settlement. Beyond lay Knockaphuca, the hill of the Pooka, a mischievous spirit. Then a turn to the left at Kealfadda bridge and a wending way home. It was only twenty minutes from Crookhaven.

Back home in Dunmanus West, Sophie prepared an evening meal. Then, she made a call to the Paris apartment of best friend Agnès Thomas, to wish her a happy fortieth birthday. A message was recorded at 6.32 p.m. French time, 5.32 p.m. Irish, meaning Sophie had driven straight home from Crookhaven. She was recorded asking Agnès, who had been out celebrating, to call her back, but it was after midnight when her friend got the message, and too late to do so.

On the Sunday evening, Goleen postman Tommy Hodnett rumbled his green van into the vicinity, a special Christmas service. 'I called at 6 p.m. with mail for Alfie Lyons and put it in the postbox near the gate. I noticed lights in Sophie's house. There was light in an upstairs room and also lights on downstairs.' He assumed it must be Josie Hellen in the house, to whom he often dropped Sophie's post, mainly bills. By 7.30 p.m., Sophie was making a call to Josie – aimed at fixing up for coal bought and other requisites, including the housekeeper's IR£4 an hour for cleaning.

But Josie was out, her daughter Catherine said. So was handyman Pat Hegarty, phoned next – whom Sophie hoped would do some work on her fireplace. It was his daughter Joanne, at 7.50 p.m., who took the holidaymaker's message in his absence. Sophie had taken off her boots – her house-keeper recalled that she generally placed them on the stairs but never took them up. Next, Josie called Sophie back, having arrived home from socialising. It was 9.45 p.m. The two women regretted missing each other – Josie said she had a headache – but arranged to call over to Sophie around noon on Monday. Sophie apologised that she had not called over to Josie, and asked her to bring handyman Pat with her, if possible, to look at the fireplace the next day. Sophie was 'in great form', according to Josie, and the call ended after fifteen minutes.

*

Earlier that same Sunday, Jules Thomas met Mark Murphy's van as she drove in towards Schull, at around 2.15 p.m. She saw Bailey in the front passenger seat and 'presumed Mark was bringing him home to my place'. Bailey had been briefly in Brosnan's Spar to get the Sunday paper.

When Jules returned, the pair had salmon for supper. He 'began to relax' before they headed yet again for town at about nine o'clock. Jules drove into the car park of the Spar supermarket, since Main Street had no available spaces. 'We went into The Galley pub and had a few drinks,' she said. 'I was in the back where musicians were playing and Ian was coming and going to the front bar. I can't say what drink Ian had. I had three small bottles of wine.'

However, shop assistant Mairead Murphy contradicted this account. She said she saw Ian Bailey sitting alone in the corner of O'Regan's, a different pub, 'tapping away' on a bodhrán. 'He was on his own. It was about 9.30 p.m. He made a phone call, I presume to Jules. He had a few pints taken. He was cheery. He left O'Regan's.' Mairead and two other girls later went to The Galley, and saw Bailey there, this time with Jules about. 'We sat down. I saw Ian talking to Dave, owner of The Galley. Jules was sitting in a corner of the front bar. There was a group of lads playing traditional Irish music in the back.'

Venita, wife of Dave and co-owner of The Galley,

corroborated this story. She first saw Jules drinking on her own. Some time later, Ian Bailey 'arrived in the side door'.

Venita's husband, the host, remembered them at a table. 'I do not know what time they came, but they were the last couple to leave.' The last drinks order rung into the till comprised a wine, long-neck bottle and a measure of spirits. 'It was a busy night, with about sixty customers in and out.' Almost all had left by 12.30 a.m. During the music session, Ian Bailey played the bodhrán and recited his poetry. 'Generally, Bailey would attend these sessions, suss out the band and, if he thought they were favourable, get the bodhrán . . . I remember giving him a towel to put around the stick to muffle the sound. He was the last of the customers to leave, with Jules.'

Galley barman John McGowan remembered that Bailey 'played the bodhrán and sang while we were cleaning up, between midnight and 1 a.m.' He was in good spirits but not drunk, he said. This clashes with the account of Bernadette Kelly, who sat beside the bodhrán man with his 'posh English accent' yet scruffy look, 'stale drink marks around his mouth'. She didn't know Bailey, who 'appeared to have a lot of drink taken'. He and Jules left with a pint bottle of Guinness, maybe two.

'Bailey was after five to six pints of Guinness and maybe one or two shorts,' McGowan said. 'Jules had three to four vodkas.' If he clashed with Jules's own account of what she was drinking, the barman independently confirmed the final order: 'The last time I served him, I gave him a drop of whiskey, a pint bottle of Guinness and a small bottle of wine. He drank the whiskey, a Powers, in one go.' When paying for the drink, Bailey counted out coins. 'He spent some time at it', and was twenty pence short, but gratefully availed of festive forgiveness.

Next, stated Jules, 'Ian went and brought the car from the car park to the front of The Galley, and I jumped in.' She waited in the alley alongside the bar because of a 'freezing east wind'. The big man was set to drive, with bodhrán and stick chucked onto the back seat. It was distinctly cold, already below zero.

Unknown to Bailey, a garda car had spotted him. In it was Sergeant Gerard Prendeville. He was aware that Bailey had been banned from driving, but he didn't know if the ban had yet run out. 'I remember observing Ian Bailey sitting in the white Ford Fiesta he and Jules Thomas use,' the policeman said. 'He was alone in the car, seated in the driver's seat and parked on my left, between the supermarket and Brosnan's car park. There was nobody on the street and it was very quiet . . . it was my intention to stop Bailey if I met him driving. From what I have seen in the past, if he was out for the night with his friend Jules, she would normally drive home and I took it as unusual to see Bailey in the driving seat alone. So, with that in mind, I drove up to the top of the town, to a place known locally as Paddy Mac's, and turned around at that junction. I then travelled back down to town.' Prendeville hoped to intercept Bailey as he drove past him along the road out of town.

By the time Prendeville returned, 'Bailey's car was gone. I turned right and went down the pier road. There was no sign of Bailey. I presumed, therefore, he had gone ahead . . . and either by accident or design avoided me.'

Jules recalled that 'we came home the usual way, along the bog road'. Of the garda car that had passed her as she stood in the alley, she said, 'Had he waited fifteen seconds, he would have seen me get in.'

Had Bailey been challenged and failed a breath test, he would have been arrested on the spot and forced to spend another night away from home. Instead, he had successfully negotiated an escape from Schull, wittingly or unwittingly, the law thwarted.

*

At around 9.20 p.m. that Sunday evening, Shirley Foster, Alfie's wife, went to close the downstairs curtains. She noticed that the outside light near the kitchen door was on in the next-door holiday home. She could only see the gable end, but it signalled that the Frenchwoman was installed and even *en fête* for Christmas. Pleased at this sign of life, Shirley closed the curtains. She and Alfie then went to bed early together and watched a Tom Cruise movie about a murder in the Marine Corps, *A Few Good Men*.

Sophie would stay up at least another hour. There was the phone call with Josie that ended about 10 p.m., with a chair drawn up to the fireplace. As that heat died down, she ascended the white staircase with its black gaps between the steps, to reach the back bedroom.

Safely ensconced, she made a phone call after 10.30 p.m. to her husband in Ambax, southwest of Toulouse in the Haute-Garonne. Daniel said he was on another call to Unifrance executives and asked could he call her back. She agreed, though surprised he was working on Sunday, and so late. Within twelve minutes, Daniel rang. It was nearly midnight now in France as they chatted. Sophie said she had been out and about, recounted the trip to Three Castles Head – and, although she had expressed uncertainty about her return to France when chatting to the Ungerers, she now told Daniel she would be flying into Toulouse on an Aer Lingus flight at 8 p.m. on Christmas Eve.

Delighted, he promised to collect her. They were due to spend New Year in Dakar, Senegal, end-point of the famous car rally from Paris – which was more his style of holiday. Sophie sounded tired, he noticed, but, she nonetheless told him about her time with the Ungerers, and how Yvonne seemed jealous when she walked in on the wine tasting. Husband and wife laughed together.

Daniel told her tenderly that it would be nice to have her back for Christmas. It was now nearly 12.30 a.m. in Ambax, an hour earlier in Dunmanus West. He got the impression Sophie was already in bed for both of their calls. They hung up, separating for the last time. It was certainly cold in Ireland, freezing, and Sophie had taken a hot-water bottle up to bed. Always an avid reader, which she said helped her sleep, she probably got through a few pages of a paperback before turning off her lamp, which she perched on top of a noir novel in English – *Nightfall* by David Goodis: 'Jim Vanning has an identity crisis. Is he an innocent artist who just happens to have some very dangerous people interested in him?'

Late the next day, detectives would find Sophie's cordless phone casually tossed just a foot from her abandoned mattress.

*

Halfway home, Bailey made an unexpected stop, leaving the engine running but exiting the car. He had consumed an enormous quantity of drink and likely needed to urinate.

'We drove out to Lissacaha and took the turn before Lowertown Creamery,' Jules said. 'We stopped at Hunt's Hill for five minutes. I stayed in the car and Ian got out. He asked me to get out, but I refused as it was too cold.' Instead, she huddled head down into her coat and plunged her hands deeper in its pockets. The meek heater had at least not been halted by cutting the ignition.

According to Jules, Bailey said he was drawn to the full moon and the sight across Dunmanus Bay as far as sparkling Kilcrohane on the far Sheep's Head Peninsula. And also because the impressive height meant 'you can get the Christmas effect from the lights in the occupied houses'. Jules said, 'When we were looking across the terrain, Ian remarked, "Is that Alfie's house across the way? There's a light on there."' He then got out of the car.

The passenger window was becoming almost frosted. Jules continued to wait, before a crunching across the front of the car, coming nearer, led to the driver's door opening. Bailey heaved himself back into the driver's seat. He turned to Jules, who shuddered at the cold air he'd let in. 'He said he had a weird feeling or premonition that something bad or evil was to happen over by Alfie's house – it was like a dark cloud over the area. 'He said he was going over to where he saw the light.'

CHAPTER 5

The Body and Barbed Wire

Animals were active that night. Foxes were heard screaming in Toormore. Domestic dogs – whether affected by the full moon, other dogs, foxes or the distant scent of strangers – set up a caterwauling. Local man David Bray at 12.45 a.m. noted that a wolfhound at home was unusually upset. Another of that breed, owned by Martin Breuinger, was strangely disturbed from midnight to 2 a.m. Derry and Geraldine Kennedy's dog was 'barking mad' from 10.30 p.m. for fifteen minutes and then for 'three hours practically non-stop' until 1.50 a.m.

*

Shirley Foster rose at 8.20 a.m. on Monday, 23 December. She had not been out of the house all Sunday and now had things to do. She made breakfast, whereupon Alfie also rose and got dressed. He had briefly been up an hour earlier to put on the heating and make tea, before coming back to bed. He had also been 'up a few times during the night to go to the toilet'. They now chatted amiably about things still needed for Christmas.

'At 10 a.m., I decided to do the shopping and take rubbish to the dump,' said Shirley. She left the house, loaded the boot of their white Peugeot 305 estate with bulky black plastic bags and drove away. 'I passed down by the back of the house', meaning Sophie's, which was at the top of the shared driveway. 'The gate was open which I thought very unusual. Her car was parked beside the house.' Shirley drove further down. 'At first, I saw something on the left-hand side of the roadway, with something like a piece of white material caught onto the wire.' Shirley also spotted something lying underneath.

'I stopped the car and had a look. I could not fully decide what it was at that stage . . .' Initially Shirley thought someone had fly-tipped a shop's mannequin or an 'inflated doll' onto their property. 'As I drove by, I could see it was a body.' Terrified, she drove another fifteen yards and stopped. 'I was leaning on the horn to try and draw Alfie's attention and I was screaming.' She turned off the engine, tore out the keys, bolted from the vehicle and ran 'back up through Sophie's field' – to the left of the driveway going in. The side gate by the pump house was open and she struggled breathlessly towards the height, 'shouting and screaming to alert Alfie'. She went 'around her [Sophie's] back door and up home'. Alfie had come out, and she panted out the need to 'ring the guards'.

What is it?

'A dead girl.'

What! Where?

'In the driveway.'

Alfie led her inside and dialled 999. A girl dead at the entrance to their home. Blood everywhere. Dunmanus West – hurry. Alfie rang off and tried to calm his shaking soulmate. By degrees they collected themselves, and she agreed to indicate what she had seen. They went out together, down and around the curve of the drive, until Alfie could discern something. He went down a little farther as Shirley hung back, saying, 'Don't touch it.' Until he too hesitated, crouching to peer from eighteen metres away.

He could see the red-painted nose and face, the matted crimson mass of hair, and blood about the shoulders. It was pale and mutely still, this ill-clad corpse. He ran back up to Shirley and they both rushed home, locking the back door, then looking out the front windows at the silent morning. Sitting there was Sophie's car. *She has to be warned*, thought Alfie, still not realising who it was lying dead. Then he saw that the upper gate leading to Sophie's back door was wide agape between their properties, though usually the gate was stiff and needed to be lifted to open. That's not like Sophie, so who would have left it open? Alfie felt a sudden chill, believing the killer was possibly still around. Turning, he called urgently to Shirley. Had she opened it?

She replied, 'The bottom gate was open.'

No – this gate *here*, near us.

She came to look, staring. No, she whispered, she had not.

Alfie eventually screwed his courage to the sticking place.

Sophie still had to be warned. He went outside, watched from home by Shirley, through the open gate, and up to Sophie's house. He thumped heavily on the glass of Sophie's window, then on the back door. There was silence. He banged again, covering his fist with the sleeve of his jumper. Then he stood back, looked up, down – and then he saw it. A smear of blood beside the steel door handle. Alfie recoiled in shock, and his own blood drained from his face. He did not approach that door again, not that he was confident his legs would carry him. The silence yawned deeper. He retreated, still facing forward, then turned and fled for his own property. He forced himself to stop, look back, and wait while some distance away. Still, she was not answering. The windows were gaunt, the roof stark, the Fiesta fierce by its simple presence.

*

The 'nine call', as emergency services say, was patched through from the national switch to Bandon garda station, where it rang at 10.10 a.m. Garda Eugene McCarthy picked up and heard the despatcher's 'Go ahead, caller' before Alfie's urgent babble. McCarthy took pencil notes on a 'flyer' pad, asking that the directions be repeated. A body, yes. Your name and contact please, sir? Was an ambulance needed?

Alfie didn't think so, a doctor maybe.

'On our way.'

The garda put down the phone, then immediately rang Schull station. Sergeant Gerard Prendeville – the man who had nearly caught Ian Bailey drink-driving hours before –

was shocked by what he heard. He also had the details repeated, then called out to Garda Billy Byrne to get the squad car out *now*. He rushed to join him, fitting on his cap. Next, Alfie Lyons was ringing Schull directly, speaking to Garda Martin Malone, who confirmed a car was on its way and warned him not to touch the body. 'It appears to be a young girl,' said Alfie, who was now 'composed and calm'.

Garda Malone recorded that Alfie Lyons 'had no idea of identity of the person killed', but was pleased to hear that Sergeant Prendeville was coming: 'Gerry, I know him well.' The garda took Alfie's number. Then he radioed to his colleagues in the car, learning where they were, and hearing mention that an undertaker would have to be put on standby. He rang Alfie back, 'to reassure him that help would be with him' in minutes. Garda Malone spoke to Shirley and asked if she was all right. She answered that she was.

At 10.38 a.m. the white garda car, of blue and yellow decals, nosed downwards into the lane, cutting left towards the two houses of three. There was still evidence of frost. The driveway entrance, curving right, was blocked a hundred metres away by Shirley's abandoned vehicle. The gardaí rumbled along as far as they could, their nearside vision blocked by briars and foliage that increased in height as they approached. The car stopped and Sergeant Prendeville got out. Ten metres up the driveway lay a body, and the figure was wearing boots. A tent of white clothing was yanked to one side by barbed wire. Prendeville edged to the left as he moved up to see. Instinctively, he took off his cap. He walked closer to look at the remains: a brutally attacked female, life extinct. There was an exclamation of horror as Garda Byrne appeared at his side, seeing the same repugnant sight: the congealed blood, exposed midriff and more, the white top that was red and pink in places, ruched up as far as the breasts, which were still covered. The right arm was cocked out, as if nudging. What remained of the face was turned to the left, snug to a jagged rock like a giant shark-tooth, blood about its crevices, a mess on the grass. The left arm lay straight beside the torso, while beneath the triangular tent of entangled clothing, pubic hair was visible through torn leggings. Someone appeared to have arranged a large concrete block beside the left leg. It was like the crudest of paperweights, weighing down a folded blue blanket. What on earth was that? It was not a blanket, but a dressing gown.

The two gardaí stood back, mouths dry, and at least one might have blessed himself before a hoarse cry was in the air. 'I'll go up,' said Sergeant Prendeville, answering a 'hello' from the hill where Alfie was holding his ground. 'You secure the scene.'

He pointed down as an afterthought. 'Hair or something in her hand.'

CHAPTER 6

Taking Stock of Slaughter

Alfie and Shirley were 'extremely distressed and nervous' as Sergeant Prendeville spoke to them. He rang from their home for backup, telling colleagues to send a doctor and to notify headquarters. He was informed that a GP and a priest had been contacted. He knew a pathologist would be needed, but didn't say too much in the presence of civilians. Ending the call, he asked the couple what they knew. They were starting to think about alerting the Frenchwoman, they said, because there was no answer from her house.

What Frenchwoman?

The one there next door, with the Fiesta.

Her name, though?

Sophie.

And the rest?

They hesitated, then gave her maiden name. 'I'm not sure of the spelling.'

In the shock of the moment, it still had not fully occurred to Alfie and Shirley that the body could be that of their nearest neighbour. Asked when they had last seen her, the pair looked at each other in sudden surprise. They hadn't exactly, not lately, but they knew she was there, from the car, the lights, and the housekeeper saying beforehand.

Was she with anyone?

They honestly didn't know.

Had they a key to the house?

Perhaps, yes, somewhere – but the housekeeper would have one. Josie Hellen.

Prendeville said he would knock on Sophie's door for himself, but the guards might need to get in there later. 'We'll also have to take statements from you both in a little bit.'

The sergeant didn't waste much time. Alfie remembered to tell him about the blood near the handle on Sophie's back door. He also said he would ring the house: he had Sophie's number. The sergeant replied that he would thump on a window, but Alfie should let him know if he got any response on the phone.

Was that their car down there? Very good, and you were driving?

Shirley nodded.

You can move it in a bit. He would have to go down to secure the scene. Medical and scenes-of-crime people would be arriving; he had to wait for them.

The sergeant left and, after failing to rouse any occupant of the holiday home, went down to Garda Byrne, noting the Peugeot serving as a useful natural barrier. Dr Larry

O'Connor was just arriving from Schull. It was 10.55 a.m. and his was the first name entered and timed in Billy Byrne's notebook, regulation protocols now in place.

The medic didn't take long. The state of the body – dilated pupils, rictus mouth, absence of respiration, above all the horrendous head damage – told him she was dead and he certified as much. She had been for some hours, he said, the frigid body already stiffening with rigor mortis. He wouldn't like to guess how long. It was a matter for the pathologist. The doctor had left the scene when Fr Denis Cashman turned up at 11.55 a.m., also alone, an austere changing of the guard. The priest from Goleen was told not to touch the remains. He already knew this, having been twenty-eight years a priest, attending murder scenes in London. He could not anoint, as such, nor sprinkle holy water. Fr Cashman understood the restrictions; still, he had his breviary and would say the Last Rites. He stood close to Sophie, bowed his head, and forced himself to chant aloud, 'Saints of God, come to her aid. Hasten to meet her, angels of the Lord.' He did not know who she was or if she was even Catholic. He then began the 'Our Father'.

'I simply prayed. The guards joined in the prayers. It was only the three of us. There was nobody else around at that time.' Despite Fr Cashman's long experience, he had never seen anything as 'brutal, shocking and horrific'. There was a rock, a concrete block, 'and obviously it had crushed her skull and her beautiful face'.

As the priest pattered through the final blessing and came away, Garda Pat Joy from Schull station arrived to take photographs, accompanied by Garda Martin Malone. It was already noon. They met Prendeville and Byrne, saw the terrible state of the body, the feet wearing no socks in brown boots. 'I observed severe injuries to the head,' Joy said. "There were also bloodstains on the white leggings. Part of the top of the leggings was entangled in barbed wire on the ditch.'

Garda Joy saw a rock beside the head and a nearby cavity block, with bloodstains on both. He realised the block came from the opposite side of the driveway. 'There was a hut built around an electric pump; the top row of blocks was not cemented', and the block beside the body had been wrenched from there – where Shirley Foster had run into the grassy field in front of the house. There were a number of bloodstains on the upper bars of the nearby gate. 'It would indicate that some struggle took place along its length.' Had the dead woman then sprung to the ditch, trying to climb over the barbed wire, and been pulled back, her dressing gown coming off as she was hauled down, leggings snagging? Garda Joy's photographs, taken from all angles, would help to establish what happened.

More gardaí arrived, with Superintendent J.P. Twomey taking charge. At 12.15 p.m. Garda Malone left to get a sheet of plastic to cover the remains. He went all the way back into Schull. As he left, housekeeper Josie Hellen turned up to meet Sophie, as previously arranged. She was stopped by gardaí. Josie explained why she was there, was told of a serious incident, that she could go no farther. There was a person deceased. She asked if it was Sophie. The gardaí did not say whether it was a man or a woman, but the silence told all; Josie clamped her hand to her mouth in horror.

It was thus of pressing concern to gardaí that they needed someone to formally identify the body. Such was her state of upset, they didn't like to ask Josie, but her husband was soon in the vicinity. 'At 12.35 p.m. Finbarr Hellen of Dunmanus West identified the body. He stated he knew her, since she bought the property a few years previously.' He left in terrible shock after three minutes to try to console his weeping wife.

Garda Pat Joy then accompanied Sergeant Prendeville to Sophie's house, and was shown what appeared to be a bloodstain on Sophie's back door. He photographed the red smear. 'We then arrived at Alfie's, and he enquired whose body it was.' Joy said, 'I informed him it had been identified as that of the French lady.' Alfie was shocked, stupefied, though at some level he must have suspected. He 'put his hands up to his face and turned his face upwards', recorded Prendeville.

The scene became busier as time wore on. The local radio news bulletin at 2 p.m. announced a suspicious death in the Toormore area, but gave no further details of the victim or location. All remained quiet in the little hamlet of three houses, two now empty, with Alfie and Shirley huddled in the other.

Shortly after 2 p.m., Shirley went down and asked the guards, perhaps in a state of shock, if she could move her car to go to the dump, where she had been headed that morning. The police were cautious and had a good look through her garbage, just in case. She was then escorted past the remains, now concealed beneath a little mound of blue plastic, a guard on Shirley's left as she stared straight ahead. Garda Malone then saw her drive off, bound for the tip and some last-minute shopping. Life goes on. The log of arrivals and departures gained another entry.

Shirley drove around a left-hand bend 'so that you couldn't have seen the houses' from the far side. About halfway down a long descent was a white Fiesta, in it Ian Bailey was driving 'determinedly' towards her.

'I more or less had to flag him down to stop. He seemed in a great hurry. I wound down the window.' His partner Jules was present, she noticed. 'I said you cannot go that way, because the police have it fenced off. He said, "I know, I'm on assignment." He knew where he was going, obviously. There was nowhere else you could go on that road. In fact, he seemed in a hurry to get past me.' Bailey didn't require any assistance, 'no information'.

At 2.20 p.m., Garda Malone recorded the arrival of one 'Ian Bailey of Lissacaha North, a freelance reporter'. Malone went up from the lane to stop him. Nothing of the scene was visible from the road. 'I saw a white car at a junction. I spoke to Bailey and told him to leave the area, which he did. I noticed he was well dressed and had a long coat. Malone had expected push-back to his instruction to leave, but, instead of pleading for basic facts, Bailey meekly complied. 'He departed too quickly and I was suspicious of him,' Garda Malone said. He asked no questions at all. It was distinctly odd, given Malone's experience earlier that year with the same man. On that occasion, the garda had met Bailey in Ballybrack, Schull, where a man fell over a cliff – and Bailey had assiduously pumped him for information.

Garda Billy Byrne strode up behind Malone to support his colleague, calling out that the area was sealed off, yet giving no reason. He too noted Bailey's coat, but also a scarf and gloves.

*

It was some time after 2 p.m. when local cheesemaker Bill Hogan spotted Shirley Foster standing in a queue for bread at the bakery in The Courtyard. She was shaking uncontrollably. He took her aside and tried to calm her. She didn't say much, just that there had been an accident and it was a terrible sight, a woman dead. But word would soon leak out about the general location of the suspicious death – because some people in the queue knew Shirley's locality and put two and two together. Meanwhile, the garda calling-in of the rental car registration by radio had produced a name: Sophie Toscan du Plantier.

So far, the local officers had done everything right. But matters were about to get a little shambolic. The Technical Bureau team, the expert white suits, were based in Dublin. They wouldn't be at the scene before nightfall; lights would be needed. The next-of-kin had to be informed – and garda headquarters was trying to find a French speaker to pass on news to their counterparts in France. The French ambassador to Ireland was told as an interim move; François Mouton could get things moving at his end. But, most of all, a forensic pathologist was needed so the corpse could be viewed in situ, then brought away for a postmortem. The hearse was available, but where was the state pathologist, John Harbison?

John Frederick Austin Harbison was synonymous with slay-
ings, being Ireland's equivalent to famed British pathologist
Sir Bernard Spilsbury, who had metaphorically buried Crippen
and a dozen other killers. Harbison, too, seemed to revel in
his sang-froid; queasy gardaí noticed that at autopsies he sometimes seemed to involve them too closely in his work
necessary as it was. He also enjoyed being theatrical when
giving evidence in murder cases: the court clerk would stand
before him, routinely intoning, 'Take the testament in your
right hand and repeat after me, *I swear by Almighty God* . . .'
Harbison would explode, 'I will not!' – startling the clerk, who
sometimes glanced to the judge for help – before adding, 'I
will affirm.' He needed no Bible; his own promise to tell the
truth was sufficient; the white-bearded old atheist wore his
science on his sleeve.

But he was slowing down even as his duties grew steadily
more onerous. In the spring of 1996, he had written a
protest to the minister for justice that his office was under-
staffed, 'overwhelmed with work. I am battle-weary'. The
refusal of government to retain the contracted services of
an assistant, Dr Margaret Bolster, who'd covered the south
of the country in his absence, was highly undesirable. Now
it was Christmas and he was off-duty, as arranged with the
Department of Justice. It happened to be his sixty-first
birthday on the day Sophie's body was found, and that
week he certainly wasn't going to darken the door of his
rooms in Trinity College, a place where papers were piled
high and human skulls lay jumbled in jutting drawers.

The guards were ringing his office and the phone went
unanswered. Superintendent J.P. Twomey also 'rang Dr

Bolster, pathologist, but could not make contact with her and left word on her answering machine that she was required'.

Eventually someone had the temerity to ring Harbison at home, a cardinal sin since he was on leave. 'We're very sorry to disturb you, doctor, but – Harbison was adamant: not on duty, the responsibility of others to ensure cover over Christmas. He had told them time and again. They needed another pathologist.

Next, an apologetic call was made to Scotland with a view to obtaining someone suitably qualified. They would have to fly to Cork. But it turned out there were 'high winds at Prestwick airport', ending that option. All seemed insurmountable – how to obtain a pathologist at short notice. Harbison had to be called back and practically begged. He was understandably furious at, yet again, being left in the lurch. High winds! He had never heard the like.

The gardaí offered to drive him down, as soon as he could possibly assist them – but this touched another nerve: Harbison had never had an official driver. He had always to pilot his own Citroën, a choice of car reflecting this Francophile lover of fine wines. But a Frenchwoman, you think? He was becoming mollified, already calculating. When was she discovered? Murdered in the night, and five hours to West Cork. The body had been steadily shedding temperature at a constant rate since death, and a rectal thermometer would give count-back to an estimated hour of death. But time was very much against them, even if someone were to magically produce a helicopter. It was not his fault, but he would see what he could do. First thing next morning, best would be to fly – when was the earliest Cork flight?

The gardaí were grateful. However, behind this feeling lay an absolute horror – that the body of the poor woman would have to lie out on the frozen grass for another night, invigilated by shivering gardaí in greatcoats, stamping their feet, vapours rising under arc lights. And then, after all that, there would still be no estimated time of death. It was ugly beyond words. Even shameful.

*

Sophie's mother was watching the 8 p.m. news on 23 December. Marguerite Bouniol's blood ran cold when she saw and heard that a French national *avait été retrouvé assassiné à une centaine de kilomètres de Cork*. Murdered! That was where Sophie was! The frantic calls began. Once more, the telephone rang and rang in the empty house at Dunmanus West.

Meanwhile, Daniel Toscan du Plantier had seen the same television news while relaxing in Ambax. *Ça ne peut pas être Sophie* – or could it? He began to feel dizzy, his palm clammy as he picked up the phone and dialled Sophie's number. The line was busy; that was reassuring. He was being silly; he'd try again later. He sat down in an armchair and tried to think straight, until jangled out of it by an incoming call. It was the French ambassador to Ireland, speaking gravely. '*J'ai de mauvaises nouvelles, j'en ai peur . . .*' Daniel's world promptly fell apart.

But it would be hours still before Sophie's parents heard the devastating truth. They rang her brother Bertrand and checked with friends. It isn't known how they did not connect with Daniel, nor he with them. The local police were rung, but knew nothing. As the hours passed, Marguerite was becoming overwrought. Husband Georges did his best to assuage her anxiety. Someone rang the gardaí and was told that it was not operational practice to disclose to callers the name of a deceased; the relevant family would be informed through official channels. A safeguard, of course, but it felt like a rebuke. Then, they hit on the idea of calling Sophie's housekeeper. What was her name and number? They fumbled with the prefix for Ireland, to be added to the digits. Finally, the line was buzzing rhythmically at the other end. Josie Hellen answered in a small hushed voice. 'Was Sophie alive?' Georges asked. The answer was hollow, full of pain – no, she was not. An abyss of agony engulfed them all.

An hour later, a car left the sullen suburbs of darkened Paris, bound for the blurred lights of the autoroute. And in the middle of the night – in the middle of France – a boy was woken. The teenager had been staying with relatives in Sologne, 280 kilometres south of Paris. He wept piteously, was comforted by his father Pierre Jean Baudey, but could not be consoled. Pierre-Louis' childhood was over.

CHAPTER 7

To Cover and Discover

That Monday, Ian, or Eoin, Bailey was due to file a story for the *Sunday Tribune*, 650 words about the dawn of the internet in West Cork. The noontime deadline came and went. Richard Curran was the business editor. 'It was Christmas week, and I was not working either Wednesday or Thursday, 25 and 26 December. I had informed all freelance reporters that deadline was noon on Monday 23rd.' Eoin Bailey was writing an article on computer link-ups in pubs. He did not meet the deadline. 'The report was eventually phoned through . . . I remember, because I was worried, and would have to come up with a replacement if it didn't arrive at all.'

Tom McEnaney was in charge of the technology page, named 'Cyberspace'. 'I was reasonably relaxed. When Monday morning came and went, and the copy had not arrived, I began to get nervous. I attempted to contact Eoin, unsuccessfully.' Eventually, Bailey filed his *Tribune* story over the phone to a copytaker at 5 p.m on the 23 December. 'I can confirm it was Eoin, as I had the call transferred to me,' McEnaney said.

*

It was 1.40 p.m. when a call came through to Ian Bailey at The Prairie from Eddie Cassidy of *The Examiner* (formerly *The Cork Examiner*) – there had been a suspicious death. It was a woman, exact location and name unknown. 'That was all I gave Bailey. I did not tell him it was a French national, as I did not know that myself at that stage.' Could Bailey work on finding out? The call lasted just two minutes. Bailey would later claim it was the first he'd heard of the Christmas tragedy. Which makes what happened next all the more remarkable.

Bailey immediately got in touch with Dick Cross, southern correspondent of the *Irish Independent*. Cork-based Cross recalled, 'He said he had a picture of the body and the guards hadn't arrived yet. He had been to the scene and there were no guards. I kept a logbook and wrote in the time of his first call at 1.45 p.m.' There was a follow-up call, noted at 1.55. Cross didn't do photos, so gave him the number of Pádraig Beirne, group photographic editor of the *Irish Independent* in Dublin.

Beirne was a highly experienced newsman who had a reputation for not suffering fools. He was called by a 'photographer from Schull' about 1.55 p.m. Bailey informed him that not only had he a picture of the body – but one of the victim in life. Was he interested? Beirne said that depended: what was it like, and how did he come to have it? Bailey answered that he had *taken it himself*, adding that she was 'a very good-looking woman'.

Could Bailey wire it? No, he had no machine. Beirne said he would make arrangements – someone would be in touch to pick it up – this 'pick-up' portrait that seemed destined for the front page.

Bailey, imagining both glory and riches, now hopped into the car with Jules, who brought her camera. They drove straight to Dunmanus West, a scene that was still a secret. They encountered a traumatised Shirley Foster along the way and were then curtly dismissed on arrival by Garda Malone at 2.20 p.m. It was not clear how Bailey had known where to go, since Cassidy had informed him only of a dubious fatality, asking him to find out where it was. The only guide was 'Toormore', an area of thirteen townlands.

Turned away by officers on the spot, a frustrated Bailey now hoped to discover who the victim was. He had a sudden brainwave and sped off to Toormore Post Office, incorporated into Nan Jermyn's little shop near the Schull–Goleen road. Here, he learned of the deceased from the postmistress – by simply asking what was the name of the foreign woman who lived near Alfie Lyons. Nan knew, and showed the entry in the local phonebook – Sophie Bouniol. It was enough, and it was good.

Bailey headed home, where he filed his first piece not to *The Examiner*, but to *The Star*. It was at around 2.40 p.m. He didn't bother to confirm the name with gardaí before filing. He knew other journalists were active, ringing the four Ps – police, priest, post office and people who might know, especially about identity and location. He was right. One even rang an auctioneer.

It was after 3 p.m. when Bailey was called at The Prairie by Mike Brown, the Reuters journalist ultimately tasked with getting the promised pics for the *Indo*. 'I rang Bailey from my mobile, looking for directions. I asked him had he got pictures.' But Bailey's story from earlier had changed. Much to Brown's surprise and consternation, Bailey told him there wasn't a photograph of the woman in life.

Brown continued to The Prairie nonetheless, arriving around 3.45 p.m. 'Bailey, after introductions, got into my car and we drove to the scene. I asked him did he know the girl and what happened. He knew her name, and told me he knew her to see, but not personally. The two of us arrived at the scene and Bailey met Eddie Cassidy and Dan Linehan, the latter a photographer. It was 4 p.m., and there was not much light left, about half an hour.

Two news teams were now on site. Gardaí were still tight-lipped at the tape, 120 metres from the hidden body, offering no confirmation of anything. Meanwhile Shirley's Peugeot was back, parked in the upper part of the lane. Escorted home by a garda, she disclosed to Alfie that she'd met Bailey at the wheel of Jules's car as she headed out earlier. Alfie was amazed, replying, 'I thought he was banned from driving?'

*

Superintendent Twomey had also returned to the scene, after notifying Coroner Colm Quigley of the fatality. He also learned that Professor Harbison would be coming, but arriving late. The superintendent now encountered Eddie Cassidy, whom he knew.

The journalist took swift shorthand notes. 'Twomey came up to the cordon, about 150 yards from the body, gave me details of the townland and said a neighbour had found the body. He told me it was a tourist, but was reluctant to give any name. He possibly mentioned it was a Frenchwoman.'

Next, Brown and Bailey arrived. 'It was my first time speaking to Bailey in person,' said Cassidy. 'He gave a name, Sophie Bouniol. I took what he said as fact. I had less than ten minutes' conversation with him. He was holding a folder and I noticed at that stage that he had the guts of a story done, that a murder inquiry was about to be launched.'

Photographer Dan Linehan was meanwhile busy. About 4 p.m., he snapped a picture of Bailey approaching Eddie Cassidy, who was in conversation with Twomey. Bailey was wearing a long coat, a folder under his left arm. Cassidy said of the victim, 'The superintendent told me she had a head wound and her clothes appeared torn.'

'Woman Battered To Death Yards From Home', clarioned *The Star* on Tuesday morning, Christmas Eve. It used Bailey's early story, featuring the name Sophie Bouniol. He pinned identification on 'postmistress Nan Jermyn [who] said the woman was well liked'. The victim was a 'professional Parisienne', Bailey somehow knew.

Gardaí had confirmed the name late the previous night, too tardily for *The Star*. But it got into some other daily titles, brushing aside the maiden name. This was now officially the murder of Sophie Toscan du Plantier.

CHAPTER 8

Doing What's Necessary

Professor Harbison was met by Detective Jim O'Riordan as he walked into the arrivals hall on Christmas Eve amid welcome home signs and seasonal decorations, his countenance in stark contrast to most travellers returning for the holidays. The bushy-whiskered old sawbones wore a green coat and carried a voluminous leather bag, eyes darting about over the stringed glasses perched on his nose. It was shortly after 9 a.m.

Soon they were on their way to Dunmanus West, arriving about 11 a.m. There, Harbison had the plastic sheeting removed from over the victim. His notes show no emotion: 'I observed the dead body of a female.' He carried out a careful visual inspection, from the most horrific head wounds to scratches on the arms. He noted everything, over several minutes.

The hearse was next, crawling almost soundlessly down

the lane. The undertakers were met by O'Riordan, and they removed a dark-brown basic coffin, stored in the rear. At a signal, they moved it forward, placing it on the ground side by side with Sophie's remains.

Gardaí were combing through Sophie's field, her rental car was being dusted for fingerprints, and the house entered and searched. All photographs and mapping had concluded. It was finally Sophie's time to leave.

Detective Garda Eugene Gilligan delicately detached the white leggings from the barbed wire. Under Harbison's instructions, Technical Bureau specialists proceeded to first gingerly lift the head though they had some difficulty because of congealment, before covering it with a plastic bag. The same was done with other extremities. Then the whole body was swaddled in white plastic. In their last duty, three white-suited specialists respectfully lifted Sophie into her coffin. Left behind was 'a slight depression with blood in it where the head had lain', the crater created by the pounding force of inflicted blows. The casket was lidded, then raised solemnly and moved towards the hearse, those watching doffing their caps and lowering their heads in respect.

Hearse driver for Arundel's undertakers Dominic Sheehan was also a part-time farmer, helped on this occasion by one Michael Collins, a man who bore the same name as the victim of the most notorious killing in these parts. Seventy-four years earlier, at the height of the Civil War, Free State commander-in-chief Michael Collins died in ambush from a wicked head wound.

At 10.40 a.m., Sophie Toscan du Plantier left her holiday home for the last time, bound for Cork University Hospital and the impersonal business of autopsy. A car of detective gardaí followed directly behind, discreet escort for the deceased. Family members from France were meanwhile flying into Cork for the very grimmest of Christmases.

*

Back at The Prairie, cleaning was getting underway in preparation for Christmas Day. Ian Bailey agreed to go shopping for supplies. 'I was going to do it myself,' said Jules, 'but Ian said he would go. I didn't make out a shopping list, but told him to get cleaning stuff, fuel and layers mash for the hens. He took the blade of the saw to get it replaced. I told him to get bleach to clean the bathroom. It gets into an awful state from mildew, and I use a lot of bleach to get rid of it. I wanted to have the house clean for Christmas.'

And so, Ian Bailey joined the hordes of recalcitrant men across Ireland splashing the cash that Christmas Eve – even as detectives were inside Sophie's tidy property, taking photographs and making diligent notes, seeing a passport on a table. They picked up a wallet in gloved hands to find ten IR£20 notes with sequential numbers, all brand new and uncreased. The money from the bank ATM on Saturday. She hadn't spent any of it.

Billy O'Regan of the Drinagh Co-op in Lowertown remembered Bailey coming in before noon on Christmas Eve. He visited the newspaper stand and picked up *The Examiner*, studying its coverage of the killing – Eddie Cassidy's stuff – before placing it down again. 'He was carrying a saw and asked me would I change the blade as it was cutting crooked. He said he had a lot of cutting to do. He was going to town and asked if we could have it ready when he came back.' O'Regan noticed scratches on both Bailey's hands, 'particularly his left', as the latter hoisted the tool onto the counter. The customer looked rough, as if his hands were 'torn' from cutting briars.

O'Regan dutifully replaced the blade in the yellow bow saw that Bailey had brought. Bailey returned after half an hour, asking for two bales of briquettes and layers mash. He was told to go 'out the back' to see Denis O'Callaghan for the latter. When he did so, O'Callaghan similarly noticed scratches on the back of Bailey's left hand, akin to briar scrapes. He described them as multiple light scratches. Bailey was 'very pale and agitated', not his normal self – and O'Callaghan had known him for years. He asked if he was all right, and Bailey replied, 'I hope to be in a couple of hours.' The co-op worker found this response strange and didn't know what he meant. Bailey disappeared from there, back into the main shop, carrying his goods.

When Bailey next came up to O'Regan at the counter, he had a one-litre bottle of 'Happy Shopper' bleach in his hand. The shopkeeper again spotted the scratches. O'Regan did not take any great notice of Ian Bailey's behaviour, but thought it strange that he was having a blade replaced that was not required. In fact, it was 'perfect' and 'as good as new'.

So good was the blade, in fact, that O'Regan put it onto a shelf for resale. And it sold.

*

'I told him to bring cleaning stuff, and he only brought bleach,' said Jules. And so it was that on Christmas Day, after attending the annual Schull swim, Bailey called to his nearest neighbours, the Jacksons, who lived 'a two-minute walk away', to pick up some items he'd requested when he met them earlier at the charity plunge.

Delia Jackson, daughter of homeowners Brian and Ursula, recalled that Bailey 'was looking for washing-up liquid and a toilet roll'. She was told that, with the girls home and a friend of Ginny's staying for the holiday, Jules had 'miscalculated' on toilet paper. Brian and Ursula said Bailey was in 'a right sweat' when he arrived at their house, pale and perspiring. He 'could not wait for a drink and immediately took a naggin of whiskey out of his pocket, which was nearly empty. He was very agitated'. They insisted that he have a mince pie. 'While he was in the house, we had a general conversation and the murder of Sophie came into it. He stated that he had met Sophie on a couple of occasions. He was the only person I knew that had met Sophie.' As he left with his supplies, they gave him a Christmas card which contained the playful message, '*Keep clean!*'

After he was gone, they puzzled over Bailey's behaviour. Bailey and Delia had worked together at a fish factory. Brian recalled: 'The first time I met him, he came around to our house to visit with my daughter. On that occasion, I learned that his hobby was destroying religious artefacts, which I thought strange, but gave an idea of the sort of person he was. He has a reputation for walking the lanes with his "thinking stick", a big branch . . . mainly at night. Ian was fond of a pint, so he would often call around in the evening, on his own, and have a pint of beer or a couple of pints.' Brian's more mainstream hobby was home-brewing.

The Jacksons spoke together about Bailey's unusual clothes and nervous anxiety earlier that day at the Christmas Swim. Brian and Ursula had noticed something peculiar: Bailey was not wearing his usual distinctive boots, part of his trademark attire. He had on a long black coat and wide-brimmed hat, but not the tan-coloured boots. They also found it strange that he was wearing 'runners' but not any socks. Like others who saw him at the swim that day, their suspicions – and alarm – were beginning to mount.

Despite the shock to the community two days before, spirits had been high down on the pier, with folk wearing red-and-white furry hats or paper crowns from crackers. The intending bathers were cheered on, with those in the water already blowing and spluttering, some shrieking real meaning into the name of Roaringwater Bay. There were fully clad onlookers dispensing whiskey to the hardy souls about to brave the waves, and to those – shivering, crouching – who had just come back. Bailey was a loner among the crowds, and declined to take a dip himself, although he had gone in on past occasions.

Florence Newman had her father's 8mm video camera, recording the jollity. The lens panned onto Bailey. She asked him for a poem. For once he appeared reticent. Pressed, he mumbled a few words before quickly adding the Irish phrase 'Sin a bhfuil', that's all, folks. He was wrapped against the cold, ill at ease, wearing those runners or trainers, without socks.

There was a fleeting view of Bailey's hands, but the footage was low-resolution and betrayed little. He appeared slightly unsettled, not the great declaimer of a few nights before.

Ursula Jackson had often told him his verse was rubbish, 'dope poetry', because he had once smoked a joint at her house. Florence, behind the viewfinder, remembers that 'to the best of my knowledge he was not a wearer of runners or trainers'. She recalled, 'I shook hands with him and noticed markings on his hand, kind of parallel lines, maybe four or five or six across the back of his hand. There was a uniformity to them. The timeframe caused me to wonder, that's all. I just thought it was a curious thing. I told my family and I just sort of wondered aloud.'

Later, this videotape would become garda exhibit no. 71, but for Florence and her father, Donal, a postmaster who had founded the Christmas Swim, it was 'simply a recording of the swim and associated activity and spectators'.

*

On 7 January 1997, Daniel Toscan du Plantier, who did not travel to Ireland that December, described his late wife to Commandant Jean-Louis Chaumet and investigator Christine Amiel of the judicial police, acting on an Irish request for assistance:

I am the husband of Sophie Bouniol. She was my associate, but, in 1988, she left work and our relationship became more intimate. We began to share our life and, some years later, we married. Sophie was very dynamic. She was an impulsive woman, and would not be in the habit of letting herself be walked on. In fact, she was a tough character with a strict moral code, who feared nothing. She rather avoided the world of society and gossip, and preferred the chic and popular quarters where she felt more at ease. She was passionate about African art and had produced a programme on African bondage. I have to say that, like all couples, disputes arose because Sophie was not an easy person to live with. She would not hesitate to leave her home and go to her cousin Alexandra, who lives in Geneva. She was equally very close to Agnès Thomas, who was indeed a confidante. If our life as a couple was sometimes not without hitches, she still decided to have a child and had ceased to use any contraceptive.

She expressed the desire about four years ago to get a house in Ireland, in a wild and isolated area, in keeping with her character. I therefore bought, at her request and in her name, I think for 400,000 francs [IR£42,000], a house situated in immediate proximity to the Fastnet lighthouse. Personally, I only went there once, about three or four years ago, but I was able to appreciate the beauty of the place. Sophie had told me how she loved long walks in the Irish countryside. As with her books, it was a favourite pastime. She used to go there three or four times a year to holiday for a week with friends, relatives and children. She was mother of a boy from a previous marriage, Pierre-Louis Baudey, about fifteen. During her absences, the house was maintained by a woman called Josie.

Because of her professional life, Sophie had only been able to go to our Irish house once this year, in the spring, much to her regret. She had therefore decided to holiday there at the end of December, during a slack period in her work. In her Irish house Sophie would sleep wearing a night vest, T-shirt, pyjamas or other such. There was no history with the English people who lived there. She had some neighbour problems with the Irish, who lived in the other house, in relation to an enclosure. Sophie had such a temperament that she was not the type to offer no resistance. Equally, and in the same vein, I'm saying that because of her character, my wife would not hide from any noise outside, but rather go out to investigate. I had been able to verify that several times. Equally, because of a certain philosophy and moral code above the usual standard, I believe her to be completely incapable of having had an affair within the marriage. To my knowledge she did not have any other particular relationships in Ireland. She used to frequent the local pub whose ambience was gratifying to her, as in Paris, where she used to frequent the popular cafés.

I have absolutely no idea [of] the perpetrator of the crime and do not see any possible motive for an attack, other than being an act of violence. I do not have an immediate wish to say anything more. I do not have it in mind to return to Ireland. I'm ready to receive here in Paris any [Irish] police officers dealing with the case, if they deem it necessary.

CHAPTER 9

The Source of It All

My first trip to West Cork to cover the story will always stay with me: Bailey sat up front in Martin's van as I lay squeezed into the back. We hurtled from the slope at Schull, where Martin and I had met Bailey, the bouncing battering my back, heading for the house where horror had been committed. The discomfort could be endured, because, for the next fifteen minutes, Bailey showed me how good a hack could be. He effortlessly had it all, delivering the most impressive 'fill' I have ever obtained, before or since. Martin was hurrying, the light fading.

As Bailey carefully enunciated remarkable particulars of the crime, *pronounced* them indeed, I felt slight pangs of guilt at having misjudged this tall, powerful man at first sight, simply because of his dishevelled appearance. I hadn't expected his flow of facts.

Bailey said for starters that Sophie had used the surname

Bouniol in West Cork, a new one on me – I'd only seen Toscan du Plantier in the paper. He stalled my attempted question like a teacher: 'B o u,' he said, pausing, 'n i o l.' A moment later: 'Her maiden name. She was a different person here. Her husband never came. Daniel, a big noise in French cinema. The Unifrance conglomerate.' He confirmed her age.

I was astounded that she'd supposedly been on her own. What was all that about?

'She would come with different people. Girlfriends, men. They're starting to do questionnaires,' he said, 'to see if anyone noticed someone new about the place. Taking advantage of the big increase in traffic.'

I mentally shrugged at that – it still seemed a pretty small place to me.

'She came in from the airport and had a rental car. Silver Ford Fiesta – oh, turn right here, just past that stream.'

On and on it went, this impressive oratory, moving inexorably to a fine focus onto the night of the crime. I was filling my notebook fast, whipping over a flap to divide the next page in two with a vertical line, jotting journalism in the left column, then the right. It was not exhausting so much as exhilarating – like a feathers fisherman suddenly struck by six big mackerel on the line all at once. I struggled similarly, writing furiously to try to reel in all these glorious flashing features, pure underbelly of what had occurred. I fought to get it all down.

Bailey spoke of the lights going on and off at the murder house, and mentioned the times. I was mentally there, seeing them extinguished. He described how two wine glasses had been left on the draining board in the kitchen.

Just a minute, catching up, were they used?

'Not sure, they were upside down. But she'd brought wine, red.'

Then the body, the nightclothes, a concrete block.

Wait – a concrete block?

'Yes, he killed her with a concrete block. About the head,' he said.

I swore swiftly. This was new. 'And was the block broken?' I looked at the back of his own head as he talked to the windscreen. He had never once turned around to glance at me.

Martin suddenly whomped into a lower gear to start on the base of a hill.

'No, and it was there until yesterday. They also took away a big stone that he left beside the body.'

He – some Hercules. Those blocks are heavy, and this story was getting heavier, in all senses. I was becoming laden down with searing details, pen-filled pages flipped over to reveal new white undersides, starting on the next virgin tablet, recording wonders.

My head was spinning. Even the engine seemed to protest. We were ascending. At some level, below the high engagement and the exertion of both car and man, I knew something for certain: these particulars – better than that, slices of life, of death – could only have been provided by someone at the heart of the investigation. Authoritative Bailey had some copper completely in his pocket.

'Then she ran down the slope, obviously to get away, and fell by the gate.'

Okay, another slope; I guess I would soon see it for myself.

'Bending left here,' said Bailey to Martin.

I distinctly remember suggesting at this point that I would not feel right transmitting this material under my own byline. It was all his stuff, supremely impressive, and he deserved the credit.

Bailey ignored me. 'You'll see the house soon. I told you she had a young son? Pierre, I believe. I've been asking round.'

Pierre, I wrote. Also the French word for 'stone'. 'Six, seven?'

'Teenager – younger end, fourteen maybe. Former marriage,' Bailey blandly recited.

Then into that aspect, and for once, he knew little.

*

We mounted the brow of a hill.

'Stop here,' he commanded, slapping Martin's shoulder.

We glided to the left and halted.

'Down there,' Bailey said.

Martin popped the boot and I slid out awkwardly in a slow-motion Fosbury flop. My liberator was already out of the car, frenetically working at his bag, clutching cameras, ready to get to work. I went the other way, to the brow. I could see dark figures below in the cleft, very obviously at the scene of the crime. At the same time, it was hardly a hive of activity – no tell-tale knot of a media scrum on safari. A touch of dusk had begun to creep into the canopy overhead. We were still over a hundred metres from the scene. I turned to Bailey, still sitting in the passenger seat, though he had lowered the window. 'Come on,' I urged.

'What do you mean?' he replied.

'Let's go,' I said, jerking my head towards the police, with whom he obviously had a close relationship. All he had to do was vouch for me – smile indulgently at the gardaí and suggest with his honeyed accent and paternal words that the kid was all right. Bailey was only six years older than me, but I was already feeling small in his 6 foot 4 inch shadow. 'You know the drill,' I said to him, one hack to another, this time indicating with my thumb. *Come on, get out*, I thought. *Shift yourself.* After all, we had commissioned him for the day; he was our fixer. He had to make the introductions.

But Bailey held back. 'Oh, no, I've given you all I can. You're on your own now. I'll wait 'til you come back.'

I found his attitude jaw-dropping. What a time to turn slack, when he must have worked his butt off to assemble all this material in the first place. But there was no changing it – and Martin wasn't helping. 'Come on,' he called brusquely over his shoulder, a Sherpa hurrying to base camp before the light faded. I had no choice: I had to leave our leading man, now seemingly transformed into a difficult prima donna. Notebook out, pen rammed into its spiral spring, I slogged after my colleague.

When we got to the crime scene, wary guards came straight up, tightly buttoned uniforms. I made practised efforts to break the ice, using the universal open-handed gesture – *I come in peace.* Despite my cheery demeanour, careful declaration of who I was, production of a press card, with casual deployment of notebook held at the ready, all I got back was, 'Garda Press Office.'

'Sorry, lads.' I thought to myself, *I will give you another chance.*

Trying again then, with greater sincerity, 'I believe the lights were off?'

Still no dice: 'You'll have to contact the Garda Press Office.'

That's fine, understood, guard: 'But what time did the body leave?'

'Dublin, you have to ring Dublin. Press office only.'

'No bother, garda – can the photographer just go down there a wee bit and stop at the patrol car?'

'No, he can't. Are you listening to me? Will you step back to the roadside, please?'

Jesus, what had I done to offend? I shot a desperate look back to the brow of the hill, where the figure of Bailey lounged unconcernedly. He seemed to be smoking, making idle small movements, removed from it all. *I am drowning here*. But I didn't have time to feel any animus towards him. I was too busy trying to frame fresh guard-unlocking strategies. All to no avail. 'Just looking for a bit of help, lads.' Practically begging. 'Come on, please, I've a job to do. Checking stuff. Just one or two things.'

They stood impassive. Silent. But at least not openly contemptuous. 'We have our instructions.'

When Martin and I had finished at the scene, not that it took long, we tramped back up to Bailey's place of advantage.

'Well, anything extra?' he asked magisterially as we arrived. Doing the teacher thing again, now ready to examine homework.

I shook my head, and not just in answer but in frustration too, angry at myself somehow, but not at him. I couldn't blame him for showing off. I should have got something, damn it.

I slunk dog-like into the back of Martin's van – my stomach

77

tightened in failure, feeling fairly worthless. Of course, I had
to let Bailey keep the passenger seat while Martin drove. Such
was his importance – the source of it all. Martin three-point
turned, and we skidded off the way we had come. Only
thinking about his precious photographs, I bet.

I told brilliant Bailey with a trace of bitterness that I
could really have done with him down there; I had got
nowhere. 'Look, I'm just going to file all this in your name;
it's all your stuff,' I said.

His reaction was as immediate as it was shocking: 'No,
no, you won't do that. All that's for you. I'm freelancing
for a Sunday. You just send that in yourself and you'll be
doing me a favour.'

This was impossible to understand; the man was
maddening. First dispensing charity, then stitching you up,
then all noble again.

Still, we had to get to the East End Hotel in Schull to
begin transmitting this material – *his* material – to Dublin.
The paydirt was in Bailey's insights: Sophie wearing nightclothes, but also boots – which had been laced up – and
no socks. Her bed was slept in, the clothes rumpled. He
even had that. She had closed but not locked the back door
of the house and there was a half-burned candle. 'Gardaí
discovered blood on the back door. It might have started
there,' he ruminated. It was all fresh material that had not
appeared anywhere, and it was extraordinary. I earnestly
wanted to know who was handing out these sweets to him
to pass on to me, but I knew it was pointless to ask. Even
among themselves, *especially* among themselves, journalists
never reveal their sources.

It was on the journey into Schull that Bailey asked my views on the crime. It was dark now. 'Come on, you're the crime reporter,' he said smoothly, as I slouched in the windowless rear, my bag buckle biting into my back.

Much mollified at being suddenly shown some regard, I reflected on my criminology classes, many court cases and in-field experience. Not needing much encouragement now, I said to him, 'All right, well, look at the crime signature here – it's complete overkill. Her skull crushed with a rock and block. You said it yourself. That's not premeditated, Eoin. It's a rage killing.'

Bailey stared fixedly into the murk, the headlights throwing hedgerows into relief.

'How many houses are there on this peninsula? Four hundred?' I asked.

Still nothing, listening.

'Half of them will be holiday homes, empty in December. That leaves two hundred, yeah? How many of those are retirement places? Take out another hundred. You agree, Eoin? People too doddery to do anything. So, you have to be looking for a man in the prime of his powers, aged twenty-five to forty. How many of those are there around here?'

He must have thought I was asking a rhetorical question, because it went unanswered. Shadowed scenery swooped by. On I went regardless, since I had been asked my opinion: 'The guards will have this wrapped up in a fortnight. It is one hundred per cent a local killer – look how hard that house was to find.'

Bailey, attentive or not, still said nothing. Despite my elegant Ellery Queen impression, the love had been suddenly switched off, it seemed. He wasn't interested in my amateur imaginings.

'Well, what do you think yourself?' I ventured, slightly irritated. 'You're the man on the ground. What are people saying to you?'

Another silence.

'Eoin, come on, what are you hearing?'

Martin was all ears too. Bailey at length adopted a dripping, judicious tone: 'Well, I think there's a lot more to it than meets the eye. It could go on for several weeks.'

I was troubled that Bailey had all these glorious details, this inside account, and yet no particular theories of his own, no suspects, and no point at which he agreed with my relatively simple analysis. Because the crime itself seemed basic and explicable: rage, rage in every blow; loss of control. A dreadful, deadly spark in one terrible moment.

We were now on the main road. I suggested a joint byline, with his name first. Or, if he really wanted – for whatever reason, taxman maybe – mine first and his second. He still wouldn't have it; he wanted me to put my name on what he had chiselled out and quarried. I thought his attitude beyond unusual, given he'd already said that, as a former journalist in the west of England, he intended to increase his freelancing here in the new year. He should have been delighted at this exposure. There was obviously likely to be a gain, something to show other newspapers.

'Look,' I said, 'a killing is a terrible thing, but it's an ill-wind that doesn't blow somebody some good. You have to hustle it.' Me, lecturing him. I said that if he had been thinking of returning to journalism, he could not have planned a better outcome than the 'murder of a minor celebrity on your back doorstep'. In fact, I was fascinated at this extraordinary coincidence, inviting Martin to agree that it was astonishing. 'This fella couldn't have arranged it better,' I said, as the lights of Schull came dimly into view.

For some reason, Bailey wasn't grinning or enjoying the joke. He didn't say anything. It was rather staggering to me that he was so completely cool that he didn't for a single moment marvel at this phenomenal turn of events.

The indifferent silence was so striking that I began to wonder if I was too giddy. Is this how self-possessed super-star journalists see the world, that even the most preposterous and outlandish event, occurring near their own home, is something to be reported on so matter-of-factly, with detached panache? The detail Bailey had helped weave into my spiral notebook was bewilderingly good – and, in a strange way, humiliating. How did I ever dream I could make it on Fleet Street, when this was the quality and calibre of someone who had jobbed there, but mostly stuck to an English regional beat? I was just his inferior, that was all there was to it.

I wrote and transmitted copy from the hotel and we brought Bailey back to The Prairie, whose lights cast the glow of civilisation into the gloom. It was late, and it seemed Bailey had had a beer or two while waiting for us to file from the East End Hotel. Now he made to get out, easier in himself but, before he left, we made sure to ask for detailed directions back to the main road. Worn out, we weren't taking any chances with getting lost in this moon-scape of strange folds and shadows. 'Thanks a million, Eoin,' I said. 'I'll call you in the morning.'

The next day we naturally bought the paper. The headline in *The Star* was splashed as 'Sophie: Killer May Have Left Prints – Key Test on Wine Glass'. [To my undying shame]

From Senan Molony in West Cork

Fingerprints from wine glasses may hold the key to finding the killer of beautiful French socialite Sophie Toscan du Plantier. Gardaí hope they will reveal if the TV producer had a visitor in her remote holiday home in West Cork on the night she was brutally murdered. The results of forensic tests are expected from the state laboratory and gardaí believe these could lead them to the killer.

On page four there was a byline picture of me on the telephone, as if dutifully calling in all Bailey's legwork. The only piece I could truly call my own was a slot headed 'Locals Keeping a Veil of Silence', which was not much good to anyone – a farmer saying, 'She would wave to me from the car, or offer me a lift, which I would never take. She was a real lady . . . she lived a quiet life, and that's that.' The real meat was in Bailey's material: 'Gardaí want to know whether she was awoken by her killer, demanding admittance . . . blood on the back door . . .'

I segued into brief analysis at the end of a spread inside: 'The sheer ferocity of the death blows which rained down upon the victim holds some indication as to motive. Robbery and sexual assault are not thought likely to have been the authors of the crime, leaving only an offence of passion – jealousy or hate.' Bailey had told me his information was that the victim had not been sexually assaulted, but I certainly couldn't use that without checking it the next day, and putting it to the press office. I realised straightaway that it was operationally sensitive – and anyway readers would indulge their own prudery or prurience on the issue when it was left unsaid. I took the information at face value, but was also keeping something in reserve. The newsdesk would be mooching in the morning, asking what else I could get. For now, I wrote, 'Whoever killed Sophie probably feels very pleased with themselves . . . in all likelihood miles ahead of a garda investigation which has very little evidence to go on. Officers must hope that the same cockiness and pride will eventually lead to the undoing and unmasking of the mystery man who could commit so foul a deed.' It was the best I could manage.

We didn't see Bailey that next day, learning instead something of Sophie's last movements and venturing farther south to follow the tyre furrows of her Fiesta. Before heading back to Dublin, we finished off our trip in style by driving out to Mizen Head, Ireland's most southwesterly point. I insisted on using one of Martin's cameras, all nicely pre-set so the dumb reporter couldn't muck it up, to picture him at Ultima Thule, beyond which none could travel. He was truly the mileage champion of *The Star*, thumbs-up in triumph. That might sound callous, but every job needs its lighter moments.

At that early stage, on a more carefree day after the previous embarrassment, I still had absolutely no idea how much mileage this case was destined to generate.

CHAPTER 10

Murder, He Wrote

Our stringer was perplexing, but nobody could deny he delivered the goods. On Saturday, 28 December, he provided *The Star* with an extraordinary angle, this time under his own byline, Eoin Bailey:

> Miss du Plantier may have held the most vital clue of all in the palm of her hand as she lay dying in the boreen beside her house. She had a clump of hair in her hand from the head of the attacker. Traces of skin were also found under her fingernails suggesting she scratched her attacker in a desperate fight for life.

This was news gold. Reading it in a Dublin café, I couldn't help but be impressed. Bailey had the key to the whole horror. Sophie had left a legacy to investigators that would pinpoint the person responsible for her death. It was nothing less than a farewell Christmas gift to the forensics folk. I felt a kind of elation as I sipped my coffee. *They're actually going to nail the bastard*, I thought. It could be within days. Whoever it is, there'll be a great trial at the end of it; Irish and French media down the Four Courts, head-ducking to avoid swinging TV cameras, an international media posse in full hue and cry.

I read it again. 'Clump of hair in her hand.' *From the head of the attacker*, no less. *Traces of skin under her fingernails. She scratched her attacker.* It was remarkable how Bailey had obtained details of the postmortem within three days of it being carried out, since he had filed this extraordinary exclusive only the day before. Bailey was just too good. How on earth was he accessing this level of information?

We'll have to go down again, I thought. If it was kicking off like this, there would surely be further developments. I'd have a word with the desk on Monday. It would be its own reward to be on the ground when hopes were suddenly soaring high. It warranted the full treatment, with interviews and descriptive pieces ahead of the inevitable and sensational break in the case. I knew instinctively that not only would the *Sun* and *Mirror* be down in Schull next week, but also the French dragoons – *Le Parisien, Paris Match, Le Figaro, VSD* – as well as television crews. I was looking forward to the trip, lifted by this news of hard forensic evidence.

But how to explain his uncanny accuracy with a story printed in *The Star* on St Stephen's Day – filed when I'd been tucking into turkey the day before. Bailey had the main live news item: the hunt for Sophie's killer was intensifying. He wrote: 'Ms du Plantier had been beaten to death

85

with a blunt instrument. A postmortem revealed that she died of multiple head injuries and was not sexually assaulted.'

As far as I knew, Bailey and the rest of the press had been kept firmly away from the body, unable to see around a corner to over 130 metres away where it lay covered with plastic. When I had got to the scene myself, I hadn't been able to prise anything out of the guards, even when asking basic questions. The formal forensic truth of this nugget – 'not sexually assaulted' – would still take weeks to establish. Yet, I couldn't understand how Bailey appeared to know more on the day after the postmortem than the pathologist who had actually performed it.

The advice to me from *The Star* newsdesk, meanwhile, was to wait a few more days before returning for a recce. I could cover the unfolding case from Dublin, ringing local personnel and the Garda Press Office. My stories began to reflect a plain-vanilla perception of events.

The Star of Friday, 3 January 1997 contained another story from Bailey: 'DNA Plan in Search for Killer'. A number of men were being asked for hair samples, to enable comparison with 'a clump of hair found in Ms du Plantier's hand after her desperate struggle', he wrote, while stating that 'obtaining a genetic fingerprint from the hair will take weeks'. Bailey further suggested: 'Although film-maker Sophie arrived alone from France, she could have been followed to her luxury holiday home.' Yet gardaí were keeping an open mind, just as 'her marriage to second husband Daniel has been described as open', he wrote. The holiday home was in both their names, he (wrongly) continued, before adding suggestively: 'Mr du Plantier has so far not asked to visit the murder scene. His wife went by her maiden name in West Cork . . .'

Murder, he wrote, and it went on and on, sometimes in terms approaching casual misogyny: 'Gardaí now believe Sophie did not have sex on the night of her brutal slaying, but she could have had a visitor. She may have left the luxury converted farmhouse with this person to walk them to the gate, and was bludgeoned to death there.'

Introducing terms like luxury to describe the farmhouse was also suggestive. In truth, it was anything but. The family considered the house impossibly cold, and Sophie needed an electric fire in her bedroom, supplemented by a hot-water bottle on her last night alive, having discovered that one of her walls was weeping damp. Undoubtedly the château at Ambax was more in the five-star line, becoming a 'sanctuary' for the grieving husband.

Bailey's spicy reportage continued: 'It has now emerged that two local men could have heard Sophie's cries for help. They were returning home in the early hours when they heard what they thought was the sound of a wailing fox. But it could have been the screams of the dying woman as she was savagely beaten.'

Bailey's ownership of the story was strange to the point of domineering. And there was something irredeemably tacky, even lewd, about his preoccupations. I had increasing misgivings about the outlandish, libidinous nature of his claims. Bailey wrote about Sophie's 'tangled love life' for more than one newspaper. She was 'twice-married Sophie' murdered near her 'isolated hideaway used . . . as a love nest' in one of his early reports to *The Star*.

He also suckered the *Sunday World*, which ran a front-page splash just six days after the murder, 'French Lover Killed Sophie': 'An evil French brute tracked lovely Sophie Toscan du Plantier to Ireland and murdered her for Christmas, gardaí believe.' Plus: 'Locals say she always brought a number of male companions to her fabulous West Cork home', with careless suggestion of a troupe of lovers all at once.

A *Sunday World* reporter from this time recalls: 'We were onto the Garda Press Office the following week, and the fella says, "Sure, what are you ringing us for? You whores have it all solved."' Meanwhile in the *Star* and *Tribune*, Sophie supposedly 'planned to divorce her second husband Daniel and rejoin her first'. Soon it was falsely claimed that Sophie had been married three times, while she '"would often visit with a different man each time", said one local, who asked not to be named'.

I was perplexed by these reports. This wasn't what I was hearing.

It was becoming garish. On 8 January 1997, *The Star* splashed 'Woman Among Sophie Suspects'. Labelled 'Exclusive' in a white-on-black headline on an inside-page report, Bailey revealed that a woman – a 'young mother' – had been subjected to DNA testing. Bailey's authorship was concealed under the name 'Emer Healy', a non-existent person used by *The Star* as a flag of convenience. I suspected it was Bailey. He said the guards had called the woman a suspect, yet he had also managed to obtain an interview. 'I am very upset,' she said. 'I had my hair roughly pulled and hacked from my head with a blunt razor blade. That was

SOPHIE: THE FINAL VERDICT

upsetting enough, but what has really made me angry is to see myself being referred to as a suspect.' But any idea that a woman had wielded the concrete block against another of her sex was simply preposterous.

Further stories kept rolling out from Bailey, as he cast the suspect net further afield and away from Cork. I had a growing unease about the tone and content of these stories being published in our paper. They seemed far-fetched yet contained supposed insider information that defied explanation. I vividly remember approaching Dave O'Connell on the desk, on more than one occasion, demanding to know why we were confusing readers by publishing contradictory stories in each edition – by me as crime correspondent in Dublin, reflecting signs pointing to a local killer, but also from Bailey in West Cork indicating a French element.

Dave looked apologetic, lolled his head and made expansive hand gestures, mumbling excuses. Covering all angles, etc. While I protested against it, motivated by the idea that we should impart the truth as best disclosed and not send readers down rabbit holes, the printed delusion grew worse. 'The belief in West Cork is that there is definitely a French connection,' wrote Bailey, going on to finger a 'Breton writer' and a 'Paris-based artist', pointing suspicion away from Ireland. Next, detectives were supposedly 'trying to trace a Paris-registered white Citroën van seen leaving West Cork on Christmas Day'.

It was only much later that the full truth about the approved publication of Bailey's articles emerged – exonerating Dave, and explaining an otherwise incomprehensible doublespeak that I had never before – and, thankfully, since – witnessed in my professional career.

*

I wasn't the only one who was becoming aware of Bailey's tenuous grasp of the truth in his published articles. 'Miss du Plantier had a taste for the fine cheeses of West Cork,' reported Bailey in the *Sunday Tribune* on 26 January 1997. He anonymously quoted a cheesemaker who had met Sophie several times, calling Bill Hogan a 'local trader', without naming him.

> 'She told me how much she loved being here and how she felt at ease. We shared a glass of wine and some cheese,' said the local trader. 'And suddenly she seemed to relax. She told me, "You won't believe how complicated my life is in France. I would love to come here, but I have a lot of complications to sort out,"' he said.
>
> At this point, he said, she confided in him: '"I have decided to leave my husband."' The local man was surprised at her frankness.

Reading this claim of a marital split, Bill Hogan, an affable New Yorker, was furious. He had never said that. It didn't happen. He was not so much 'surprised at her frankness', as astounded and angered at Bailey for making it up and putting words in his mouth that he had never said. Bill had no idea about Sophie's private life.

He protested to Bailey about the invented quote. But

SOPHIE: THE FINAL VERDICT

Bailey calmed Bill down, talking him round. 'He said he was trying to flush people out. He was the best reporter in Ireland, and he was going to solve the crime.' Hogan let the matter drop, because Bailey was so convincing, going on to warn about larger, sinister forces at work. French cinema was corrupt. There were wheels within wheels.

Bill Hogan told the author that Bailey 'had a theory about Sophie's husband, Daniel, a very powerful man, with all types of connections, including the Corsican mafia, who had backed his films financially. He interrogated me on my knowledge of Sophie, and I told him what I had told the guards. I think it was on the third or fourth visit that Ian said he had to go to France to solve this crime, that he was going to do investigative journalism in France to prove that the husband had done it.

'Ian Bailey called to me again the following Monday [3 February 1997]. He said to me that he could not go to France, that gardaí think he is the chief suspect and that if he went to France, he was afraid he would be arrested. I was upset, and I shouted at him, "What do you mean? You're the reporter, not the suspect!" The outburst provoked an extraordinary reaction.

'Ian whacked himself on the forehead with his hand and his head went backwards. He straightened himself and he said that he would "go down for mental like that guy from Sligo", which was a case in previous years to this. He went on to say that he couldn't remember what happened that night; that maybe he should visit a psychiatrist to get hypnotised, to see what really happened. I got him right out of my house at this stage, and called the Bandon gardaí. The same afternoon I was visited by two or three gardaí and I told them what Bailey had confided.'

Bill Hogan remembers that he had said to himself 'that Ian had done this murder; that he killed her, he was a murderer'.

The 'Sligo case' to which Bailey referred involved a man called John Gallagher who shot dead his ex-girlfriend, eighteen-year-old Anne Gillespie, and her mother, Annie, fifty-one, in the grounds of Sligo General Hospital in 1988. Then aged twenty-two, Gallagher was tried for murder but was found insane. Twelve years later, he escaped from detention at the Central Mental Hospital and went on the run. He later returned to the Republic from Northern Ireland, and was sent back to the secure institution. But, after a fresh psychiatric assessment, Gallagher was deemed sane – and freed. It was how Irish law stood at the time.

The *Sunday Tribune* front-page lead story of 19 January 1997 featured a joint byline, with a journalist called Sophie Rieu reporting on the French aspects of the case, and Bailey covering Irish angles.

Sophie Rieu must have experienced my sense of bafflement when our individual reporting collided with Bailey's version of events. In the same article as a Bailey invention about impending divorce, she quoted by name Valérie Bouffard, 'a close colleague of du Plantier at Unifrance', who rejected the idea that the couple were on the point of separating. On the contrary, 'they wanted to have a baby', Bouffard said. 'Sophie had even decided to call the baby Thérèse if it were a girl.' This chimed with husband Daniel's statement to French police that Sophie had stopped taking contraception. Daniel said he was happy to have a child, and knew of her hope for a girl, to be named Thérèse, a sister for Pierre-Louis. Indeed, Sophie had spoken to her housekeeper, Josie Hellen, about how she would love a baby girl.

Sophie Rieu also quoted Pierre-André Boutang, president of the Arte television channel, for whom Sophie had made documentaries. Boutang pointed out that Sophie had sold her Paris flat in 1995, 'a sign, he believes, that her relationship with her husband was healthier. He says "It was one of the places where she liked to be when things were not going well at home. Her husband's public life was very demanding. Almost every evening he had to attend a gala or a cocktail party, and she did not like being in the limelight. She was a very private person".' Besides, Daniel remained on very good terms with both his ex-wives, Marie-Christine Barrault and Francesca Comencini. 'These two women were even invited to every social gathering,' Rieu reported. No wonder Sophie might sometimes want to be elsewhere.

But Bailey had to have it his way. He had written one loaded story for the *Sunday Tribune* on 12 January that began: 'The husband of murdered French film-maker Sophie Toscan du Plantier is to be brought to West Cork to assist gardaí in their enquiries.' The story was wholly untrue, even as Bailey sneered about 'Garda speculation that the killer is still in the vicinity', saying that they had a 'hunch' – merely – that the killer 'might be a local'.

Well warmed up by now, the next story by Bailey to appear was perhaps the most grandiose of all: Daniel Toscan du Plantier 'had taken out a large amount of [life] insurance on his wife, and he was the beneficiary'. It was an absolute lie.

Sophie's dearest friend Agnès Thomas saw Daniel on 30 December 1996 at Sophie's funeral in rural Mauvezin, near Ambax in southwest France, where he linked arms with her son, Pierre-Louis, as they followed the coffin.

Daniel was 'devastated', and felt guilty only at not being present to protect his wife when she was fatally attacked. 'I feel responsible. I should have been there,' he sadly confided in Agnès, his agony enduring.

CHAPTER 11

False Leads and Forensics

While Bailey was intent on filling acres of newsprint with lurid accounts of Sophie's life and death, the official investigation into the murder was ramping up. The state pathologist had been busy uncovering scientific evidence as to the cause of her horrific demise.

Professor John Harbison had before him on the gurney Sophie's mortal remains. The body had formally been identified by Garda Pat Joy as 'Sophie Toscan du Plantier, otherwise Bouniol, believed to be thirty-eight years, of Château de Lamézan, Ambax, near Toulouse'. It was 1.57 p.m. on Christmas Eve. In the presence of several gardaí, with fifth-year medical student Robert Lowe acting as morgue technician, the postmortem got underway.

Sophie's clothing was described aloud to a garda notetaker as it was removed. Then Harbison reported on the body. 'The dead woman had long hair which had become entangled in vegetation. It was obvious that she had severe head injuries because there were gaping wounds on the right side of the forehead and the right ear was severely lacerated at its lower edge. There appeared to be abrasions, and not mere blood-staining, of the right cheek. Beneath the lacerations on the right side of the forehead I could see [brain] tissue and noted there was depression of the skull extending from the right eyebrow back as far as the temporal bone.

'I took scrapings from the fingernails of both hands and placed them in plastic bags held by Detective Garda Joy,' wrote Harbison. 'In doing this, a number of hairs, almost a dozen, were adherent to, and even wound around, fingers of the right hand. Because of dried blood, these were removed with difficulty and some of them parted. I found one long and one very short hair adherent to the back of the left hand.' The police present were evidently pleased and extremely hopeful about what these vestiges revealed.

Harbison, in his preliminary report, delivered on the same day as the autopsy on Christmas Eve, concluded Sophie had died from multiple head injuries, fractures of the skull and laceration of the brain. 'There were gross injuries of the head, neck, arms and hands,' he wrote in a later more detailed report, though he briefed gardaí orally as he went along. 'These hand injuries, including fractures, constituted defensive wounds, indicating that she put up a considerable fight.' A cut which broke the left index finger could have been caused by a 'sharp weapon', but generally they were bludgeoning, blunt injuries.

The report notes three times that a Doc Marten boot could have been used to kick or scuff the body. Gardaí separately had an incomplete boot print in mud from the scene to back up this theory. Harbison, who was used to heinous crimes, saw 'consistent superficial abrasions of parallel nature' among the skull injuries. The likely cause was some surface sliding along the skin. 'I did suggest that they could have been caused by impact from footwear with linear markings, such as a Doc Marten boot.' In the neck area, there were up to nine similar abrasions. 'These resemble slightly the imprint of a Doc Marten boot, but could have been inflicted by some weighted object passing across the skin of the neck.' Next, 'on the back of the right wrist was another collection of closely spaced linear abrasions suggestive of the imprint of a Doc Marten boot'.

The garda boot print was somewhat consistent with the sole pattern of that company's classic 1460 eight-eye boot, which had metallic eyelets, but it did not exclude other brands of boot. It was not, however, like the sole of Sophie's own footwear. Harbison said of the body: 'I pulled off the left boot without untying its somewhat strangely located bow knot. There were several thistles embedded in the laces and the sock band around the top. The boots were made in Italy of the Fiorella brand.' Bailey reported on the subject of boots in the *Sunday Tribune* of 2 February 1997: 'This week detectives in West Cork took shoe and boot samples from a number of local people to match against footprints found at the scene.'

Harbison dealt economically with the fact that Sophie's body had lost all temperature before it was removed from the scene, meaning there could be no working-back to establish a reliable time of death. 'When I visited the scene, the body had lain scantily clad in the open for twenty-four hours since its discovery,' he wrote, 'and probably several more before it was discovered.' But he went on to address the question to which investigators desperately wanted an answer: when was she killed?

Her body 'still had the remains of a recently ingested meal in the stomach', seemingly fruit pulp, slightly yellow in colour, but consistent with oranges. There were some in a bowl in her cottage. Harbison made the point that 'if Ms du Plantier had died after breakfast on the 23rd, her body would still have been warm to the touch', never mind the advanced rigor mortis seen by a GP later that morning. But 'if it were her evening meal, she would have died within two or three hours, and if she had lain all night in the open, would therefore have been cold and stiff on discovery, the weather being cold and frosty . . . The circumstances would therefore seem to favour death the previous evening or night'.

Harbison had twenty-two years' experience, sometimes dealing with bodies found much longer after death. It is noteworthy that the French authorities would exhume Sophie's remains in France in July 2008, nearly twelve years later. A team of expert medical examiners found nothing wrong with any element of Harbison's main findings; in fact, they concurred with them all.

Separately, Harbison had found no outward sign of injury to the genitalia, but a whole series of swabs would be sent to the laboratory for detailed analysis, the results expected in six weeks. In a handwritten summary, separate to his thirteen-page report, Harbison signed himself State Forensic

Pathologist, before penning the additional words *Specialiste en Médecine Légale* in flawless French.

Unfortunately for the early hopes and aspirations of the investigators, the idea that Sophie had pulled hair from her attacker proved misplaced. Forensic scientist Geraldine O'Donnell reported weeks afterwards that she 'mounted for microscopic examination the five hairs taken from the right hand . . . it is my opinion that they were consistent with having originated from Sophie Toscan du Plantier's head hair'. Sophie must have touched her own caving head wounds at some point, hair coming away stickily in her hand. The finding was deeply disappointing. The guards would have to find the killer through other avenues of evidence.

*

Detectives were following all lines of enquiry, attempting to establish Sophie's final movements. Questionnaires were sent out to every household in the vicinity – officers hopeful that any small clue would help them find Sophie's murderer, who remained at large.

Seeds of confusion as to her movements in the lead-up to her death – and who she may have been with – were starting to be sown. A man named Seán Murray claimed to have seen Sophie in her rented Fiesta at a garage in Skibbereen on the day of her arrival. He told gardaí on New Year's Eve that he had a 'strong feeling' it was Sophie on that Friday before Christmas. At some time before 3 p.m., a Fiesta called into the garage for petrol, turning off the main N71 road. It had a 1996 Cork registration, and he thought it was 'blue or grey', wrong for Sophie's silver Ford, but he was sure it was a rental because the hubcaps were missing. 'I am in the motor trade and I would recognise a hired car.' The driver was an attractive woman with 'longish' gold-blonde hair, tied in a ponytail. She wore little make-up, and was aged in her late thirties or early forties.

What Murray said next was arresting. 'There was a gent sitting in the passenger seat . . . next to the pump. I asked the lady what she wanted. She did not appear to understand.' The gent said something to her; then she smiled: 'Full, please.' Murray filled the car with unleaded petrol. The man handed over a banknote to meet the cost – 'an even tenner'. He was tall, his head nearly touching the car roof, and much the same age as the lady. Murray did not get a good look, but thought him dark. He might have had a beard. He never spoke 'but looked Irish'. The car drove off from Hurley's in Skibbereen, towards Schull. 'I remember thinking them home for Christmas. The driver was French, without a doubt.'

But there *is* a doubt. Sophie's silver rental, photographed after her death, had all four hubcaps. On the other hand, the passenger seat was tracked back a little when compared to that of the driver, its back support a good deal more reclined. Neither footwell was clean, but the driver's was noticeably more used. There was no paper detritus anywhere – certainly no receipts. A 1996 'tenner' amounts to an overfill of the Fiesta's tank if it had been anywhere near full when the car left Cork airport that same day, as would be standard for a rental vehicle.

Murray said gardaí later told him they had a statement – Kitty Kingston's – from another filling station when there was nobody else in Sophie's car as she stopped to buy firewood. But Murray now recalled the woman asking, as she bought petrol, if Hurley's sold firewood. He did not put that detail into his original garda statement. 'I can't understand why nobody ever came back to me,' said Murray. 'I've no doubt the woman I saw was her.'

The puzzle showcases the potential for error in all witness accounts. However, it did raise the question: was Sophie ever travelling with a man? And, if so, when and who was he?

On Tuesday, 21 January, Bailey reported on a case conference at Bantry garda station, 'to pool information and leads, and analyse evidence from France'. He wrote, 'Inspector Liam Horgan said last night: "We are open-minded. We are not saying that it is a local or a French national that we are looking for."' Bailey also reported that gardaí were 'checking on all flights and ferries into and out of Ireland, trying to discover if one of her male friends was with her when she travelled to West Cork'. Seán Murray, if he was right – a huge if – would have Sophie with a companion as she travelled to West Cork, the man waving his tenner out the window.

Then, there was the Bailey bulletin that 'Gardaí have interviewed a number of foreign men living in the remote area . . . Interpol and the French police are checking out possible suspects'. And no wonder, because Bailey said that Sophie was 'known to have had a complicated private life. She and her husband had an open marriage, and had relationships with other people'. It was odious exaggeration, and yet he reported that other possible suspects 'include a number of robbers, embezzlers, drug dealers and even a paedophile who had been found guilty of abusing children'.

*

The gardaí had been busy in France too. Bailey had falsely reported in the *Sunday Tribune* of 26 January that they had come back 'empty-handed', and that interviews had been refused because gardaí 'did not have the proper authorisations'. There was an overtone of an investigation adrift: the gardaí had 'excluded no-one', and, worse, Daniel du Plantier 'who said he was too busy to journey to Ireland to identify his wife's body, told members of the French press corps that he personally intended to oversee the investigation' – this from the man whom Bailey had practically ordered extradited in handcuffs in a previous report.

There was Bruno Carbonnet, Sophie's one-time lover, with whom she'd had an affair during her marriage to Daniel. Bailey had correctly reported that she had brought him to the house in Dunmanus West. He had also alluded to Bruno as a prime suspect. But Carbonnet had a solid alibi for the murder weekend, having signed a receipt in relation to a new phone, while also dining in the company of friends who would vouch for him.

Carbonnet was interviewed very early on – 28 December – by Police Lieutenant Jean-Luc Rondele of the judicial police at a station in Le Havre, where he lived. Sophie and Bruno's affair had ended in 1993, and his account thoroughly checked out. Bruno Carbonnet was disregarded as a suspect on several grounds.

Detective Superintendent Dermot Dwyer would repudiate all Bailey's claims of hopeless bungling: 'We eliminated every possible suspect in Paris. We left nothing undone.'

*

While Bailey had been largely left to his own devices, I was back in Dublin and working on other crime stories and fresh murders: 'Call girl clients are being begged for help by gardaí, desperate to track down the killer of Sri Lankan sex worker Belinda Pereira . . .'

Below this story was another by Bailey, with the startling headline 'Mine Search for Murder Weapon'. I read on: 'Gardaí are searching a disused mine for the weapon used to bludgeon 38-year-old [sic] Frenchwoman Sophie . . . They have also extended house-to-house enquiries. And they are questioning a greater number of people. But so far they have not made any breakthrough. They hope forensic results will help their investigations. The murder continues to attract major media attention in France.'

It was nonsensical. There was a rock and block beside the body – weren't these the murder weapons? Once more, I was perplexed. What was clear was that my original esti-mation that gardaí would have it wrapped up in a fortnight was looking less and less likely.

Unbeknownst to me, by then work was intensifying for investigating officers. Was a major tip-off from a member of the public the key breakthrough they had been waiting for in the search for Sophie's killer?

CHAPTER 12

The Clue at Kealfadda

Garda Noel Banbury picked up the ringing phone in the public office of Bandon garda station just past midday on 11 January 1997. There were never many calls on Saturdays. When the caller spoke, he paid immediate attention.

'Hello, my name is Fiona. I have information about the murder.'

He asked her to continue.

'I saw a man at Kealfadda bridge on the Monday morning, about 4 a.m. I don't know who it was, but that's it.'

The caller was briefly persuaded to give further fragmentary details until she abruptly hung up. Banbury recognised the potential significance of the tip-off. 'I immediately contacted Bantry garda station and asked to speak to the incident room. I passed on to Superintendent Dermot Dwyer exactly the information this lady gave me.' It wasn't much, summed up in garda flyer no. 435: 'An unknown female, who gave her name as Fiona, rang Bandon GS at 12.05 p.m. on 11 January 1997 and stated that on the Sunday/Monday morning [of the murder] at 4 a.m. she observed a lone male near the knitwear shop on the Schull–Goleen road. He was wearing a long black coat and some kind of hat. He appeared to be wiping himself and stumbling along. She stated that she will probably ring back with her identity in [the] near future.'

The call was not recorded, but could be traced. A special effort showed it led to a public telephone box in Cornmarket Street in Cork city. Whoever placed it, codenamed Fiona, was taking precautions.

Senior officers were excited, since the location given for the sighting was the end of the twisting hill road leading from Sophie's holiday home. A squad car was sent, with gardaí instructed to carry out a discreet search for any discarded personal items, especially clothing. They were to look carefully up to two hundred metres west from Kealfadda bridge, in the vicinity of Sylvia Connell's woollens shop. Sophie's road was known as Kealfadda, since it was parallel to the long stream, *caol fada*, that empties into the sea below the main road. The area, like others, had already been screened, but this would require a scouring.

Officers in the meantime had to keep an open mind: one possibility was that 'Fiona' was personally connected to the killer, despite her assertion that the man she had seen was a stranger. Gardaí could not think of any likely Fiona in the local area; it was indeed probably an alias. The caller's elaborate secrecy seemed to heighten the significance of Banbury's contact – even though nothing of note would be found in the search ordered at Kealfadda. But there were no more calls from Fiona. It was beyond frustrating.

*

Undeterred in their efforts, the guards were certain that someone knew something. They had been to Three Castles Head, and interviewed Yvonne Ungerer on Christmas Eve. Bailey too had tracked her down, acting on local gossip, highlighting her in print in the *Sunday Tribune* on 19 January as one of the vital last witnesses. Bailey heard from Yvonne about Sophie's eerie feelings on her walk – which prompted his own disclosure to Yvonne of his unease on Hunt's Hill the night of the murder. She told gardaí in a statement on 22 January: 'I have been thinking about what he said to me [about] a premonition as he was looking at the place where Sophie lived, by moonlight . . . a black or foreboding feeling. He couldn't explain it, but said these premonitions he had usually came true.' Now Bailey would be forced to admit to the guards his strange stop at Hunt's Hill on the night of Sophie's murder.

The national television programme *Crimeline* was set to broadcast on Monday, 20 January. It would feature a recon-struction of Sophie arriving at her holiday home, visiting Schull and driving to the end of the Mizen Peninsula, all aimed at jogging memories and bringing forward new witnesses. Any trivial piece of information could unwittingly prove crucial, even though officers had already taken over a thousand statements.

Actor Anne Cahalane, who played Sophie in the recon-struction and bore a strong physical resemblance to her, had been hearing odd rumours about Bailey, whom she didn't know. It was a coincidence that the woman cast as *Crimeline* 'Sophie' – who lived in Dublin – happened to also have a holiday home in Schull. She was aware at the time of talk beginning locally about a peculiar English character – and how he was viewed as a viable suspect.

During filming, amid directors, technicians and people carrying call-sheets, Anne donned a blonde wig and instantly became Sophie, alive once again at Three Castles Head. A handful of spectators were at the reconstruction, watching enthralled, until a voice called a cut to the cameras rolling. Then, it slowly became Anne Cahalane's turn to feel a deep sense of unease.

A man, who turned out to be Bailey, 'came bounding over the fields' during the break in proceedings and began 'enthusiastic' conversation, telling her he was a journalist covering the story. He had an English accent. He told her that he knew Ms Toscan du Plantier and had met her on this very walk. He was smiling, looking into her face, searching for a reaction.

Anne didn't know what to say, struck silent as she was by his claim that he knew the victim, with local talk of the suspect at the forefront of her mind. He was 'animated and quite excited'. Her partner Peter Wilson, who had been keeping an eye on her, soon came over. He said hello to Bailey, who wore a long green raincoat and wellingtons. Bailey said he was a journalist working on the murder, repeating what he had told Anne.

'He told us he knew her and had met her on that walk, of that I'm absolutely sure,' said Anne. 'I have no doubt Ian

Bailey came over to talk to us because he knew we were reconstructing the Sophie case.' He might have claimed an 'inside track', but certainly 'an insight,' she said. Wilson's impression was that Bailey had said at Three Castles Head that he knew the Frenchwoman other than from meeting her on the walk there. The conversation was brief because Cahalane and Wilson had been cautioned by gardaí not to talk to anyone about what they were doing, its purpose, or any aspect of the crime. Wilson now told Anne he needed a quiet word, and Bailey read the signals to clear off.

After he left, Peter reminded Anne that they been asked by their garda liaison to stop filming in a bar in Schull, two days before. Intended to represent O'Sullivan's in Crookhaven, Wilson had been playing the barman. Ian Bailey and other gawkers had turned up at the bar, and filming was only resumed when they were safely off the premises.

Eventually the reconstruction was in the can. The subsequent *Crimeline* broadcast recorded a viewership far above the average. The Irish people were already hugely engaged with the case, and the broadcast brought a torrent of telephone calls to the special number featured on screen.

In addition to a general appeal for public assistance, Chief Superintendent Noel Smith looked squarely at the camera and especially requested that a caller named Fiona get back in touch. He asked her to contact Bandon garda station 'in complete confidence'.

*

The next day, a Tuesday, Fiona did just that. She repeated the information she gave in the previous call ten days earlier.

Gardaí attempted to keep her talking, asking questions, imploring her to come to Bandon to speak to detectives in person. But Fiona was jumpy. She terminated the call after less than a minute, having added nothing more to the details she had given about the sighting at Kealfadda bridge. Garda engineers laboriously traced the call. This time it led to a public phone box in the village of Leap, County Cork. This was two-thirds closer to Schull than the Cork city payphone of the first call, but still thirty-three kilometres away.

Gardaí had to fervently hope Fiona would call again. All personnel at Bandon were briefed to pay special attention to anyone identifying themselves by that name and to get her out of public view as soon as possible if she happened to come into the station. Next, arrangements were made to record all calls to the number Fiona had twice dialled, since it was not the special number shown on the *Crimeline* programme. That led to Bantry garda station, where public calls were automatically available on playback. Efforts were made to bring Schull garda station up to speed. With all bases covered, they waited.

Three days later, on 24 January, Fiona telephoned Bandon again. She would not be coming in, she said. She had already told them all she knew. 'Could she give any better description of the man she had seen? they asked. But seconds later she was gone again. Once more, the trace team got down to work, expecting to run up against another anonymous phone box. But no, hours later their diligent efforts turned up trumps. The call had come from a private house in Schull. There were cheers in the incident room. Breakthrough!

The pinpoint lead still had to be verified, without alerting the person who had placed the calls. Gardaí from Schull station were asked to come to Bantry, one by one, to listen to the recorded voice of the female on the phone call, believed to be one of their townsfolk. They were not told the name.

Garda Kevin Kelleher was the third or fourth guard brought in. Unlike the others, he wasn't the slightest bit puzzled. 'I recognised the voice as that of Marie Farrell of Crewe Bay, Schull. I confirmed this voice. I was asked how well did I know her, and said I knew her to speak to.' The information matched with the registered occupant of the house. They were in business.

'I was subsequently directed to approach Marie Farrell, the person who had been making calls,' Kelleher said. 'My memory was that I was to confirm she was Fiona, and if so, to introduce her to Detective Gardaí Jim Fitzgerald and Jim Slattery.'

On 28 January, four days after the traced call, Kelleher paid a visit to Marie Farrell at her shop, Tara Fashions, on Main Street. The 'two Jims' were at Schull garda station, as prearranged. Kelleher had a ruse in order to get Farrell away for a private conversation. 'I told her I wanted her to view some footage in my house – the only place I had a VCR machine to play the Christmas Swim video,' recently requisitioned from Florence Newman. Marie Farrell agreed to follow. 'I brought Marie into my sitting room, sat her down and went over to the video recorder. I put on the tape of the Christmas Swim.

'A short time into the tape, I remember I was standing at the television, and I asked Marie Farrell, "Are you Fiona?"

Her answer was, "Fuck it, I should never had made that phone call from home." That reply stands out in my mind to this day.'

Kelleher told her that two detectives were waiting to speak to her and she agreed to meet them. He left the room to call Schull station, asking the others to come to his house. 'While waiting on them to arrive, my recollection is that Marie was worried about Chris, her husband, finding out that she was out that night.'

The two detectives arrived within minutes and were introduced. Kelleher went out to make tea for everyone. 'I can't recall if the video was still running when the lads arrived, but no reference was made to it while the two Jims were speaking with Marie.' There was also nothing being written down by either detective. The encounter was as informal as possible.

'During the conversations I recall Marie Farrell making reference to Ian Bailey. The context she said it in was her sighting of Ian Bailey at Kealfadda bridge.' Kelleher's strange syntax hardly conveys the drama of the bombshell moment when the guards finally had a name for the man seen stumbling along the road on the night of the murder. Breathtakingly, it was Bailey, the man scooping the world on a headline-hogging crime.

'She agreed to show us the location. Marie was told she had nothing to worry about, that the gardaí understood her situation, but that we needed her help.'

CHAPTER 13

Positive Identification

Marie Farrell appeared a golden witness at first. She put Ian Bailey at Kealfadda bridge in the early hours on the night of Sophie's murder. From early on, however, the reliability of her statements became shaky.

She gave several versions of events. The sighting was pulled back from 4 a.m. to 3 a.m. She had been the passenger in a car, driving back to Schull, when she saw the figure at Kealfadda. She wouldn't say the driver's name because she did not want her husband, Chris, to know. Yes, it was a man. An old flame. She had five children to think about. Detectives understood that the man was also married. Still, her refusal to name him robbed them for the time being of a vital corroborating witness.

Kevin Kelleher accompanied Marie Farrell to Kealfadda, where she pointed out the exact spot: the second reflector stick fifty metres west of the bridge, beyond the junction of Sophie's road with the main artery. The stranger had been moving his hands up and down his face, as if washing, or smacking on aftershave. Marie said she now knew it to be Ian Bailey, whom she had seen as a stranger outside her shop in Schull on the Saturday. She also claimed that Sophie had come in to browse in her shop that Saturday, but bought nothing. Later, she claimed that Sophie had bought a brown Carraig Donn sweater, but there was no such garment found in the house and no equivalent till transaction.

The man at Kealfadda was on the opposite side to her car, towards the sea rather than the hills, in the place for traffic heading in the other direction, and he was walking towards Goleen – farther away from both the holiday home and The Prairie. She looked diagonally across at him on the right. The man seemed to be shielding himself, with both hands up. But the guards had to think that the reaction might simply have been produced by the dazzling glare of the headlights, which were on high beam.

Later Marie gave an account placing the man on the other side of the road. He was still walking west, but 'on my side of the road'. Subsequently too, she gave courtroom evidence that she had been driving alone. Her old boyfriend had simply dropped her back to the Nissan vanette she had parked at a rendezvous in Goleen, she said. She had then driven back to Schull by herself. The man had since died, she added.

*

Marie Farrell had also given gardaí a statement in her own name in January 1997, reporting the presence of a suspicious man in Schull. This was while simultaneously acting as their anonymous informant on the phone. She had phoned gardaí on Christmas Day 1996 under her own name, to describe a 'weird-looking character' she saw outside her shop four days earlier, on Saturday, 21 December. It had been preying on her mind since the murder, she said. She mentioned him 'taking long strides', a line entered in the station message book by Garda John Lordan. In her formal statement, made after a garda follow-up, the man walked towards the Allied Irish Bank, as Sophie had done after leaving Brosnan's supermarket. 'On the other side of the street, near McCarthy's butchers, I noticed a man pacing up and down the footpath. What drew my attention was his clothing. He was wearing a long black coat down to his ankles, a black flat beret. He was very tall.'

While some seize on the beret as a Gallic indicator, in fact, Bailey's hair sat strangely at this time. Moreover, Marie's account of the stranger is independently mirrored by that of eighty-year-old Dan Griffin, a retired publican, who told gardaí on 28 December that he had seen a man in Schull that same weekend. 'He had a long black coat down almost to his ankles. He had a black beret on his head. He was walking fairly lively, aged 35 to 40 years.' The brisk gait was noticeable because Dan's regular afternoon walk was much slower. 'I suffer a lot from arthritis.'

Dan went further: 'The man I saw was over six feet tall. He was taking very long strides.' Dan saw the man again within a fortnight, 'same height, same long step'. This time, he was linked arms with a lady and facing towards the old man. 'I saw the hair was very black and heavy, which may have appeared to me [as] a black beret when I first saw him. I now know the man as Ian Bailey. I have since spoken to people, including my daughter Bernie, who knows him.'

Marie Farrell had a further sighting of the suspicious man the next morning, Sunday 22nd, when she was on her way to a stall she operated in Cork city. It was early: 7 a.m. in one account, 7.30 by another. On the way into Schull from her home, farther west, she saw the man from Saturday now walking out of town. He thumbed for a lift, even though they were going in opposite directions. Marie noticed he was 'wearing the same clothes, had the face stubble and was no different from the day before'. She still didn't know who it was. Ian Bailey had spent the night in Schull at Mark Murphy's impromptu party. If this was Bailey, he must have given up thumbing and gone back into Schull, to return to the house where he was seen hours later by Tony Doran. This would mean he had made two abortive attempts to leave the party address, the other having been at 2 a.m. Mark Murphy would eventually drive him home that Sunday.

*

Marie's shop had a long Christmas closure, and she and her husband travelled to England by ferry to buy stock, which they packed into their vanette. Returning home and unloading everything, she reopened on Friday, 17 January. This explains the long delay between her first and second anonymous phone calls, on 11 and 21 January respectively. The Cork city one had been placed on the way to the ferry.

The next was after she came back, and caught the *Crimeline* programme on Monday, 20 January.

That Friday, 17 January, she saw the stranger again near the post office. 'I got an awful shock. I thought I'd never see this man again.' He was dressed differently, in a mauve mackintosh and green wellingtons. There was no 'beret' this time. 'I noticed his face was thinner and drawn, clean-shaven.' Marie dashed back to her shop and rang the garda station but there was no answer. She was about to drive there when two guards walked in with a questionnaire. She gabbled out her tale and 'they left immediately, and returned ten minutes later'. Was this the breakthrough as to who the strange man was? Unfortunately, no. 'They told me they couldn't find him.' The guards left.

Shortly afterwards Marie went down the street to get some groceries. She walked into Brosnan's. 'I immediately saw the man again. I left the shop – the two guards were there again.' She urgently told them, 'That's him,' pointing inside. She did not know his name. As Garda Mick McCarthy went into Brosnan's, the man was coming out. Marie made herself scarce, hiding. 'I didn't want this man to see me, or see me talking to the guards.' It was Ian Bailey, the same man Marie said she had eyed at Kealfadda bridge, if only for a few fleeting moments.

So far, so good. All this was complex, but comprehensible, even if Marie's Christmas Day call had suggested that the Saturday stalker of Sophie was 5 feet 10 inches – or six inches shorter than Bailey, whom at least one other witness also estimated at that lesser height. But people guess when unexpectedly asked for heights by guards. In any case, more significant contradictions in Marie Farrell's accounts would ultimately undermine her, but the Kealfadda sighting was everything for now – even if Farrell was already inconsistent.

*

The most Marie would say about her own companion the night Sophie died – Sunday into Monday, 22–23 December – was that she had met him in Goleen, where she left the vanette, getting into his vehicle, after she had worked at her stall in Cork city. They went out around Barleycove 'and stayed there for some time' – yet there were no sightings of the pair by the dark and empty trailer parks, or along the beach. 'I practically lived with this man one time, and Chris and I had had rows over him.' She had lied to her husband, saying she was meeting female friends that evening for a Christmas drink. She and her former lover had 'chatted about old times and things like that'. She was 'in an awful state' after being discovered by gardaí as the witness who had seen the man at Kealfadda, 'and the person [she was out with] is also married, and he is very worried'.

The figure from Kealfadda bridge was expanded upon in something Marie Farrell blurted out to her fourteen-year-old babysitter Leah Quinn, which might – if repeated – have led to the rumour of the man washing his boots that ran through Schull. Leah later told gardaí that 'a couple of weeks after the murder of the Frenchwoman', Marie told her that she was coming home 'from a friend's house, in the early hours . . . and saw Ian Bailey down by the river *washing his hands*'.

CHAPTER 14

Media Frenzy

The *Crimeline* programme propelled the murder back up the news agenda, and the day after broadcast, Tuesday, 21 January, I was down again in West Cork with 'Wallop'. Jim Walpole was an exceptional photographer with whom I'd worked on many murder cases. We were back in the East End Hotel in Schull – which would become Hack Central – and out again as soon as we had dumped our gear at reception.

There were limited local mutterings about Bailey, speculation merely, but we were blissfully unaware of them. I'd been covering a Mountjoy Prison riot and then had been in London for an underworld court appearance – with the paper relying on its West Cork stringer, the man of the murmurs, for the latest Sophie stirrings.

We took the Toyota through the fading light to get establishing shots in town. We would also need pictures of people who knew anything, and senior police who might pose. Along with this would go a story; something along the lines of the 'valley of the squinting windows', or a town under shadow, siege or suffering; essentially a form of 'holding copy', with the real work to be done the next day. We'd been told by the newsdesk not to contact Bailey: he had told *The Star* he was 'bought up' for the next few days, under the exclusive control of *Paris Match*. Fair enough, best of luck to him. In the meantime, we had our own leads to explore. It was also important for me to make face-to-face contact with gardaí I would be attempting to raise by phone when I got back to Dublin. It's harder to refuse a few words when you have previously met the guy.

The following morning we were out and about in the countryside. Aha! – there was the *Daily Mirror*. Our two cars slowed opposite each other on a hillside pass, with windows coming down. There was grinning and jeering among rivals, with jaunty 'Jumbo' Kierans saying he had been wondering how long it would take *The Star* to count the pennies from the piggybox and decide to 'send'. Next came a bit of feeling each other out, as to what each might know, with neither side revealing much – and each car then ostentatiously revving away, as if on a mission, just to unnerve the other.

There were also actual French-registered cars, besides rentals – denoting magazine writers who had taken a ferry to Ireland before the run to West Cork. They would be writing longer, descriptive pieces of the pain-in-paradise variety, because of an inherent Gallic aching for Ireland's rugged beauty. These *littérateurs* would come mechanically bounding around blind corners, hidden by shoulders of rock, because of course they were attempting to drive on an unnatural side of the road. It was somewhat alarming – *'Pardon, monsieur!'*

And then, a leak – a major break in the case: where it came from I had no idea, but it was gigantic, a show-stopper. A man had been seen washing his boots at Kealfadda bridge. The news seemed to have an instantaneous and simultaneous effect across West Cork. Brakes were jammed on, steering wheels wrenched aggressively around, all accompanied by a scrunching of gravel.

'Move it, Jimmy!'

The response: 'I am moving it! Where am I going?'

I fell again to rapid road-atlas reading, as if from a rally car. 'Next right, two hundred yards . . .'

Kealfadda, the long stream, halfway between Schull and Goleen. Washing his boots. Summoned by a collective homing instinct in the blood of journalists, the cars came into a conclave at the bridge, parking alongside on a lip of land known as 'the causeway', where the water runs out to the sea. There we all were: the *Sun*, *Mirror* and *Star*, and a couple of French publications, such as *VSD* magazine and *Le Figaro*. What did we know? It was time to pool information. The same was common to all: a man, washing his boots, *ici*. But when, on what day, *à quelle heure*? Was it *dans la nuit*?

The muscular, bearded Frenchman in front of me delivered a smile and an exaggerated shrug: *'Sais pas.'*

We were all at a loss. The person who saw him, I asked Jumbo, was it a man or a woman?

A young Sophie in the arms of her father, Georges, left, while baby brother Bertrand is held by mother Marguerite, central Paris, 1960.

Sophie as a child with her uncle Jean-Pierre Gazeau.

Sophie in her late teens and, later in life, with husband Daniel Toscan du Plantier.

The last photo, featured in an issue of *Paris Match*: Sophie captured by CCTV arriving at Cork Airport.

Sophie's West Cork house from the air. She fled down the front field and died near the entrance to the property, marked above.

Sophie's bed as she left it on the night she died, with the cordless phone, on which she had spoken to her husband, within easy reach.

The bloody location after Sophie's body was removed from the scene.

ROCK

NIGHT ATTIRE SNAGGED ON BARBED WIRE

CONCRETE BLOCK

DRESSING GOWN

DRIVEWAY

GATE

A sketch of the body as found on Monday 23 December 1996, with the leggings stretching to a snag on barbed wire.

Photographer Dan Linehan's picture on the day the body was found shows Ian Bailey, third right, approaching Eddie Cassidy of *The Examiner*, who is talking to Superintendent J. P. Twomey (cap). Photographer Mike Brown, who was directed to the scene by Bailey, is to the left. Sophie's house is seen, with that of neighbours Alfie and Shirley behind.

Two upturned and washed wineglasses sit beside the Belfast sink in Sophie's cottage, vessels which were used for wine or water. Bailey erroneously made much of them in the aftermath of the murder as suggestive of company.

A blood smear thought to have transferred to the back door as it was closed by Sophie's killer after the slaughter.

The Schull squad car at Dunmanus West.

Technical Bureau officer John O'Neill stoops to pick up the cordless phone Sophie used to call her husband from her bed.

Daniel du Plantier, Sophie's husband, links arms with her son Pierre-Louis at her funeral in Mauvezin on 30 December 1996.

A family remembers: Parents Georges (second left) and Marguerite (centre) at a blessing of Sophie's commemorative cross, installed a year after her death. In the black hat is her aunt, Marie Madeleine, with Sophie's cousin Alexandra Lewy alongside.

Yvonne Ungerer, who saw Sophie on the eve of her death.

Sophie's best friend, Agnès Thomas who worked with her at Unifrance.

Barman Dermot O'Sullivan in Crookhaven, where Sophie took tea.

Josie Hellen, the housekeeper who looked after Sophie's home.

Finbarr Hellen, who identified Sophie's body.

Fr Denis Cashman, who gave the last rites to Sophie the day her body was found.

Sophie's near neighbours Alfie Lyons and Shirley Foster. It was Shirley who first spotted the remains.

Garda Sergeant Ger Prendeville, who almost arrested Ian Bailey for drink-driving earlier on the night Sophie died.

Delia Jackson, to whose family home Bailey called on Christmas Day to borrow household cleaning items.

Detectives at a case conference in Bantry, Cork. Supt J.P. Twomey (left), Detective Superintendent Dermot Dwyer (centre) and Sergeant Liam Hogan, who arrested Bailey (right).

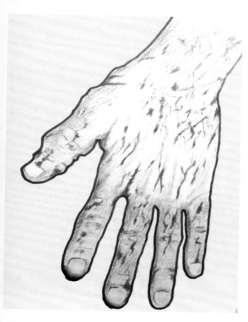

A drawing made for gardaí of cuts and scratches on Bailey's left hand. Supplied by witness Roger Brooke.

A garda sketch of the hairline injury observed on Ian Bailey's forehead after the killing.

A caller named 'Fiona' told Gardaí she had seen a man near Kealfadda Bridge at around 4a.m. The woman was identified as Marie Farrell, shown at the bridge in spring 1997.

Front page of the *Irish Sun* the morning after Bailey's arrest.

Bailey arrives at Bandon on 1998 re-arrest. Detective Jim Fitzgerald, right.

Jules Thomas's 1987 Ford Fiesta parked in Schull in 1996. Did Ian Bailey use it to drive to Sophie's house that fatal night?

Schull-based Garda Kevin Kelleher was instrumental in identifying mystery caller 'Fiona'.

He didn't know either, and shot back, 'What did he look like, anyway?'

Not that I could tell. It seemed we had all absorbed this scant information by osmosis. None could say its source.

I noted that Caroline Mangez of *Paris Match* was not there. She must have been elsewhere, probably with her stringer Bailey, possibly interviewing the bridge witness right now! This is what cut-throat competition is like: paranoia is quick to descend. What was meant by boots? Hiking boots, desert boots, Docs or wellingtons? Nobody knew. I peered at the clear brackish water with its hint of brown, lapping towards my feet over golden grains of rock and sand. It was deceptively bucolic, because the deep sea rushed to meet it yards away. At the end of the causeway, there was fathoms of water. I thought briefly of Bailey's 'Mine Search for Weapon' story; what killer would seek a pit-shaft when the sparkling ocean beckoned?

Paddy Clancy of *The Sun* was asking more immediate questions to anyone who would listen: Where was he seen? On what side of the road, and from which direction? In what way was he behaving? How was he dressed? It was a complete guessing game and nobody had any answers. But Jimmy was doing his thing: taking shots from different angles of the bridge, which was little more than a slight camber on the road, although there was an arch. He moved about, lining up his lens, patiently waiting for other photographers to wave in apology and move out of the way. Then, he moved down onto the causeway to shoot some frames looking back up, where the brook splashed below the passing cars, one of which now mysteriously glided down to our meeting point.

It was a squad car, with guards taking a look at us. Still, they were not inclined to talk, though they had a certain smugness about them, as if they wanted us to know they knew something. They moved down to where they could turn, then drove away again – a helpful reminder of where we had to go next: Schull station and maybe even Bantry.

As we drove away, I put it to Jimmy, who was frowning over the dashboard, 'We don't wash our clothes in rivers any more, Jimmy. Most of all, if you were the killer, you wouldn't do it on the bloody main road, whether night or day. Why not upstream, nearer the house?' Talking it out, trying to think it through, attempting to Rubik's-cube the meaning into place.

What did those cops know, the ones who wouldn't even wind down their windows when smiled at, their car being approached with a friendly wave of the hand? A moment of your time, if you would be so kind . . . But no, we were on our own, trying to reason things out. And up against the rest of the media pack. I couldn't get it out of my mind, this washing of boots at Kealfadda. Surely, he didn't have the boots in his hand? And either way, why take that risk, even in the darkest depths of December? Was it because your soles might sell you into captivity by means of a long trail of tiny traces towards your dwelling? Or could it be that you simply couldn't go home – that someone might see you cleaning them with a brush in the small hours over the sink?

I filed the story before being called back to Dublin: 'The Clue at Kealfadda'. Had a man – Sophie's murderer – been identified? Or was the figure merely a shadow, still effectively draped in darkness? Gardaí were remaining tight-lipped at a crackling rumour that lifted local hopes, but it was startlingly obvious that their mood was appreciably buoyed. Game on.

I didn't know the identity of the informant, even whether it was a man or a woman, and I certainly didn't know what they'd actually said. Or, in Marie Farrell's case, exactly what she didn't say. Her story would emerge in many written statements now that the guards had traced her, and she would later give evidence in court. However, she never officially deposed that the man she saw had been *washing his boots*.

CHAPTER 15

Sorting Out Suspects

There were originally fifty-four 'persons of interest' drawn up as possible killers of Sophie Toscan du Plantier. Gardaí threw the net wide, true to their oft-announced policy of keeping an open mind. The threshold was low and the focus 'broad rather than narrow'. First, they reviewed all well-known local clients and added anyone to the catalogue who had committed crimes against the person, from common assault to sexual offences, to robbery and much in between.

Next were those who had committed burglaries or had trespassed, carrying out crimes against property . . . not forgetting peeping toms, which straddled the two. The sieve even sifted out an old boy who had a habit of stealing other people's gas cylinders, which were generally left outside. People were tipping off the guards about individuals who had no convictions at all, about whom they simply had the creeps. There was one lonely man, recently broken up with his partner, who paid unexpected calls to at least two women living alone. He was polite, a little tongue-tied, and never got around to the point of his visit, until it dawned on the women that he was only there for company. His name was added to the list. So too were the names of practically anyone who had seen Sophie that weekend, including those from the supermarket. Alfie Lyons was closely interviewed, although he had a solid alibi from his wife Shirley, who had found the body, and he was infirm in any case.

Foreigners, of whom there were forty-one in Toormore alone, and particularly any French, were fair game. Interpol enquiries were made in search of any past convictions. One German had gone home since Christmas and died by suicide, causing a posthumous probe. Rumours swirled, which gardaí later categorically said had 'no foundation', adding that the gossip had caused great distress to his family.

Barman Dermot O'Sullivan was grilled in Crookhaven. Dermot aroused garda suspicion after telling officers Sophie had visited the family pub on the Saturday, not Sunday. Was he giving himself an alibi, this muscular young man who happened to speak fluent French? It was an innocent mistake, but Dermot was soon involved in a series of interviews about how he knew Sophie, his weekend movements, and his sojourns in Paris. His past French employers and associates were then thoroughly investigated by the Sûreté. Dermot's story eventually checked out completely and his simple mix-up of days was accepted. Nothing sinister had emerged, and he was no longer a person of interest.

All handymen who had ever worked in Sophie's house were probed, as were those with indirect access to a key, such as Finbarr Hellen, and even his teenage son John. Former owners, even anyone who might have had a hint that Sophie was there that weekend, were carefully examined: such as the husband of Sally Bolger, the woman who had checked on the horses and spotted Sophie's car. Hair samples were taken from several men.

*

All 'domestic' incidents were reviewed, producing more names, with alibis investigated for everyone, generating a widening ripple of enquiries. Questionnaires were issued to houses across the area, specifically asking about strange characters hanging about, or being nosy near a house.

Jules Thomas was one of those bewildered to be asked about lurkers. Sergeant Oliver Goggin and Garda Pat Faley had called to The Prairie and filled out the standard form, asking questions and entering replies. 'I then asked if she knew of any incidents involving acts of violence or prowlers in the past twelve months,' Goggin said. 'She replied, apart from her own personal experiences with Ian Bailey in the past, no.' Jules knew that the guards were aware of the bad beatings at his hands.

It was an acid answer, but other issues gave equal pause. Detectives were surprised when cross-referencing their returns to find that Jules and Ian said they spent Sunday night in The Courtyard, rather than The Galley, where others had seen them. The couple also claimed to have spent Saturday night together at The Prairie – but questionnaires from the Murphys were placing Bailey at their home in Schull. The discrepancies would have to be resolved. Since Bailey was absent when Jules commented about 'violence or prowlers', Sergeant Goggin called back to the house the next day, 14 January, to see him.

'I interviewed Mr Bailey in relation to the questionnaire. I observed Mr Bailey was hyper, excited and nervous. He did not seem to be able to sit for long, constantly jumping up from the table and getting coffee on several occasions. He also appeared very excited about his own investigative enquiries into the murder. Mr Bailey strongly believed there was a French connection, but would not elaborate.' It would be made known in France in the near future, he said. Goggin was suspicious. He would learn that 'a few days after, Bailey relayed a message to Schull garda station that he had stayed in Schull on Saturday night, 21 December, at a friend's house'.

This correction came after Bailey paid an urgent visit to the Murphys, realising that the guards were aware of the discrepancies in his responses. Patricia said, 'I answered a knock on the door and it was Ian Bailey.' His partner Jules was with him, but remained sitting in the driver's seat of her small white car. Surprised, Patricia asked Bailey how he was. He answered, 'Don't talk to me; what a year '97 is so far.'

Patricia added, 'He was hopping on his feet. He said, "Did you tell them that I was here?"', meaning Saturday night, 'and I replied, "Yes I did – do you mean you didn't tell them yourself?" And he said, "No." I asked why, and he said, "I couldn't remember." He didn't tell me what made him remember now. He went on to say he killed turkeys and cut a Christmas tree and got scratched and marked, and then said, "You see, Jules was away." I understood from this that Jules was absent that Saturday. Jules started the car and he went to move away. When at the gate next door, I said to him, "I can't believe you didn't tell the guards you were here, or where you were." I don't know if he replied or not.'

All these stray pieces of information were quickly moving Ian Bailey up the leaderboard of suspects, as the list shrank rapidly through process of elimination. The many enquiries – 'jobs' in garda-speak – soaked up time. Not to mention the major garda mission to France to follow up leads in Sophie's native land. The winnowing was steady, but to the outside world it appeared very little was happening. Until the thunderclap of a first arrest.

CHAPTER 16

The Arrest

On 10 February 1997, American football and film star O.J. Simpson – acquitted of a notorious double homicide – was dramatically found guilty of 'wrongful death'. The judgment arose from a civil case brought by the families of murder victims Nicole Brown – Simpson's ex-wife – and her friend, Ron Goldman. The bereaved families would receive a measure of justice, in the amount of $25 million awarded against the former Buffalo Bills running back known as 'The Juice', who would die in 2024.

That same Monday saw movement in the hills of West Cork. A garda car containing three detectives, led by Sergeant Liam Hogan, quietly arrived at The Prairie, Lissacaha. It was 9.25 a.m., overcast with a light drizzle and temperatures were below ten degrees. Gardaí Denis Harrington and John Paul Culligan got out of the car and went to the front door. Jules Thomas appeared, wearing her dressing gown. 'He's not here,' she said, when asked for Bailey. 'He's down in the studio. What's this about?'

They thanked her and returned to the car. Doors slammed and the squad car drove on a farther short distance to the run-down two-storey building in which Bailey had lived before moving into The Prairie, but where he often still worked and occasionally slept, usually if there had been a row. Once more the gardaí got out, and Sergeant Hogan performed a three-point turn so that the car was now facing back towards Schull.

He watched the pair of officers go to the rear of the house via the side. There was rough ground behind and nothing doing in front. Sergeant Hogan, looking left, scanned his eyes over discarded objects at the front of the house. Bailey would later allow that the house 'needed quite a lot of work, but it wasn't derelict', although one garda succinctly called it 'a kip'. It was a long wait 'til, at last, to Hogan's relief, Denis Harrington reappeared. He returned to the car and reported, 'We have him.'

Ian Bailey, bleary on a Monday morning, had been arrested on suspicion of murdering Sophie Toscan du Plantier contrary to common law. Bailey said that he had been busy writing when the officers called. He was now getting dressed, Detective Garda Harrington told the sergeant, tapping twice on the roof of the squad car in satisfaction, before returning to the dwelling. Hogan noted that 'minutes later, he and Detective Garda Culligan returned to the car, having with them a male whom they introduced as Ian Bailey'. The new arrival was handcuffed.

Culligan helped Bailey, who ducked his head, into the

back seat on the left-hand side, with Harrington going around to the right. Culligan recited Bailey his rights, reminding him that he did not have to say anything, but that anything he did say could be used against him in a court of law. Did he understand?

'I do,' said Bailey, before croaking confidently, 'You are making a big mistake. You've got the wrong man.'

Hogan promptly took those remarks down in his note-book, then started the car.

As it bumped away, Bailey asked to be allowed to speak with Jules, since her house was on the way. 'I want to tell her where I'm going.'

There was a moment of murmured consultation, then they acquiesced.

The squad car crunched to a halt outside Jules' place. Once more the two guards got out, doors slamming, with Bailey sitting cuffed alone in the back seat, Hogan diagonally in front. 'Some minutes later, Jules Thomas came from the side of the house and went to the rear-left passenger window of the garda car where she spoke to Bailey.' He made small talk about a phone bill that needed to be paid. Jules Thomas then moved forward into the open window and placed both her hands on Bailey's left arm. She said, 'Remember they have nothing on you, and I will swear to that in court. I love you.' Hogan had his notebook out and was taking it all down. 'I love you,' repeated Jules. 'Remember, they have nothing.'

Hogan noted that 'Jules Thomas was very pale and agitated', but the three gardaí remained impassive. There is no record of Bailey's demeanour, though he lifted his chained hands in farewell. The car moved off, beginning the long journey to divisional headquarters at Bandon, well over an hour away.

Yet it appeared this Jules encounter had strengthened the arrested man's sense of martyrdom. 'En route, Ian Bailey spoke freely, saying that we were making a big mistake, telling us that it was disgraceful that the person who killed Sophie was out there walking about,' wrote Hogan. Despite his formal warning, Bailey continued to say he had nothing to do with the crime, that he was just working as a journalist. 'In the course of our discussion, he told us how he had been contacted by a reporter called Eddie Cassidy who worked for *The Examiner*. He said Cassidy told him a woman had been killed between Dunmanus Castle and Toormore and asked him if he knew of it. He told Cassidy that he lived near there, and agreed to go to the scene to cover the story. He told us how he had been acting as a freelance journalist in the area – this was how Cassidy knew about him. Ian Bailey told us that he got Jules to drive him to the scene.'

Detective Garda Harrington casually asked Bailey what route they had taken, since they were now navigating themselves. 'He outlined that he went directly to the scene, being driven there by Jules Thomas.' There was a pause. Detective Garda Culligan, looking out the window, asked him how they had managed to drive directly to the scene without asking anyone for directions or enquiring any further about the incident? Bailey drew in his breath, then heaved a sigh. 'He replied that he just went there on a hunch that it was the Frenchwoman residing beside Alfie Lyons that had been killed.'

The car continued to bounce along, but Sergeant Hogan

had been listening closely. As the wipers gently thwacked against the cold morning mist, he now threw a killer question over his shoulder. It suited the dreary weather. 'I asked him how he could have known that the Frenchwoman was at home at this time, as it was only a holiday residence?' He was pointing to the odds stacked against her presence in dark December.

'Ian Bailey then said he thought he should say no more until he spoke to his legal adviser, and asked if he would be given access to one at Bandon.' Culligan reassured him of that. Bailey now finally shut his mouth and moped for the rest of the morning. The squad car arrived at Bandon garda station at about 11.55 a.m. and the prisoner was processed into custody.

*

'Ian Bailey's been arrested.' Dave O'Connell again.

'Jesus Christ. For Sophie?' I could not believe it. Then dawning realisation. 'Oh for God's sake!'

Of course Bailey could be the perpetrator. How had I been so blind? Had I not outlined a catalogue of criteria for the killer to Bailey himself? How did I not then see that he ticked every box? Once again Bailey had effortlessly shown me up as a rather rubbish crime reporter. A Pollyanna.

I would later discover that an unsuspected greater purpose was at work in *The Star*'s publishing of increasingly erroneous Eoin Bailey stories. A quiet approach had been made by the upper echelons by gardaí, informing us that 'Eoin Bailey' was a suspect – but that they would be most grateful if we would continue to publish his contributions because they were

monitoring all such output to see if he would further incriminate himself.

My head was a whirlwind. So much was becoming clear.
His standoffishness at the crime scene, his refusal to introduce me to gardaí, his knowledge and yet detachment, all
made a horrible sense. I sat at my desk, hands behind my
head, blowing out a long sigh of sheer bewilderment.

But no time to waste, we had to get down to Schull. I
reefed open my drawer and grabbed the tiny bag of absolute
essentials for an overnight trip. I was off again, with Wallop,
photographer Jim Walpole. Bailey had been arrested under
Section 4 of the Criminal Justice Act, which specified that
he could be questioned for six hours from time of arrest,
extendable for another six by a garda superintendent. Time
enough to get down there. I also foresaw a court appearance
in the morning.

My mind was still reeling as we drove. Was Ian Bailey the
mystery man seen washing his boots at Kealfadda? I hadn't
remembered him wearing boots, just the bulking size and
height of him, and the impression on first meeting him that
he had been dragged through a bush backwards. One thing
was for sure, I wouldn't now have to compete for space every
day with Bailey's bonkers notions. It was an end to the Bailey
byline, even if he was released without charge. Only the solid
conviction of someone else entirely, and their going down
for life, could ever have him back in newsprint, no doubt in
that case with an authentic account of 'My Mis-Arrest
Misery'. I started wondering about how much garbage I might
have been fed. The amazing 'fill' in the aftermath of murder
now seemed revolting. Jesus, I couldn't get over it.

He would hardly have pushed that wine glasses angle – that two that had been left on the draining board – if he had been inside the cottage. And all that 'French connection' nonsense! The only connected person was likely Bailey himself. It must be, I thought at that time, when the findings were not yet known, that the hairs found in Sophie's hand had been forensically linked straight to him. That's why he had been arrested.

Wallop, who'd never met Bailey, was worried that it could be very bad for the paper if our stringer were to appear at Bantry District Court the following day charged with this atrocious killing. We would never hear the end of it. He'd have put the red into 'red-top', he said. I agreed. There would be a backlash, of course: '*Star* Reporter Charged in Sophie Murder' was a headline easily imagined on the front page of a rival paper. There would certainly be an internal inquiry if our stringer was going to jail. You couldn't make it up, except that Bailey simply must have done. I thought of some of those imputations we had cheerfully carried against Sophie's husband, for which there might now be a libel bill. It didn't bear thinking about, but it was all we could discuss. 'It's going to be bedlam,' offered Wallop, and I was nearly sure he was talking about West Cork when we arrived, and not a meeting of newspaper executives to be held in a Dublin boardroom.

I phoned back to base when we stopped to refuel. The good news was that they had received a wire picture of Bailey arriving under arrest at Bandon. Mike Brown, the Reuters man, had received a tip-off that Bailey was going to be detained that morning. He immediately phoned Bantry garda station and asked to speak to detectives Culligan or Harrington. Told they weren't there, he was satisfied the arrest was being made. Mike was on his way to Bantry when he got another call on his mobile: 'It's Bandon.'

'Whaaat?'

'Bandon garda station – that's where they're taking him.'

Mike wheeled about in time-honoured fashion, his BMW eating up the miles driven in the wrong direction. And yet he would be stood on a wall with a great downward angle when it mattered. 'I took the photograph of Bailey outside Bandon garda station which appeared in the national papers,' said Brown, referring to next-day editions, including *The Star*. 'The only paper that named Bailey was *The Sun*. It closes down for the day around 9 p.m. They would have written the story and used his name on the assumption that he was going to be charged.' It was a gamble.

The Sun could be in financial danger if Bailey was released and someone else identified for the crime. Its headline over Mike's picture was 'Newsman is Held in Sophie Probe', which at least had the virtue of being accurate. The sub-deck, as expected, sneered: 'His reports used by *Star*'. The caption to the prisoner's picture at Bandon then read: 'Under arrest . . . Eoin Bailey', still using his assumed name.

As we continued our journey south, I started turning over the murder again in my head. Sophie had been talking to her husband on a cordless phone beside the bed on the night of her death. But she ended up outside the house – and hadn't used that phone to call 999. It pointed to a knock on the back door, and to Sophie being satisfied with the answer when she shouted out 'Who is it?', in order to feel secure enough to open that door in the first place. Therefore, my belief remained that she knew her killer, however casually. Secondly, it was a rage killing. She was felled in a tornado of blows, possibly compounded by the *need not to let her live*. Because she knew who her attacker was – and would identify him if allowed to survive.

Sophie was arguably murdered by a self-absorbed neighbour, who really did believe there was every chance of sex in the early hours. Only that way of thinking could propel the perpetrator in her direction. That was the psychopath the police were looking for – someone who had a sexual motive, and who was probably already in a relationship with *another* unsuspecting woman. He hadn't gone straight home if that vital clue was correct: washing his boots.

There was one major problem with the Bailey arrest. Why would he be at Kealfadda bridge, two kilometres south of Sophie's house? Bailey's address was another three and a half kilometres east by road from her place, or 'a mile as the crow flies', as he later put it. If he had carried out the monstrous act, wouldn't Bailey have sought to clean up, as best he could, on his way home, going east? *Unless he had a car.* If he was driving, and not on foot, then at least the bridge sighting could be comprehensible. He might park on the causeway where a vehicle would not be visible from the main road.

Even still, to wander farther abroad after carrying out a grisly killing was improbable on first consideration . . . unless the sea came into it, the point at which Kealfadda's long stream emptied. It was an ideal spot to deposit incriminating objects, if there were any. Again, I thought of Bailey reporting on the search for a murder weapon, in addition to the stone and block. Those detectives hunting down the shaft of a disused mine. He had also mentioned a poker more than once. It had seemed lurid to me, part of his hard-to-believe reportage that I had protested against. I didn't know of Harbison's fleeting mention of a 'sharp weapon' in his yet unpublished report. But if there really had been another implement, then Kealfadda was not just a natural laundry – it also offered permanent disposal. Did something fly in a glinting arc through the moonlight to end in a satisfying splash?

In fact, Bailey had written as much, on page four of *The Star* on Saturday, 4 January 1997: 'There is growing speculation that the weapon used to kill glamorous film producer Sophie could have been thrown into the raging Atlantic just a couple of hundred metres from her home.' Was this a covert admission, or just disinformation?

And yet, if the killer had been driving, then surely his engine growl ought to have been heard that night by Alfie Lyons and Shirley Foster as it approached the house? Yet Alfie said he heard no cars. These questions all swept into each other, sloshed about in counter-currents, and seemed to offer few easy answers.

*

As Jim and I hurtled towards Bandon, Jules Thomas was also arrested at The Prairie for separate questioning, a couple of hours after Bailey. By this time there was a crowd of media waiting outside the garda station and TV cameras from Cork filmed her being brought in, head covered – as she had requested – by a green coat.

Jim and I arrived in Bandon that evening and stationed ourselves outside the garda gates with a French and Irish throng, camera lights occasionally banishing the gloom. The Section 4 detention, if extended by a further six hours, was due to expire at 11.30 p.m. Or so we reckoned. Initial enquiries earlier that evening – as squad cars came and went – were aimed at finding out about an extension, and then a possible charge in the heel of the hunt. That would be a sensational new line for the morning papers, the holding line otherwise reading 'was being held last night'. If officers could be lured into answering simple questions, then they might be led on to tougher ones, such as whether or not there had been any admissions, or if a court appearance could be expected. Some of those garda cars entering the yard, when parked out of sight around the back, carried evidence bags. The arrests had been accompanied by warrants, executed at both The Prairie and the studio, with long hours of an after-noon search by members of the Technical Bureau.

*

Detective Garda Eugene Gilligan, who had been involved in the case from early on, and who untangled the barbed stretch of leggings as Sophie's body was removed from the scene, thought he knew what he was looking for. 'I was given a list of garments that he was seen wearing [in the bar on the night of the killing],' said Gilligan. There was nothing at The Prairie that was evidential, so they transferred to the studio. 'We were told to look for a dark blue or black over-coat, hat, and big boots.'

A quantity of clothing was seized from both properties,

but little was considered promising. Gilligan commented: 'At the back of the studio, we found a fire scene. And it was a fresh fire.' The scorched earth had been noticed that morning by arresting officers. There seemed to be the remains of a mattress in the blackened patch. 'My view at the time was, why do you burn beds, the bedding, your own clothing, just outside your back door?' said Gilligan. 'But unfortunately, any DNA, blood evidence, that whole thing was gone. No hard evidence. Very disappointing, but certainly it was a deliberate act. There's no doubt about that.' Gilligan would go through the ashes and detritus with a fine-tooth comb. 'I removed big items, including mattress springs. Then I found small items – clothing, coat buttons, jeans, even boots,' meaning the barest remains of such items. Metallic eyelets, deemed to be from boots, were listed among the recovered fragments.

*

Chief Superintendent Noel Smith was now overseeing the separate rounds of questioning at Bandon, being the highest-ranking garda officer in West Cork. He had appeared in uniform on the *Crimeline* programme, with its reconstruction of events, calling for information from the public about anyone in the area who had sustained marks or cuts, or had bloodstains on their clothes. The gardaí had information, he said – not mentioning the stout defence put up by Sophie indicated by the pathologist at the postmortem – that the attacker in this case would have sustained at least minor injuries, such as scrapes and scratches. As *Paris Match* put it, 'A clawed man was wanted.'

Had the prisoner at Bandon been maimed and cut in Sophie's last minutes, I wondered. I racked my brain as to how Bailey had first appeared to me – dishevelled to be sure, but what, if anything, else? I was now not entirely sure.

Meanwhile the chief superintendent might have been pleased to introduce himself to Bailey in detention. Bailey had previously called Smith on the telephone, days before *Crimeline* aired. On Thursday, 16 January, he rang Bantry garda station seeking Inspector Liam Horgan, who was not present. 'The caller then asked me if I was Noel Smith. I confirmed I was. He identified himself, and told me he had information from France about the murder of Sophie Toscan du Plantier. He said Sophie had received threats from a Breton writer. I enquired whether the threats were verbal, or in writing. He replied that he had no more. I asked him when the threats were made. He told me he didn't know. The information had come from friends of Sophie's husband. He promised to contact me again if he had anything further on the alleged threats.'

Finally, late into the evening, Chief Superintendent Smith had to go out and face the media at his door. 'There was the whole French press corps represented, and everyone thought he was going to be charged,' said Daniel Caron of RTL, a French TV channel. In a halo of television lights, Smith said there would be no charge or court appearance because 'Mr Bailey has left, free'. He had been released sometime after 10.30 p.m., in the last hour of permitted detention, although a woman remained in custody.

There was quiet media consternation – nobody had seen him leave, or had even conceived that he would be allowed to. It was 'to everyone's surprise', reported Caron. Why had there been no solid development? It wasn't explained, but clearly there had been no admissions. Smith sympathised with the media's plight: 'You thought I was going to be carrying a head out here, I suppose.' More seriously, he added that a file was being prepared for Ireland's Director of Public Prosecutions, whose job it would be to assess the evidence and whether or not it warranted a criminal charge.

Jim and I were as crestfallen as the rest of the scrum. Bailey had somehow been smuggled out. There was nothing for it but to pack up and head for the hotel – although some cars containing news teams were already revving out towards Lissacaha to try to catch Bailey at home. 'He's never going to say anything tonight,' I told Jim, both of us knowing it was too late for the morning paper in any case. 'Bet they've dropped him somewhere. There's no way he's going home.' Something in the chief super's demeanour had already indicated as much; he also sweetly suggested we stay in Bandon to avail of the last hour of licensed serving. Better a sit-down and a glass of consolation, after long hours of standing and waiting, than desperate extra effort on a wild-goose chase. Kind of him, but we had to get to Schull, where the office had booked our hotel.

Bailey had headed in the opposite direction, in fact – to Skibbereen. He intended to spend the night at the home of a friend, Russell Barrett. An artist, Barrett had worked with Jules Thomas a few years earlier on murals at the Mizen lighthouse, helping to turn it into a visitor experience. Barrett also ran a boarding house in Skibbereen. The gardaí at Bandon, at the prisoner's request, established by phone that he could stay at his boarding house for the night. Exhausted, and at risk of further hounding at home, as he saw it, Bailey desperately needed some peace and quiet. As for Jules, she would simply have to fend for herself.

*

At breakfast the following morning, Jimmy and I considered the lie of the land. Surely if the swabs had come back and Bailey was DNA-positive, to coin a phrase, then he would have been charged. *Traces of skin under her fingernails*. He had written it himself: *hair in her hand from the head of the attacker*. Yet he had been released, and now Jules was out too, as the radio reported. Bailey thus continued to be considered an innocent man.

Had his scratches caused the arrest? They'd been seen by gardaí and reported by locals on foot of the *Crimeline* appeal. Jim was jabbing with his toast, saying that I must have seen scratches on him when I was down here with Martin Maher; but I was in the back of the van, trying to get all Bailey's bull-run of information down on paper. Martin had been looking at the road. But no stories of the 'I saw scratches' variety – from anyone – were going to get into the paper because it implied guilt; without a charge the lawyers would never allow it. Even with a charge, they wouldn't allow it either, because it could prejudice future proceedings. No, what was needed was reaction from Bailey, and Jules Thomas too, if possible. We had to find them.

Jim downed his coffee: 'Do you think he might have stayed in Bandon? That copper was clearly suggesting we should hang around.'

A fair point. But still speculation. 'Dunno, Jimmy, it's a complete guessing game.'

All that was certain was that the paper would be demanding a splash story and two-page spread for the following day. This case had gripped Ireland. We had to produce the goods. A file was going to the DPP, so our story had to be about Bailey, not mystified, worried townspeople. *The Sun* was already scoffing at us. We badly needed a result.

CHAPTER 17

He Said, She Said

I may have been surprised by Bailey's arrest and by his subsequent release from custody, but Bailey had clearly anticipated these dramatic developments, writing in the *Sunday Tribune* over six weeks earlier, on 29 December 1996, that 'an arrest might be made today'. Wrong on that occasion, he could nonetheless see the gardaí accumulating information – with officers taking hair samples from both himself and Jules two days later, and one garda paying particular attention to his scratches. 'I remember him looking at my arms and he had an immediate suspicion,' disclosed Bailey in a later radio interview.

He had felt the net closing in. His remarks to cheesemaker Bill Hogan, exactly one week before his arrest, show he knew he was becoming 'chief suspect'. He had abandoned plans to travel to France and instead spoke of not being able to remember what happened the night of the murder and a possible defence of mental incapacity. It would thus have been reasonable for Bailey to prepare his ground for the day the guards came.

Familiar with the legalities surrounding detention, Bailey may have believed he could get through custody by adhering rigidly to a rehearsed position while being economical in his answers. Indeed, Bailey bore all the hallmarks of an exam-prepped student, and now the moment had arrived.

What happened in the hours after his arrest would be revealed in time. On arrival at Bandon garda station, he was introduced to the member in charge, Garda Des Prendergast, who explained what would happen and handed him Form C 72 (S), 'Information for Persons in Custody'. Garda Culligan told Prendergast in Bailey's presence that he had been arrested because he had given a false alibi, had scratches on both hands at the critical time, and had been seen at Kealfadda bridge. Bailey displayed not a flicker of emotion. Garda Harrington also stood by as Bailey signed the custody record at 11.56 a.m., requesting a lawyer as he did so, adding that he didn't know of any. Shown a list of public defenders, he pointed randomly to Con Murphy. He then casually requested a cup of tea. It was a perfectly English display of insouciance. Bailey was allowed to have it in a cell. At 12.06 p.m., when he had finished his beverage, the prisoner was searched and his property taken and placed in an envelope.

At ten minutes past noon, Bailey was brought upstairs to an office converted into an interview room for the purpose. Jules would later be taken to Interview Room No. 1 at the end of a ground-floor corridor. And, as expected,

SOPHIE: THE FINAL VERDICT

the initial approach: Why did he give wrong information on his questionnaire about his whereabouts on Saturday night? He did not recollect everything at the time, he said. As soon as he remembered spending Saturday night at the Murphy house, he had voluntarily gone into Schull garda station to set the record straight. The detectives, of course, had ammunition to assault the credibility of this account – Bailey's checking first on the information Patricia Murphy supplied to police.

'Did you call up to Patricia?' Bailey was asked.

'I met her on the road.'

'That's not true, you called to her door.'

'I did knock on her door. I was on my own.'

'You were not on your own, Jules was with you.'

'At this point I have told you everything I am prepared to say.'

They moved on to Sunday night.

'Did you leave the house after going home with Jules?'

'I went to bed; I stayed in bed all night, until next morning. I never left the house that night, Jules will tell you.'

Even as Bailey was saying this, there were developments at The Prairie, where Jules claimed to have been interviewed for two hours in her kitchen by gardaí after Ian's arrest. It was 12.22 p.m. 'They were talking with me, and then they suddenly came out with arresting me. Talk about the wind out of your sails. I was knocked for six.'

Solicitor Con Murphy arrived at the station at 12.26 p.m. and saw Bailey three minutes later – Culligan and Harrington leaving to enable the private legal consultation. The solicitor left after twenty-six minutes, having advised Bailey to say

147

nothing, or as little as possible. The gardaí returned and Bailey availed of another cup of tea at 1 p.m., although he declined to have anything to eat. As an afterthought, he requested some cigarettes along with the tea. He generously gave a fag to Garda Harrington and they both smoked, eyeing each other before the resumption of questioning.

To the question, about his whereabouts on the Saturday night, Bailey replied, 'At the moment I have nothing more to say, on the advice of my solicitor.'

Harrington then asked a desultory question: 'Is it a crime to leave a man's house?' He was referring to Bailey's brief departure from the Murphy house on Saturday night, but it might have been intended to rattle.

Bailey couldn't help responding: 'There wouldn't be anything wrong.'

'You are persistently lying about your movements.'

'I have been arrested for the murder. I know I had nothing to do with it.' He continued to parry, adding, 'You have the wrong man in here. The man is still running around that killed her.'

Gardaí Culligan and Harrington exchanged glances in a theatrical moment. It was an interview technique to unsettle the prisoner.

They turned to Bailey's assaults against his partner, who was now on her way to the station. Bailey said, 'Most of it was because of drink and we were both under a lot of pressure. It shouldn't have happened. It wasn't premeditated.'

He was asked about Kealfadda bridge. Told he had been seen there at 3 a.m., he replied, 'I don't agree with it, being on the roadway Monday morning.' As if to firm up this passive non-agreement, he added, 'I know I had nothing to do with it. I didn't murder her.'

*

On her arrival at Bandon, Jules Thomas had a consultation with solicitor, Michael Doody, before she was interviewed on the floor below Bailey in what she called 'a blank room, with a table and a few chairs'. She received a cup of coffee but similarly declined the offer of a meal.

The questioning got underway, with again two gardaí facing the prisoner, one taking notes. There was no video recording in either case, since no country stations were then so equipped, the system in its infancy. As to Bailey's movements on the Sunday night, Detective Garda Jim Fitzgerald noted Jules' response: 'I'm a light sleeper, he never got up all night. I'd have heard him. I don't remember him getting up to go to the bathroom. Even if Ian was going to get up to go to the toilet, he would tell me.'

On went the verbal sparring, and in came another cup of coffee.

'Ian didn't get up during the night. He was in bed 'til 9 a.m.–10 a.m. Monday morning. He didn't get out of bed during the night. I would know if he did.'

To more questions: 'No, Ian was with me all night. I had my period all that week and was sleeping light. I would have known if he left the bed.'

The interview was paused. Jules went to the toilet, took a meal at 5.38 p.m. and started a rest period. She requested to remain in the room – rather than go to a cell, which was normal procedure – and this was allowed by the member-in-charge. At 6.30 p.m. she was allowed to speak privately to her mother Beryl on the phone. It may have been the hinge moment. She smoked a cigarette, then questioning resumed.

Gardaí began taking Jules slowly through the many assaults inflicted on her by Ian Bailey, at least one of which she had earlier denied ever happened – but now she readily admitted that Bailey had violently attacked her in 1993 after a concert in Cork.

Soon she found herself talking of Bailey and Sophie. 'He said that he had seen her at Brosnan's supermarket in Schull on that weekend. He did not elaborate on whether she was on her own or otherwise. He was in Schull . . . so it must be on Saturday that he saw Sophie in Brosnan's shop.' Jules was slowly becoming more frank and forthcoming.

Pressed again about the night of the murder, she now struck a wholly different attitude and, within moments, Ian Bailey's alibi evaporated: 'I fell into a sleep almost straightaway and I took two tablets for period pain. I was in a sleep, and Ian was tossing and turning and he then got up from bed. I would estimate that he got up about an hour later. He got up easy, so as not to wake me. Even though my recollection was poor, I am almost one hundred per cent sure. He did not say anything to me. I did not take any notice of him leaving the bed as this was common. I can't recollect Ian coming back to bed. I remember him getting me a coffee about nine o'clock – and as far as I honestly remember, he did not come back to bed at all that morning.

'I got up and went into the kitchen and did a bit of clearing and made a cup of coffee again, and I did not see him at that time. Ian then came back and I saw a scratch on his forehead. I have no recollection of seeing this scratch on the Sunday.' The scratch was raw and she asked him what had happened, 'as it was fresh and a bit bloodied, and he said he got it from a stick, a gouged bit of a mark. He did not elaborate on where he came in contact with this stick. Ian looked very tired. I did notice scratches on his hands . . . apart from being tired and drawn, he was otherwise normal. The radio was on in the kitchen at the time.'

With minor prompting, she carried on. Ian could have taken the car in the middle of the night. 'He could have pushed it out without me knowing, as he has pushed it out in the past and could freewheel it down. The keys are left in the usual place, and I often leave the keys in it.'

Did she now think he did it, the murder of Sophie?

'He seemed so normal and composed after talking to [Eddie] Cassidy that my suspicions were not alerted and, through Christmas, he acted so cool that I got no feeling about him ever doing such a thing.'

Asked what she had to say about Ian allegedly being seen at Kealfadda bridge on the Sunday night, a new line of questioning after the empty-bed admission, Jules wearily answered, 'I say to this that I have been duped and . . . [it's] unbelievable. I am shattered if this is the case. He would never be over there, only around the fields . . . From what was said at Hunt's Hill, the fact he said to me he was going over to Alfie's, the mark on his face, and now he is put at Kealfadda bridge – my concluding remark is that there is strong evidence to connect him with the murder of the French lady.'

She signed every single page of her garda statements,

151

certifying that they had been read over to her and were correct. Unfortunately for Ian Bailey, his partner had come unstuck with the story.

*

Hours had gone by and Bailey maintained his story of sleeping in the shared bed all night. He was afforded all breaks and conveniences, and gave a sample of blood – taken by Dr Anthony Calnan of Bandon – to be checked against his seized clothes and other exhibits. Next came fingerprints. He had an evening meal and a cup of tea in the cell at 8 p.m.

Forty minutes later. the squeeze came on – heralded by two senior officers taking over duty in the interview room. Detective Superintendent Dermot Dwyer walked in, introducing Inspector Michael Kelleher, both men in full uniform. They sat. Dwyer, soon to be promoted a chief superintendent, repeated the formal caution. Bailey had enjoyed friendly fencing with him at The Prairie, when he'd called up in civvies to ask about a *Sunday Tribune* article, but now Dwyer had his game face on. No more chats about the full moon, life in England and, from Bailey's point of view, why the French husband had to be involved. Only five days before, Bailey had enquired of him why gardaí were not more forthcoming about other leads they had. Dwyer had told him, 'Perhaps we have far more evidence than you think. But why should we tell the media?'

Now Dwyer addressed the suspect: 'You know why you are detained. I would urge you to tell the truth from the outset.' There was evidence available to gardaí that Bailey was involved in the murder of Sophie Toscan du Plantier, Dwyer said. 'Tell the truth,' he repeated.

The prisoner again denied any involvement, insisting that he was at home in bed with Jules Thomas. He was then gravely informed that witnesses – plural – had seen him at 3.15 a.m. at Kealfadda bridge. Dwyer was relying on Marie Farrell's untraced motorised male companion to make more than one witness, but didn't give any details.

Bailey took his time, then replied, 'These people are mistaken. I was in bed.'

Dwyer moved closer to him and said slowly and harshly, 'That. Is. A. Lie.' He leaned back.

Bailey said nothing.

'I must point out to you,' said Dwyer, joining his hands, 'that Jules Thomas has told us that you left the bed – and returned in the morning with a mark on your forehead.'

Bailey, shocked, mustered some defiance: '*That* is not true.'

As Inspector Kelleher stared at the prisoner intently, Dwyer again put it to Bailey that he had left the house. The superintendent's sworn account now records the sudden crumbling of Bailey's barriers: 'After a short time, he said as follows: "We got home between one and two o'clock and went to bed. I had stopped on my way home at Hunt's Hill and looked at the moon. Some time after going to bed, I got up and did a bit of writing in the kitchen. I then went down to the studio. I am not sure what time it was, but it was dark. I have no watch. I had a story to write for the *Tribune* but was told it was okay, that Tuesday would do. It was a story about the internet. I went back to Jules' house at about 11 a.m."'

Dwyer and Kelleher had their suspect out of the house.

Bailey initially told gardaí he had spent Friday 'gardening and writing'. Yet it must have been *other* writing, because it seemed he hadn't completed the long-commissioned piece for the *Tribune*. Nor had the looming deadline stopped him from boozing until long after closing time on the very night before it was due. Odd, too, that the call to night-writing had not lingered in his memory, despite being strong enough to cause him to get out of bed to compose in the kitchen – before heading out farther in the freezing dark to a studio some two hundred metres away. All to complete a short newspaper article due that Monday.

The word-length of that page-38 story is far less than an hour's work, once the notes have been gathered. Yet Bailey had vanished for a number of hours on Sunday night. He told gardaí it was just 'a very difficult story because it was about computers', and he found it difficult to write because it 'had to refer to computer language'. This necessary night-shift, complex and mentally challenging, was what made him appear weary and jangled to Garda Malone at the murder scene next day. I read his article: it was basic and leaden, with a lame intro: 'A taste for the net from the comfort of a bar is on the up.'

*

It must have been a surprise to Bailey when, during a rest period, he was suddenly visited by another senior officer, Noel Smith, and told he was free to leave. Bailey knew murder suspects could be held for a maximum twelve hours under Section 4. He'd been told as much on arrival. The duration was ridiculously short when set against the forty-eight hours of questioning provided for under the Offences Against the State Act, used to hold subversive suspects, and the maximum for Section 4 would later be doubled by amending legislation. It pointed to a lot of inadequate law for ODCs, slang at the time for 'ordinary decent criminals'. Arrest itself was ill-defined, which in turn encouraged the phrase 'helping with enquiries'.

Before the advent of ineffectual Section 4, few persons who accompanied gardaí to the station knew that they were technically free to leave at any time – and they weren't told. As Bailey gathered his things, possibly mystified himself, there was no hint from Smith about anything in the background. But Bandon garda station would have been liaising regularly with the Office of the Director of Public Prosecutions. Bailey may have been belatedly got out of the house, but he had not confessed to murder – and now he was suddenly out of the station too. Dermot Dwyer told the author, 'He was 50 per cent there [to a confession], and we had to let him out the door.'

Before Jules was released, she said, 'I now feel betrayed and abused. Allied to the fact that he acted so cool and carried out his duties in such a normal fashion that I never suspected, and if he was at Kealfadda bridge at that time, it's only shattering.' She admits that she cried. Jules was driven home by gardaí to The Prairie, where she would again spend the night alone in bed. Her mother came over the next day for moral support and, according to one early visitor, was scornful of her daughter's lover.

Yet it was soon Jules's position that nothing she purportedly said to gardaí in their written records could possibly be relied upon as the truth, even though her signature appears on every page. Meanwhile photographs had been taken of both suspects in custody – but since no formal charge was made, they were destroyed after a short statutory period, as provided by law.

CHAPTER 18

Cheers, Mate!

Outside The Prairie stood a knot of journalists. The word was that Jules was inside, probably sleeping. She'd spent nearly twelve hours in custody, although she considered it fourteen hours of questioning with the chat at home beforehand. There was no sign of Bailey, and the door was not being answered. We didn't linger, but went to check on the studio: empty. I mulled things over. There was scope for a 'Neighbours' Shock' story, although without its standard fare of 'kept himself to himself' – Bailey broke that paradigm to smithereens.

Similarly, a 'Why Can't They Catch Our Girl's Killer?' story from Sophie's family, for whom I now had numbers, could await developments. We could go back into town and try the four Ps again, see if we could find out anything about the Kealfadda spotter. We might front-up the local parish priests and post offices, any passing police and pedestrians – while a pint could be called for.

I've often thought of the pub as the fifth P. The atmosphere can be conducive to providing information on tap, but, as outsiders, it's always about striking the right attitude, not rushing anything. It means appearing almost idly indifferent to the issue at hand. Just introduce the topic and let the tongues wag, as if you aren't there. It was not yet even noon – something would turn up. We didn't have to panic. Jim drove back from the studio and we stopped briefly at The Prairie so I could post a note in the letterbox. To our bosom friend Bailey.

I scribbled something suitable on a page hastily torn from my notebook: he was our stringer, we'd worked together before and he could trust me – never mind that he actually couldn't, particularly not now. We wanted him to pose for a photograph and to give us some quotes. Having been released, both his and our only viable option was 'Nope, not me: I think you'll find somebody else killed that woman.' The note was short and ended with my mobile phone number, and the number of the East End Hotel, signing off with an upbeat 'Cheers, mate', and my name. Then I folded it over, wrote 'Ian' on top, and got out to march up the lane and pop it in the house.

Back in the car, I remembered feeling renewed annoyance. We'd been gullible enough to take this chancer's lurid stories about a French link to the murder. Now I was pretty angry. We owed nothing to this guy. Actually, we did – a degree of payback.

*

When opening his libel action against several newspapers in 2003, Bailey took up the tale of his release from custody:

I was told [in Bandon garda station] that I couldn't return to my house and that the studio/Prairie was a crime scene and was being examined. I was told there was a hanging mob waiting outside for me. It was the media, in fact. I was told Jules did not want to see me; she had accepted that I was the murderer and did not want me back. I couldn't go to my own home. I was led out of the interrogation room and through the barracks. There were officers in the corridor and I was led through them, taken out and put into a car. It was dark and there was a mass of individuals outside. I got them to drive me to Ardnamore, near Skibbereen, and it was nearly midnight. Before I left the car, the gardaí said they wanted me to sign something, and I did because I wanted to get away from them. I went up to the house and knocked on the door. Russell [Barrett] was not there. He had lodgers and others staying there. I tried to sleep but my mind was racing. I felt abused – the gardaí were saying cast-iron witnesses, et cetera.

Bailey continued with what happened the next day. 'Another occupant went out and came back to tell me my name and photograph was on all the newsstands. *The Sun* had it. The London *Times* also, and my name was on radio and on RTÉ. That was a thunderbolt.'

Bailey rang his lawyer, Con Murphy, who said he would issue a few quotes to try to quell the attention. Bailey couldn't get through to Jules on the phone. 'I wanted to pass word to her that I was alright.' He spoke to Beryl, his de facto mother-in-law, who said Jules had no problem with him coming home.

Then Russell Barrett appeared and told Bailey to get into the back of his van:

I rode in the van and covered myself. The house was under siege when I got there. Russell drove through the press and down to the back of the house, fifty yards from the road. The lane was full of vehicles and people. Jules was relieved to see me, and in shock. We caught our breath, hugged and could hear knocking all around the house. People coming through the fields to get to the side of the house. We had to take the phone off the hook. It was great to be reunited. Jules said that she was told I had confessed. The atmosphere in the house was that I was under siege. Eddie Cassidy said I was a prime suspect gone to ground. I felt like a hunted animal. They were all coming to the house in waves . . . I had worked with the *Star* reporter before, Senan Molony. A note was passed to me and he asked me could he have a few words. It read 'Dear Ian, I hope you are feeling better after your ordeal . . .'

I am a journalist, trained in PR and media. If they want to see you, they will stay there. I thought if I said a few words they might go away. I was a press man. I had worked for *The Star*. They were in the NUJ [National Union of Journalists] and I trusted them. I took solace from the note they had sent. At this stage I hadn't seen Senan Molony. I saw him when he came down to the cottage later in the day. He was all 'cheers, mate', friendly. I decided to talk to them.

It would be a major mistake.

CHAPTER 19

The Goldfish

The note had worked. Bailey rang me in the aftermath of his release and agreed to an exclusive interview with *The Star*. I was elated – here was our Cannonball Express of copy, just down the track. Whatever he said would waltz into the paper, happily doffing its cap. I just had to make sure we weren't taken in again, that we asked the right questions. But we essentially couldn't miss; it was a scoop.

Jimmy and I drove in to The Prairie at 7 p.m., ignoring a few media stragglers outside, not that we recognised any as Irish. I hopped out: gate open, car in, gate closed; back in with Jim and around to the rear yard.

Bailey was waiting at the back door, dressed in a badly holed brown woollen knit over a blue shirt and jeans. 'Hello, hello, come in,' he said, the bright light pouring out behind him, as if all was well with the world.

He indicated a pine table, and I sat down, babbling chat

161

as I did so, showing that I too detected nothing other than the complete ordinariness of this encounter. 'And this is Jim Walpole, one of our finest . . .' I slid along a bench.

Casually laid across the table was a copy of the latest *Paris Match*, featuring a cover picture of Alain Delon, the French actor, singer and sex symbol. His arm was around a Sophie lookalike, I noticed. Ironically, Sophie had Delon's number in her contacts book, along with other stars, like John Malkovich and Gérard Depardieu. 'Delon the Seducer is Back', proclaimed the headline.

I gestured: 'Some Sophie stuff in here?'

He told me what I already knew, that he had been working with *Paris Match*.

I flicked it open quickly and had a glance: 'Sophie Toscan du Plantier: Dernière Photo'. The last picture: a colourised still of Sophie, taken from Cork airport CCTV on arrival, smiling and looking optimistic. There were pictures of 'Where the drama unfolded', and husband Daniel, hand atop his head 'In mourning'. The text was racy: 'At the bar counter behind their Guinness, men spy on each other and slyly let slip the names of locals.' Then more speculation about the *visiteur mystérieux*. I hadn't much time, so I tossed it aside and got straight down to work, even as Bailey served up tea and biscuits. 'Right, Ian, tell us all about this arrest of yours.'

Bailey had an agenda. He wanted to portray his candidacy for the crime as not only prejudiced and ill-conceived, but also accompanied by threats, intimidation and insult. I had not the slightest doubt that Bailey was using me just as much as I was using him. Here he was, future-proofing against a

SOPHIE: THE FINAL VERDICT

possible, even likely, charge of murder. His detention and prosecution were going to be unlawful and unsafe, and corrupted by police brutality. I sighed inwardly. I had no choice but to slavishly take it all down. My turn would come.

As the garda car had driven away from a last intimate moment with his loved one at Lissacaha, Bailey expounded, 'Immediately the atmosphere became very intimidating and threatening. I was abused in the squad car. I was called a fucking bastard, an English bastard, English fucking bastard, and told I would be found face down in a ditch with a bullet in the back of my head.' He gestured to the back of his cranium, somewhat creepily, I thought.

Slow down, I indicated, scrawling away.

Caught up, he had more: 'I was even shown a bullet. They took it out and showed it to me. They were shoving me. They actually stopped the car in a remote area and all turned on me, shouting at me and sticking this bullet in my face.'

What sort of bullet, Ian?

It was snub-nosed apparently, finger and thumb indicating an inch and a half tall. 'Don't ask me about calibre.'

Did they take out a gun?

'They didn't take out any gun, but they left me in no doubt that they were carrying. It was all expletives, and this Garda Culligan kept jabbing me in the side.'

No, he didn't have a first name for Culligan – John Paul, as I later found out. The driver of the car was called Liam, Bailey said. None of this information assisted me much, but I wrote it down, Bailey looking on approvingly as line after line was filled in my spiral notebook. At Bandon, Bailey said, he was made to strip down to his underpants. They were laughing at him. As the centurion and legionaries mocked Christ, I inwardly sighed. Aloud: What did they do next? Well, they handed him some new clothes and gave him back his shoes, but they had taken his belt and shoe-laces.

Ian Bailey said threats were directed at him in the garda car taking him to the station. He was at pains on this point, but I neither believed nor reflected his allegations in the subsequent story. This was the most sensitive case in the country – with another country looking on. No arresting officers in such a high-profile murder inquiry would allow such compromise as would come from making threats. Even as I was hearing it, I instinctively knew it to be nonsense – silence in a car plays far more havoc with someone's mind. The prisoner was facing into twelve hours of gruelling detention and questioning, and the cynic in me knew threats at this stage would be counter-productive; that it would be much more understandable to bully and abuse him on the way *back*.

There was much else, of real substance, that we spoke about during the interview, including Bailey's failed first marriage and his physical assaults on Jules. I later gave a legal statement: 'During the interview, Bailey told me directly, and I have the clearest recollection of this, that it was being claimed in the locality that he had become some sort of werewolf monster because there had been a full moon on the night of the murder. The only basis for this, he said, was that he liked to go for walks at night, and he had been seen doing so.' But he also dramatically mentioned a 'moonstick', a kind of staff he carried around, and said it had been put to him that it had magical powers, 'because I had done a deal with the Devil, or something'.

I asked Ian, 'Can I see this moonstick?' I had an inner vision of Jimmy taking a picture of him holding it over his head, like a warlock.

Bailey hesitated, carefully considering. 'Well, it's just a stick,' he said at last. 'No, I don't think we should imbue it with any importance.' Bailey got up, I thought for the stick, but instead produced a bottle, pouring tots for all three of us. I chucked it down in stages, just to be polite.

'They weren't suggesting this moonstick was like a divining rod, drawing you to Sophie's house,' I sallied.

Bailey made a filthy grimace. But it was he who had wandered off-topic with this lark, and it was he who had said he 'liked to go for walks at night'. I was wondering whether he was future-proofing here, too. Had someone seen a boot-washing man with a stick at Kealfadda bridge?

Jimmy cocked his head towards the kitchen clock. It was closing on 8.30 p.m. without a single word filed – I had to press on.

'Were you at Kealfadda bridge that night, Ian? What were you doing there?'

He bristled immediately. 'Completely wrong. I was here at home. That is very dangerous stuff, probably invented by the gardaí, because *I* certainly have not been told about it, not told its origin, if it has an origin, and in fact was not asked about it. So don't associate that, please, with me.' He seemed emphatic, but I could not be sure he had not been asked about it in custody. This was one man's self-serving account, after all.

And so, to cut to the chase, or indeed vice versa: 'But come on, Ian, the scratches – I saw those scratches on you myself.' I lingered on *saw* because I was essentially bluffing. 'How did you get those scratches?'

Bailey drew in his breath and very gently moved the magazine, then his glass, a fractional distance. It seemed an almost imperceptible control mechanism. 'I told them that I got a few scratches, not scrapes or cuts, cutting down Christmas trees,' he murmured. 'We have a little sideline here, at this time of year. We supply people with Christmas trees.'

I looked him hard in the eye and frowned. The scratches had been sustained on the night of 22 December, possibly early Monday 23, if the guards were right. 'But Ian,' I said coldly, 'who the fuck buys Christmas trees two days before Christmas?'

I watched, and still see vividly to this day, his reaction to that challenge. His mouth opened and closed. Then it opened and closed again. He did not say anything. He had gone from guru to goldfish, staring silently.

'This is Ireland, Ian,' I continued. 'Everybody's got their tree up at the beginning of December.' In retrospect, I should not have reasoned, but stayed quiet myself – to let the tongue-tied vacuum persist.

He was still offering no response, as if suddenly deadened. He seemed to be seeing into space, micro-nodding. Then, a second or two later, he was back, but in a flatter voice: 'The main thing is: they have nothing on me. I had nothing to do with this murder. I have given them hair samples, and so has Jules. They were trying to browbeat me the whole time, and they were threatening throughout.'

That mantra again. I stood up. It was time to go. 'Well, thanks for all this, Ian; we gotta go file it now.'

Later, Ian Bailey would cite turkeys to explain all manner of injury, from scrapes and scratches on his hands and arms, right up to a talon-swipe at his head that produced a severe cut near his hairline. So, it is important to set down here that at no stage in our interview did he ever mention turkeys. Not once. The scratches, he said, came only from cutting down Christmas trees.

Walpole called politely into a darkened corner as we left, 'Thank you for the tea.' I did the same, though my focus was trained on Bailey. Jules Thomas was behind a doorway, in a sidelong parlour. She turned about in the relative gloom, and gave me some pertinent comments that I took down in my notebook. She had obscured herself, but was talking airily, dispassionately, yet somehow almost theatrically, while putting things away on shelves. There was a tone of injury in her voice, but I didn't notice anything else. It led to a sidebar piece in the next day's paper: 'Anger over Home Raid':

> Jules Catherine Thomas, the girlfriend of Eoin Bailey, said last night she was not shown a search warrant when gardaí burst into her home and arrested her. She told *The Star*: 'They barged past me into the house. They didn't show me any search warrant. I will be consulting a lawyer, either in Britain or Ireland.' Mrs Thomas, originally from Wales, said she had been living in Ireland for the past 25 years. She claimed she was in garda custody for fourteen hours. Ms Thomas said

she and Mr Bailey had previously given hair samples for routine genetic sampling to eliminate any local involvement in the crime. 'Those tests should be out now,' she said. 'Where are they? We are innocent but our lives have been totally disrupted.' Last night Mr Bailey's solicitor issued a statement saying Mr Bailey was 'innocent of any involvement in the tragic death of Mrs du Plantier'.

*

Jimmy and I were in the car, waving a last goodbye to Bailey. I stopped myself from saying 'Cheers, mate'. Jimmy first reversed the car, then slalomed past the gable corner.

'Gate is closed,' I reminded him.

'Did you see her black eye?' he demanded.

'Jesus Christ, what black eye?' I asked in surprise. Yet again I had detected nothing.

'She had a black eye,' he said.

In a subsequent interview with the guards, Jimmy said, 'I could clearly see a woman peeping out the gap and I noticed she had a black eye. The door was closed after about twenty seconds, and I believed the woman to be Jules, his partner, because she looked like her. I knew her face.'

I was gobsmacked at this suggestion. But now I had to jump out to open the gate, and Jim fairly chucked the Toyota through the gap. We hadn't time to close the gate again, and in any case, nobody was around. I got back into the car and we hotfooted off into the dark. 'Did you get a picture of her eye?' I asked.

'No, she wouldn't come out. I just saw it for a moment.' His mouth tightened in regret.

We were both quiet for a moment.

'Brilliant copy,' I said.

'We gotta get it over,' Jim agreed, shooting for Schull. 'He was saying some mad stuff.'

We were both suddenly pretty tired.

'And he got out the hooch,' marvelled Jim.

As for me, I hadn't known what it was, just some clear spirit I was obliged to fling down the red lane. 'Some sort of moonshine to go with his moonstick,' I said, and Wallop pealed with laughter, pleased as hell now we had got the scoop. Another pause, and then I said, 'Are we going to play our game?'

He knew what I meant: a form of Rock, Paper, Scissors that had evolved on trips like these. One, two, three and we would each shout out what we thought, a one-word verdict. We never said 'Not guilty' when we interviewed these guys, because they were suspects, after all. So that verdict was 'Dunno' – meaning everything from *I don't know whether they can pin it on him*, to *doubt where I really did do it*, to *I don't know whether I would convict, based on what I know so far*. Really, there were just two options, and the other one was 'Dunno'.

'One . . . two . . . three . . .' and we both shouted, 'Guilty!'

Now we were grinning like schoolboys, exchanging glances, laughing without shame, delighting in our childish game. 'Guilty, guilty, guilty!' I said. 'The fucking Christmas trees! And what about that shit with the first wife?'

'And the guards went up to him for a domestic. Can't believe he came out with that. He's got a death wish.'

'He *had* a death wish,' I said. 'That's what brought us here. His death wish was Sophie.'

We had burned off the pure high of grabbing a great story and fantastic pictures and now we were grimly sober again. The awful reality of what had happened Sophie was never all that far from our thoughts.

*

We filed. I spoke to the newspaper's lawyer. He knocked out some content, no surprise there – including the nightstalker stuff. Editor Michael Brophy warmly came on the line: 'Really well done. Yourself and Jim have done a great job.'

I lapped it up, then Walpole and I went and got the hotel bar going with a couple of pints, and lapped those up too. After we had unwound, rubbed our necks and our jowls, and laughed again, I said to him, 'We have got to get over to England. That's where we go next, hoover up all these details about his past life. We can maybe run a couple of stories before he gets charged.' I took a long draught. 'He's going to get charged, and that will be an end to it, but even if we have to hold it all to the end of the trial, it will be worth it – we get it all in advance, and splash it on conviction; pictures, the works.'

Jim knew it too. 'This story is huge. It has legs.'

Never a truer word spoken. I knew then that it would run and run.

*

'I DID NOT KILL SOPHIE' screamed the following day's *Star* exclusive. A small box on the front page, beside a huge Bailey picture taken by Jim, reported:

> The journalist questioned by gardaí in connection with the murder of Sophie Toscan du Plantier last night told *The Star*: 'It wasn't me. I didn't do it.' West Cork-based freelancer Eoin Bailey alleged that gardaí wanted to 'stitch me up'. Mr Bailey (40) in his first interview since spending twelve hours in custody, claimed that gardaí had repeatedly told him they knew he was the culprit. He explained: 'I want to make it clear that I NEVER met Sophie and that I NEVER spoke to her. I know she was French, and I had seen her once, two years ago.'

Inside was a double-page spread, with a photograph of the misunderstood poet pouring me a mug of tea from a china pot.

Eoin Bailey Talks to *The Star* about his Arrest Ordeal

The first man arrested in the Sophie Toscan du Plantier murder hunt claimed last night: Gardaí wanted to stitch me up. 'It looks to me as if they are not looking for anybody else,' Eoin Bailey said. 'But I know that I didn't do this killing. I have no guilt and nothing to hide.'

The phrase 'nothing to hide' became the caption to the photo of the tea-pouring, with even a teaspoon and a bottle of milk offered in visual evidence.

He then told his version of what had happened when gardaí called to his house in Toormore, West Cork – two miles from where Sophie died just before Christmas.

He went on to make a series of claims about what was said while he was detained. 'I was arrested on Monday morning by two gardaí who arrived at 10 a.m. in an unmarked car,' Mr Bailey said. 'They cuffed me and told me they were arresting me for the murder of Sophie Toscan du Plantier. I was a bit speechless – I won't say gobsmacked, because I hate that word – but speechless. In the garda car, they said that I had done this murder. They knew it was me. This was the recurrent theme I was to hear for the next twelve hours. They were trying to make out that I had a violent reputation. They were determined to let me know they knew it was me, that they had the evidence.

'When I was being arrested, I had asked if I could go down the road to Jules, my partner of five years, and tell her. First, they said I couldn't, but then they let me. When I didn't confess to a crime I had no knowledge of, and definitely hadn't done, they arrested my partner and subjected her to twelve hours of questions. They told her I'd confessed – untrue – and that she was going to be charged with complicity to murder by making an alibi for me. I wanted to know about the DNA results. I gave a hair sample seven weeks ago and so did Jules, my partner. If the DNA had matched up, I'd be banged up by now.'

Mr Bailey said gardaí had once been called to the scene of a domestic between him and Jules, a 38-year-old artist from Wales. 'Jules and I had our ups and downs before and the gardaí were once involved at the behest of a third party,' he said. 'The gardaí said they had checked into me in Britain, where I had had a very acrimonious divorce from my wife. They were clutching at straws all the time. They kept suggesting different motives. I want to make it clear that I never met Sophie and that I never spoke to her. I knew that she was French, and I had seen her once, two years ago.

'When I arrived at Bandon garda station, there were photographers waiting. Someone had tipped them off and it all became very public. The gardaí could have brought us in very quietly, not arrested us even, but asked us to come in. We would have gone. I know that they were under pressure but they trampled on us . . . just like they trampled all over the murder scene. There is a forensic saying: the victim dies once, but the murder scene can die a thousand times. It was not properly preserved. I saw all this. I was rung up by a press photographer on 23 December and told about the killing, and I went up to the site to see for myself.

'When I was questioned, they took all my clothes away. Someone then went out and bought me what I call the typical guard's off-duty uniform – black shoes, jeans, a check shirt and a very fine jacket. I still have them, but the guards have all my coats and quite a few bits and pieces. I think the publicity over what has happened has put me in a very prejudiced position, not only in relation to my career as a journalist, but also, should I be charged, in relation to a fair trial.'

Mr Bailey speculated why he might have come under suspicion locally, and on some of the rumours: 'One was that my journalism career was down the tubes until this story came up, and that I needed the murder as a way to make money. There was a claim that because it was a full moon that night, I became some sort of werewolf monster. It was suggested that, even if I couldn't remember killing Sophie, I had killed her. There was also the implication locally that I had killed her and then written stories which pointed more and more to someone coming over from France to do it. And then it was said that I had forged a life insurance policy in my [ex-]wife's name for £200,000 sterling. They told my partner Jules that it was for £250,000. I have absolutely no knowledge of that whatsoever.'

*

The arresting gardaí denied any abuse of Bailey on the way to Bandon. Sergeant Liam Hogan, the driver, said, 'There was absolutely no aggression displayed by any member of the gardaí in the patrol car towards Ian Bailey. In fact, it was quite the opposite, the arresting members were most facilitative and even brought Ian Bailey at his request to meet Jules Thomas and allowed them to speak with each other. Neither I nor any other garda told Ian Bailey that someone would shoot him. I was present at Bandon when Bailey was processed. [He] made no allegation of ill-treatment or improper conduct by gardaí. I was also present on release, and when asked by the member-in-charge if he had any complaint pertaining to custody, he had no complaints. When in my presence [the prisoner] was at all times treated with courtesy.'

The other two guards said the same: 'At no stage during the journey was Ian Bailey abused or threatened and no member was aggressive towards him.'

To judge from Caroline Mangez's experience, the only one with a foul mouth was Bailey himself. Freshly clad at taxpayer expense, he had also repaid apparent courtesy with his own accusations.

CHAPTER 20

A Match Made in Heaven

Two days after my interview, Bailey had an awkward sit-down meeting with *Paris Match*, for whom he had been working in previous weeks. Journalist Caroline Mangez had been sent from Paris to cover the story, working in tandem with veteran Irish photographer Colman Doyle. Their setting was identical to mine – the kitchen of The Prairie, with Jules tucked out of sight in the parlour. It was Valentine's Day, and Ian Bailey was in mystical mood. 'He told me he was in a superior state of conscience [*sic*],' she said.

Bailey warbled on: 'I am escaping from myself. I am not any more man or woman. I am kind of androgynous. I've got visions. I've got intuitions and premonitions. Ask me whatever you want and I will tell you the truth.'

Then Colman Doyle left the house to develop some film, unhelpfully from Ms Mangez's point of view. 'That left just Jules, Ian and I,' she said. There were supposed to be some other guests for dinner, but they hadn't arrived, and Jules remained out of sight. 'Then I noticed he had a hatchet by the door in the kitchen. This was never there before.' Even as her discomfort increased, Bailey was becoming flattering, edging to romantic. 'He told me I was a very special person, that everybody who met me was highly impressed. I was scared, and didn't want to enter into this kind of conversation with him. I was uneasy. Any time that Jules came near the kitchen where we were talking, Ian would tell her to go away.

'He told me the gardaí had no right to take a sample of his blood, as he was not charged, and that he knew they would put his blood on Sophie's door [to incriminate him]. He said the gardaí were manufacturing evidence against him. He told me that Ginny was telling the gardaí lies about him. I asked about his being seen at Kealfadda bridge, and he said, "Anyone can say anything about me, people don't like me here. They consider me a marginal."'

He told Caroline that if he was ever charged with Sophie's murder, the trial would be prejudiced, and that he would never be tried because of media coverage. 'I asked him why he answered all the questions in the press. He said that his solicitor had told him to shut his mouth, but that he was always dreaming about being famous. I asked him how he could have written in one of his articles that there was material under Sophie's nails. He told me that he knew it from his intuitions . . . He said he didn't have any black coat. But he had already told me this material could have been from a coat. In late January or early February, he told me he had seen Sophie on a previous visit to West Cork.

She was working on a laptop computer in the kitchen. I later went and looked at Sophie's house – and Bailey cannot possibly have seen her in the kitchen, unless he was right outside the window looking in.'

Caroline continued, 'Ian often told me he had at times great powers and energy, and likes to dance in the light in his underwear. He told me that one of the girls, Jules' daughters, either Saffy or Ginny, had said that they felt a very bad energy about him, and wanted to split up him and Jules. Bailey said that she [Ginny] had come to him in a black brassière and was "exhibiting her tits to him dressed in this black bra". Jules was present when he told me this, as was Colman Doyle, the photographer. He told me that he used to be a very famous journalist in England, and he was proud that all the English journalists had come to him after the arrest. Even the English TV came.'

Caroline said more later to French investigators: 'He constantly asked me to sleep in his house and told me he had prepared [stepdaughter] Fenella's room for me. I always refused. I was very apprehensive. Jules told me she can't bear to be separated from Ian for more than a few days, and that they have a very strong link between them. He said that in 1997 the world was entering the year of Kali, an Indian goddess of destruction.' Mangez changed the subject: 'I asked him about his assault on Jules, which I had heard about from a source. He said it was just normal fighting between couples.'

I didn't know of Caroline's meeting, but there are similarities to mine with Bailey forty-eight hours before. He was still making accusations against the guards and suggesting corruption, that he would not get a fair trial. One difference was his claim to Mangez that gardaí would daub his blood on the back door of the house at Dunmanus West. Sophie's door was already bloody – the door handle and nearby stain had been carried away in evidence bags the same day the body left the scene – but it was perhaps telling that Bailey was prepared to hear it being falsely claimed in future that it was *his* blood. How had that blood got there? The smear was later identified as Sophie's blood.

If she had run for her life before dying at the bottom of her driveway, then it seems that the killer had gone back up to the house and calmly closed a back door left open since she fled. Why go back? Detectives theorised at one point that the lights were still on and that switches inside the porch had been nudged off with an elbow. Fingerprint dusting throughout the interior revealed evidence only of Sophie being there. Might the killer nonetheless have removed items? Housekeeper Josie, taken through the house, confirmed one thing. There was a little red hatchet missing from its usual place by the back door. Had it been picked up by Sophie as a precaution as she answered the door and put on the light? Might she then have used it, dropped it, run away?

In his conversation with Caroline Mangez, Bailey played up his magical powers, having played them down with me. Jules had kept out of the way on both occasions, but Bailey snapping at her was different. Most disturbing of all was Ms Mangez's reporting of Bailey's willingness to use sexual crudity against Ginny, aged nineteen, his perceived enemy, and in front of Jules. Mistreatment and mere 'normal' – in

Bailey's words – assault of Jules, coupled with the contemptuous sexualising of her daughter, should make it clear to anyone that Bailey was just not right. In fact, he was out-and-out a wrong 'un.

Daniel Caron of French radio network RTL was next to get in contact – and Bailey did an interview over the phone. Caron recorded this and later conversations, which were broadcast with French-language overdubbing of the audio.

Caron began, 'Do you think they have evidence against you?'

Bailey replied, 'I don't know. If there had been sufficient evidence, I would have been charged.'

The initial answer, however, was 'I don't know.' An innocent man knows there can be no actual evidence against him whatsoever.

CHAPTER 21

Turkeys and Trees

By this stage it was clear that Bailey's stories were riddled with inconsistencies. He had a history of nocturnal wanderings and domestic violence. His police questionnaire had lied about where he stayed on the Saturday night. He gave the wrong pub for the Sunday night. And he had mystery scratches on his left hand in particular, plus a nasty nick on his brow.

There was bleach bought, and the replacement of a perfect saw blade. Was the latter a theatrical prop – to suggest that he'd been cutting a lot of trees, explaining his own injuries? Also, there was a direct garda witness to Bailey's arrival on the scene on the day Sophie's body was discovered and his oddly unquestioning departure. And much more, besides a fallen alibi.

Garda Michael McCarthy thought he had detected tensions between Jules and Bailey on Saturday night, possibly explaining why Bailey crashed overnight at the Murphys' house in Schull.

'While off duty I went to The Courtyard for a drink,' he said. 'I observed Ian Bailey and his girlfriend Jules. They went in separate directions. I also noticed Jules did not appear in good form.' From 9 p.m. to 10.15 p.m., when McCarthy left, he 'didn't notice any verbal contact between them. My reason for taking notice was that Ian Bailey seriously assaulted Jules Thomas in May 1996 and I was the investigating member.'

There were published details Bailey couldn't and shouldn't have known; then the Bill Hogan encounter, and 'going down for mental'. And finally, Kealfadda – Marie Farrell said it had been Bailey that night at the bridge. It had been all more than enough reason to bring him in.

No wonder he had begun to impugn the gardaí once released. They were running rings round him on the facts – chief of which were his numerous and poorly explained minor wounds. Caused by turkeys and trees, said Bailey, when he was in garda custody. Both he and Jules spoke in detention about scratches incurred in killing birds, though they clashed on the circumstances and even contradicted each other on what day it had happened.

Jules spoke of Ian at home on Saturday afternoon. 'He had shorts on him and he was going killing the turkeys for Christmas, and me and the girls were stringing them up.' But Bailey separately associated the turkeys with Sunday, even though people who saw him playing the bodhrán bare-armed that night had no recollection, when questioned, of any scratches or cuts. He later claimed to have killed the turkeys single-handedly, rather than have any females help-fully bind the birds. In his questionnaire, he said he did 'the usual chores' on Saturday, but on Sunday killed turkeys in the yard, and had only 'plucked them in company of the Thomas family'. It was exactly because he was alone, said Bailey, and holding a turkey upside down, a knife in his other hand, that the avian victim was able to lash out, injuring him. At one point Bailey said slaughtering turkeys was 'not a job I like doing'.

It was also a job he was not good at, according to Michael Oliver, who had been Jules' partner for thirteen years and who was the father of both Saffron and Ginny.

Saffy, three years older at twenty-two, called to visit her dad that Saturday and complained that Bailey was 'lazy'. They remembered the Mancunian's 'botched job at killing a turkey close to five years ago, when, instead of breaking its neck, he pulled off the turkey's head. It was a joke in the area'.

As part of their investigations, gardaí consulted poultry farms and foresters on the hidden hazards of killing and cutting. This included a turkey farmer, Tony McCarthy. Of Bailey's claims that his scrapes were suffered through dispatching turkeys, McCarthy scoffed, 'Over the years I have killed several hundred of them and never received as much as one scratch. I would go as far as to say it would be a physical impossibility, irrespective of what way you go about killing them. My children would assist and, despite being beginners, never received a scratch. You can get hit by blood, but you can't get scratched.'

But the most devastating account came from a twenty-one-year-old friend of Saffy and Ginny. Student Mark

McCarthy said, 'Last Christmas [1996] Ginny and Saffy told me how much effort that they put into the Christmas tree and decorations. The girls were giving out about the fact that Ian Bailey was so lazy over Christmas, and they had to put so much effort into cutting down the Christmas tree. I think the girls had a few prick marks from handling the Christmas tree, but they didn't have scratches all over them. I believe Ian and Jules were involved in the killing of the turkey. I saw Ian in Schull on Christmas Day at the swim. Neither of us took part. Ian was wearing a big hat, but I could see a scratch on the right side of his temple. I remember at the time that the explanation was the turkey being killed. I thought this explanation unusual, because I have killed a few turkeys in my time and they are not that hard to kill. They are docile creatures.'

Meanwhile, in Garda Pat Faley's memo, Bailey claimed that after the slaughter on Sunday, accompanied by Saffy, he obtained a Christmas tree by lopping the top off a spruce at a plantation near the house. He claimed to still have the tree, discarded out the back. 'He stated he had cut his hands when climbing the tree.' Jules corroborated, up to a point: 'Following the cutting of the tree, his forearms were scratched, but there was no scratch on his forehead, or at least I didn't see it.'

Another peculiarity is that Bailey said he used the yellow bowsaw to chop someone else's tree, the one with the 'perfect' blade presented for replacement the next day, which was the Monday. He then told other gardaí the tree-lopping was on Sunday morning, reversing the order with the turkeys. Yet Tony Doran, at close to noon that

Sunday, had been told by Bailey at the Murphy house in Schull that he, Bailey, would be late for his professed work in Bantry 'plucking turkeys' at noon. And Mark Murphy said he only dropped Bailey home at 2–2.30 p.m.

Saffy later told interviewers the day of turkey doom was 'probably Sunday', and 'we would usually kill the turkeys in the morning'. She was 'pretty sure' three were killed by Ian early in the day, 'and I helped to hang the turkeys and pluck them'. But she too had stayed overnight in Schull, and only got home in the afternoon. She then 'went with Ian and we cut the top off a Christmas tree'. Sister Ginny, in 2002, said she was at home when Bailey and Saffy returned with the tree. 'I remember Ian had fresh scratches on his hands.' She described them as 'long thin scratches on his hands and wrists'. The third daughter, Fenella, interviewed by gardaí at a neighbour's home in early 1997, was 'jittery and nervous', unsure about some events, with a clear recollection of others. She didn't know when the Christmas tree appeared, or what time of day the turkeys were killed.

The guards consulted John Brennan, a Bantry forester of thirty-six years' experience. Brennan accompanied Garda Bart O'Leary to Lissacaha, where the latter pointed out a Sitka spruce, twelve to fifteen years old. The top had been cut off, 'used as a Christmas tree'. Brennan noticed there were no briars around or under the tree, and it had been partially denuded of branches because of the proximity of other trunks. The garda told of a man 'that got multiple scratches to both hands during the cutting and removal of this Christmas tree', said Brennan. 'My opinion is that it is highly unlikely that this would occur.' Later Garda Kevin Kelleher climbed the same tree. He sustained zero skin damage. He climbed another to the top: again, no damage. His flawless hands were photographed, yet Bailey's never were. Later the gardaí commissioned felling tests abroad, involving multiple Sitka spruce. The workers involved, ignorant of the point of the exercise, emerged unscathed.

*

Leaving aside the cause and origin of both scratches and the forehead mark seen at the Christmas Swim, the investigation sought to establish when these injuries first appeared. That meant interviewing everyone who'd been at The Galley and other pubs Bailey briefly visited on the Sunday. It meant getting detailed descriptions of the lighting conditions at the time, and cooperation from Dave Galvin, the owner, as to the number and wattage of lightbulbs in the particular area where Bailey had thrashed his bodhrán. Nobody recalled seeing scouring on his skin, or anything akin to turkey inflictions.

Gardaí were next able to obtain a Christmas letter Bailey had sent to his parents, Ken and Brenda, in Gloucestershire, in which he boasted of a large journalism cheque received, adding that 'Ginny and Nella [Fenella] are a pair of sham "tarts" who are only interested in money and having a good time'. He went on to give a later date again for both the Christmas-tree cutting and the turkey-killing: 'We shall bury the ghosts of 1996. So the Christmas tree which Saffy and I cut on Monday [23 December] stands bedecked with little lights, the turkeys lye gutted and ready to meet their eaters, stretch on the bathroom floor, prostrate turkey's cadavers [sic].'

The usual chatty missive then, and one which Bailey dated Christmas Eve, also giving the time of writing, 9 a.m. If true, it meant he had been extraordinarily busy the previous day – after an epic night out with minimal sleep – attending a murder scene, killing turkeys, cutting down a tree, reporting on Sophie's murder to *The Star*, making calls to media contacts, and still managing to file on cyberpubs to the *Tribune* by 5 p.m.

In his letter, Bailey did not make any mention of the murder, despite having been at the place of death only the day before. Instead, he told his parents: 'Things are definitely beginning to happen here for me – I am an overnight success after five years. As you know, I intend returning full time to my craft of journalism, and had been practising during November and December – Well the dividend is already paying.'

*

Roger Brooke, who had since moved to Italy, made a statement to investigators: 'On the evening of the 23 December 1996, I entered The Courtyard bar in Schull. I spotted Ian Bailey at the other side of the room.' If Brooke is right, this was Monday night and Bailey was back in Schull to continue his prodigious seasonal drinking, displaying extraordinary stamina.

'I went over to wish him a Merry Christmas,' said Brooke, a sign writer who had helped Jules with a mural for the Jameson Distillery in Midleton. They worked on it together at the studio, Ian's home. 'I approached him from his left side and, after wishing him well, I looked down and was shocked to see that the back of his left hand was criss-crossed with deep and obviously recently incurred cuts and scratches.

'This, of course prompted me to ask him what on earth he had done to his hand. His answer was "I was killing turkeys." I remember thinking that it was strange to be killing turkeys just before Christmas Day. That is usually done a week earlier.' Brooke moved abroad soon afterwards, following a break-up, but what preyed on his mind was 'seeing the serious wounds to Ian Bailey's left hand less than twenty-four hours after Sophie Toscan du Plantier was murdered'.

Brooke finally walked into a police station, ironically in Bailey's native Gloucestershire, in 2014. 'The reason was that I had read a report that Ian Bailey told gardaí that cutting a Christmas tree was responsible, which was not what he told me.' He added in an email to the author that Bailey 'always struck me as a fairly strange individual who seemed to have a very high opinion of himself, for no particularly good reason, and I witnessed his resentment towards Jules, that her talent was being praised, whilst his "poetry" was not'. In recent times I put Brooke's claim to Bailey. He replied, 'The name Roger Brooke sort of rings a bell. But I am going to make life easy for you: I've got no comment.'

*

Garda Bart O'Leary had spotted Ian Bailey in Brosnan's shop two days after Christmas. O'Leary was with Garda

Kevin Kelleher and the two, in uniform, feared Bailey would try to pump them for information, aware he was covering the crime for the newspapers. However, Bailey, who appeared 'scruffy', bolted away. The previous day Bailey had reported that Sophie had not been sexually assaulted – yet it would be another two weeks before *The Irish Times* ran an article entitled 'Du Plantier Forensic Test Results Awaited'. Garda O'Leary, like Billy O'Regan in the co-op three days before, noticed that Bailey's left hand in particular was badly scratched. He later made an outline drawing, with the fingers seriously scarred. Having jumped the queue to buy a copy of *The Irish Times*, Bailey bustled past the gardaí and left the shop, throwing glances over his shoulder as he hurried away.

The pair were suspicious and went with a questionnaire to The Prairie the next day. Bart O'Leary said, 'I noticed the scratches on both his hands in Brosnan's. All I could see was as far as his wrists. When he took off his overcoat on 28 December in Jules Thomas' house, it was then I first noticed the scratches on both hands and arms up as far as both elbows.' They each saw a nick on Bailey's forehead, and later drew that too – having no authority to photograph their subject.

*

In 1999, another witness came forward and attested to the scratches on Bailey's hands – a house guest who had stayed at The Prairie that Christmas when Sophie was murdered. Her name was Arianna Boarina.

Arianna, an au pair from Vicenza, Italy, had come to

Ireland to improve her English. She, Ginny and Mark McCarthy were housemates in Dún Laoghaire, County Dublin. She did not have the money to return home for Christmas, so Ginny had generously stepped in and invited her to spend the holiday at The Prairie. Arianna took a bus to Schull, and the young passenger was horrified to hear on the radio of a bloody murder right beside her destination.

Jules Thomas picked up Arianna at the bus stop. They must have briefly discussed the shocking killing, as the twenty-year-old visitor had been assured by Ginny that Schull was a 'peaceful' place. In a 1999 garda statement, Arianna said, 'When I arrived I met Jules' boyfriend Ian. I immediately noticed heavy marks from scratches on both his hands. They were numerous, up as far as his forearms, and they were fresh. He was agitated and drinking a lot. When I first saw Ian, he looked really rough.

'At the house it was said by either Jules or Ian that these marks or scratches were from cutting a Christmas tree and killing turkeys. In my own mind, I doubted this, as the marks were too numerous and too dense.' The offending arboreal item was in the house, decorated with wrapped chocolates, she said, and it was a small tree. Arianna formed her own opinion: they looked like they had come from 'sharp plants, like thorns, rather than Christmas trees'.

The au pair went further: 'I also recall marks on his forehead, but I can't remember exactly where. While there, I plucked with Saffy, and there was only one turkey. During that time, I remember clothes being soaked in the bath. They were dark, but I can't say what type.' Later, the clothes were gone from the bath and she could wash her hair. 'I

190

would describe the relationship between Ian and Jules as not very good, and they were arguing a lot.' She could not understand much, 'as my English was not very good at the time'.

Mark McCarthy of the 'docile' turkeys also had something to say about cactus-like Christmas trees. Early in 1997 – he could not say when – he was with Saffy, visiting her father Michael Oliver in Schull. 'The subject of cutting the Christmas tree came up. Saffron [Saffy] showed her hands, which had some small cuts, and said they were from cutting the tree. Saffron said *she* had cut it, and Ian was probably taking credit for the work done around Christmas.'

If she did all the work, then Bailey couldn't have had much skin in the game. Mark McCarthy met Bailey over the Christmas season and seemed to contrast Saffy's 'few prick marks' with her stepdad's 'scratches all over'. He also noted the cut on Bailey's forehead, the slice above the right eye that featured in a separate drawing by Garda Bart O'Leary, which Mark would not have seen. Jules Thomas was also familiar with her partner's head injury, which she regarded as relatively severe, but when questioned by her, Bailey claimed he had just got it from a stick, without explaining further. In a general sense, sticks are fallen – whereas it is branches that project.

Turkeys, tree, stick.

Saturday, Sunday, Monday.

Were other versions being played of Rock, Paper, Scissors?

CHAPTER 22

St Stephen's Day Smoke

As Bailey was being escorted into custody in Bandon on 10 February 1997, the newly discovered flame-blackened ground outside the studio was being photographed by the Garda Technical Bureau team.

It would soon transpire that the fire hadn't gone unnoticed by those living in the vicinity. Louise Kennedy attested to it in a statement she made to gardaí in the days after Bailey's arrest. The twenty-nine-year-old had gone for a walk on St Stephen's Day. 'I saw a fire burning behind the studio,' the run-down dwelling of her neighbour, Ian Bailey. 'I just thought it unusual. I thought maybe he was burning . . . you know, maybe getting rid of the evidence. I mean, I can't say that, I'm not one hundred per cent sure. That's what I thought. That's why I told the guards.' Louise was suspicious because, as she would later tell the Circuit Court, she had seen 'maybe two scratches' on Bailey's cheek on the very day the body was discovered. He had called for milk, and quoted her mother-in-law the next day in *The Star*. Bridie Kennedy claims Bailey even then was suggesting the guards were mucking up the scene.

So now, after Christmas, Louise was 'inquisitive', and looked in to see burning on the fire 'a mattress, clothes and boots'. This she told to Ursula Jackson – one of Bailey's neighbours from whom he had borrowed the Christmas Day cleaning materials – who later reported it to the guards, although Louise did not mention clothes or boots in her own garda statement. She said the studio was only three hundred yards from her home, and she 'noticed smoke coming around the side [of the studio] from the rear. I walked in to investigate. I saw an old horsehair mattress burning on the ground a short distance from the back door. One-third of the mattress was left unburnt at this stage. I did not see Ian Bailey around. I looked at it for a while, as I thought it unusual to be burning anything on St Stephen's Day. I have not seen Ian Bailey burn anything before'. She was not mistaken on the date, she stressed, while the blaze was strangely close to the back door.

Louise Kennedy sadly suffered catastrophic brain injury in a car crash in 2012, but her husband Pat told the author that the reason she walked into the rear of the studio was she thought the fire was inside the house. He said, 'I asked her what was Ian burning on St Stephen's Day as it sounded really strange, since he had moved in with Jules by then. She said that he was burning a mattress, clothes and boots. It never dawned on us to connect the fire with Sophie's death. It was only about five weeks later when Ian was arrested for the first time that Louise asked me if I remembered the St Stephen's Day fire. I have absolutely no doubt that the fire happened on 26 December.'

Brian Jackson also remembered Thursday, 26 December. He took his dogs for a walk in the early afternoon. Brian saw a small fire in the back of Bailey's garden and 'felt it odd to be burning something on St Stephen's Day'. As he later explained: 'There is quite a high hedge between, but I could see and smell smoke, and I could hear a fire crackling on the other side. I could also hear somebody walking around in leaves and branches. I heard Ian Bailey say one word.' He called out 'Saffy', presumably addressing Saffron, Jules's daughter – who was studying away from home and had returned for the holidays. Brian did not hear Saffy answer, nor see what was burning, but had 'no doubts whatsoever' as to whom that voice belonged. 'Mr Bailey has a very distinctive voice. There are not many people in West Cork with an accent like his,' he said. 'The garden I could only describe as neglected at that time, and that's why it struck me as particularly odd that anybody should bother to tidy it up and have a fire on St Stephen's Day, of all days, in a garden not touched for years.'

Bailey subsequently made a point of saying to Brian and Ursula Jackson that he had set a fire in November, not any other time, but they told lawyers that their friend Phyllis O'Meara had also seen the fire and knew when it was, agreeing with them on the date.

Jules Thomas would take responsibility for this combustion, and initially seemed to accept that it happened over Christmas. One of the handwritten pages of interview notes produced during her detention shows a question posed by Garda Kevin Kelleher: 'What about the fire at the back of the studio?' He was referring to St Stephen's Day.

The answer attributed to Jules is as follows: 'It was going for about three days. I wanted to clear out that place, and tidy it up. I burned newspapers, and clothes I used in my painting. I burned the mattress as well, as it was old and worn.' In another statement made while under arrest, Jules told Detective Garda Jim Fitzgerald: 'In relation to the fire at the back of my mother's house at Lissacaha, I wish to state that I started up this fire myself long before Christmas. The place needed a clean-up and I burned out an old mattress and there was a heap of old magazines there which I also burned.' She was not asked to be precise on dates, yet it seems 'long before Christmas' became significantly stretched upon her subsequent release.

*

Some months later, in July 1997, Brighid McLaughlin interviewed Ian Bailey for the *Sunday Independent*: 'There were rumours that he was burning clothes on the morning after [*sic*] the murder. He says he was obliged to burn the clothes because they were covered in turkey blood.' This was the first time the fact of a fire had been published. Bailey subsequently denied elements of what Brighid attributed to him. But she repeated his quote about turkey blood on his clothes in an article in April 1998 for the English *Independent on Sunday*. Brighid surrendered her background notes to gardaí, and these clearly show the comment about the turkey blood that she twice ascribed to him, set among many quotes that he readily admitted giving. But if actually said by Bailey, the remarks raise the question as to why he would burn, rather than retain, such bloodied clothes. Any forensic tests could easily and clearly establish that this was poultry blood, not of human origin. It would instead have been of much benefit to a putative defendant, indeed a powerful physical rebuttal, to hold on to such items, just in case.

The remains of the blaze yielded nothing evidential by the time the Garda Technical Bureau team carried out their investigation, just charred scraps of paper, clothing and an old mattress. The only interesting items were the eyelets thought to be from boots, the only surviving items from the footwear consumed, along with any forensic evidence, by the flames.

CHAPTER 23

The Past Is Another Country

It was February 1997, and myself and Wallop were embarking on virgin territory with this story. We were bound for Cheltenham and Gloucester, to dredge up Bailey's past. I didn't need to say much to convince the *Star*'s editor that England was the new frontier. Michael Brophy already had uncanny antennae, as I had seen many times – he was an inspirational editor.

Bailey's ex-wife was the person we were aiming to speak with. Her name was Sarah Limbrick. 'Acrimonious divorce', he'd said to me in our interview that night in his kitchen, and now it was left to us to track her down. Bailey had married Sarah, the daughter of wealthy property developers Malcolm and Gill Limbrick, in 1980. After their wedding, they moved into a large house in Churchdown, Gloucestershire, with plans to develop it into a nursing home. But the marriage ran into difficulty. They separated and were finally divorced in 1998.

We flew into Bristol, and our first port of call to the Gloucester and County News Service quickly produced the goods. Yes, they knew all about him and his former wife. Sarah was also a journalist. I was able to obtain her address: she had moved back home with her parents.

Jim and I drove up to the rather imposing Limbrick family home in Cliffords Mesne, a picturesque village with a history of falconry going back centuries, such that it was the location of an International Centre for Birds of Prey. We didn't stop, so couldn't tell whether it housed any turkeys. Malcolm, Sarah's father, answered our knock and came out to talk, carefully closing the door behind him. Was he protecting Sarah? I wondered? He said she wasn't there. What was this about? I explained about Sophie's murder in Ireland. His daughter's ex-husband. He couldn't say where Sarah was, or when she might be back. He looked at our press cards, and I got the impression that something in him wanted to help, although he remained guarded. I later found out he was a former journalist himself. In response to my questions about Bailey letting slip that he had been questioned about forging an insurance policy on Sarah, he looked me directly in the eye. 'You would be better going to Avon police.' It wasn't lost on me that an insurance scam was the very claim Bailey had invented, and seen published, about Daniel Toscan du Plantier.

Malcolm made it clear his daughter would not be granting an interview, even though I had offered that the whole household could sit in and screen out any question they didn't like. It wasn't about Sarah, I said, I was just trying to establish facts about her former husband. But no – and so the next stop was the police. Here the story is best taken up by Detective Constable Clare McGuire, who interviewed Bailey's ex-wife at the behest of An Garda Síochána. She reported to the investigation:

Sarah met Ian Bailey in the late 1970s while she was working as a journalist on the *Dursley Gazette*. Bailey was working freelance for [editor] John Hawkins, based at Westgate Street, Gloucester. They married in 1980 when she was twenty years old. They subsequently separated. Divorce proceedings were started in 1984, but not finalised until 1988, due to arguments by Bailey over property entitlements.

Sarah described Bailey as very charming prior to their marriage. However, afterwards his true personality began to show through. He had a very violent temper. He never used violence towards her directly, but would punch walls, turn over tables and throw his typewriter around the room. During the relationship he had extramarital affairs and would even lock her out of the house if she came home late. She describes him as selfish, nasty and deceitful. She found out that scars on his knuckles were as a result of punching tiles on the wall of a previous girlfriend's home.

During their marriage he cultivated cannabis in the back garden of their home. She states that he smoked cannabis and also used 'magic mushrooms'. Towards the end of their marriage, he disappeared to Wales on occasions to pick his own mushrooms. She once discovered a hold-all containing cut cannabis plants. Following an incident in 1984 during which Bailey locked Sarah out of their house, divorce proceedings were instigated.

At this time, through paperwork held by Bailey, Sarah discovered he had been fined for importing pornography by Customs and Excise. She also discovered that he had taken out a life assurance policy for approximately £200,000 sterling in the name of 'Sarah Bailey' – she never used her married name – and had forged her signature on this document. He was also found to be in possession of building society books in his own name. One account contained £30,000, of which Sarah had no knowledge. She challenged him about the life assurance policy. He stated that if he had asked her in advance, she would have declined.

Sarah describes Bailey as the type of person who liked to impress people. The only hobbies and interests she is aware of were entertaining associates at dinner parties. He was also a marathon runner, a rugby player, and was a member of the Old Cryptians Rugby Football Club.

At the time Sarah first met Bailey, she was then living at a house in Gloucester, which she owned solely. When they married in 1980, they moved to another. She again purchased this house in her sole name, but he made financial contributions. The couple then moved to Newent in Gloucester, also purchased by Sarah in her sole name.

Following their divorce, Bailey received a settlement of £20,000 from the sale of the house in Newent. He went on to purchase a house in Worcester Street, Gloucester, situated near the Kingsholm rugby ground. Part of the settlement resulted in Sarah signing the life assurance policy taken out by Bailey in order to release the monies he had paid in premiums.

Back in Ireland, gardaí wanted Sarah to make a formal statement, but she didn't wish to be involved in any way. She initially indicated she would not be a witness if Bailey were to be charged with murder in Ireland. Detective Constable McGuire, who tried again, reported that 'she is a very private person, who obviously loathes her ex-husband and is trying to forget she was ever married to him'. McGuire did finally relate to the team that Sarah had softened slightly, and that 'if Bailey was in any way responsible for a woman's murder, and if her evidence was considered vital, she may well reconsider'.

She added: 'Sarah mentioned that an old friend of hers went out for a social drink with Bailey after she had divorced him. Her friend later told her that she actually left the pub, as Bailey was acting very strangely and [he] ended up having a fight with someone. During her divorce proceedings, Sarah stated that Bailey had many confrontations with her solicitor. The solicitor also received silent and semi-threatening phone calls. She believes these were made by Bailey.'

Sarah Limbrick's position was defensive, as it remains to this day. I contacted her for this book and sent an email setting out allegations that Bailey had once tried to strangle her, a claim made by former friends of his. There were also claims of 'threats with a shovel'. I suggested that her divorce petition, on twelve grounds, indicated actual violence. I invited her to consider matters, now Ian Bailey was dead, particularly if she wished to deny the specific Irish accounts I submitted. She did not reply.

*

Pete Bielecki and Ceri Williams, former friends of Bailey and Jules, told the story of Bailey actively squeezing Sarah by the neck as she fought to breathe. 'I was friendly with Ian Bailey up until mid-1996 when he gave Jules a bad beating,' said Pete, who lived close by. 'He would visit Ceri and me at Ardravinna and we would call to Jules and Ian in The Prairie. I recall Ian telling me how he was tricked out of his house in England by his wife, her family, and their solicitor.

'There had been legal argument for quite some time and Ian discovered that his name had been deleted from the deeds of his house. As a result, a lot of arguments developed between Sarah and himself and it was in one of these, he told me, that he tried to strangle her – he lost it and caught her by the throat, and wanted to finish her off, but he came to, and stopped himself in the last seconds. He brought this up on a few occasions and would mention Jules and the three girls, saying that you could not trust any one of them.'

Ceri Williams, who had bumped into Sophie outside the supermarket on Saturday, 21 December, corroborated. 'Ian confessed to attempting to strangle his ex-wife. He told us he got very angry with her and lost sense of time, that he flipped – when he came to, he had his hands around her neck, trying to strangle her. As soon as he realised what he was doing, he stopped.' Ceri added elsewhere: 'He said he saw red, or blacked out. He felt shocked that she could have driven him to that point.'

Pete and Ceri took the strangling admission seriously, having witnessed the aftermath of Bailey's devastating violence towards Jules Thomas in May 1996. Ceri Williams contacted officers prior to Bailey's arrest. She said, 'I am aware of an assault that Ian carried out on Jules, and of Ian propositioning Ginny. After the assault, there were several occasions, shortly after, where Ian would come around Jules' home at 5 a.m. in the morning and once he pulled up all the leeks in the garden. After the assault we cut off all ties with Ian Bailey and have had no conversation with him since.'

Ceri said she had known Bailey for four years. 'A very intelligent man, can be quite witty at times, but eccentric. The assault on Jules happened in the car. After that, I had no further dealings with Ian Bailey. It was so brutal, I felt at the time I just didn't want myself or my children around somebody who was capable of doing that. I find Bailey intimidating at times.'

Pete Bielecki gave evidence about the 1996 assault on Jules in the libel case Bailey took against several newspapers in 2003:

There was a knock on the door; I answered. Virginia Thomas was there in a very distressed state. She said that a doctor had brought her to me. I could hear a car on the other side of the hedge. Her mother had been badly assaulted by Ian Bailey – could I take her to the hospital? I said, 'Yes, of course I can.' And she went and told the doctor it was okay for him to go. I quickly got dressed, went down [by car], and walked into Jules Thomas' house via the kitchen. Young Fenella was stood in a state of complete shock. She saw me. She burst into tears. I gave her a hug, and said, 'It is okay. We will sort your mum out.' Jules' bedroom was off to the left-hand side of the lounge. I could hear what I can only describe as almost animal sounds. Terrible distress.

Jules was curled up in almost a foetal position at the end of the bed, making these terrible moans. Her hair was completely tousled. I think she had hair in her hands. She was pulling hair in her hands. Her eye was purple. It was huge. There was blood coming from one point. There was what appeared to be antibodies, sort of pink, draining from the other side. Her mouth was swollen. Her face had gouges in it, and her right hand – I think it was her right hand – actually had teeth marks. She had teeth marks on her hand and arm. It was as if somebody had had their soul ripped. It was like their spirit had gone. It was absolutely the most appalling thing I have ever witnessed.

Later, Pete came back from the hospital, where Jules remained. She later stayed with friends, one of whom was an Irish Army captain, and he photographed her injuries in their back garden. Jules had decided to go to court to get a barring order against Bailey. Pete Bielecki said, 'I went down and stayed at The Prairie with the girls, because Mr Bailey was obviously in close proximity.' The perpetrator had always flitted between the studio and The Prairie, but was now confined to the studio.

Ceri Williams was due home from Wales the day after the assault, but Pete didn't want to leave the Thomas girls, so he couldn't pick her up from Cork airport. They had a phone call. Ceri told him he must stay 'until such time as we feel it is the right time for you to leave'. He ended up staying for three weeks.

Pete testified that he slept on the sofa downstairs and had a hammer. 'The girls insisted that I keep it under the pillow, in case he [Bailey] tried to enter. He is rather a large man and I'm not sure how well I could have handled it.' He corrected himself: 'I do not consider him a man. I no longer considered him worthy of my friendship in any way, shape or form. I've seen my mother receive domestic violence, but I have never seen violence the likes of that.'

It was six months before Sophie died when Pete finally moved out, Jules having returned to her daughters in the meantime. But he was utterly disgusted to soon hear that she had forgiven Bailey and the brute was now back, bigger than ever, in pomp at The Prairie. Also revolted was close friend of the Thomas girls, Mark McCarthy: 'I remember reading an article in the *Sunday Independent*, where Ian Bailey said he did not have a violent nature and that he was a peaceful and calm person. Ginny had told me that Ian had hit Jules several times in the face and ear while he was driving the car. This happened in June 1996 [*sic*] and I saw the injuries to her face. This shocked me, and I was glad when they split up. But Jules took Ian back a few months later.'

The car row had flared because Jules did not want intoxicated Ian to drive them home. Besides, he'd been banned – convicted of drink-driving. But she was angrily refused the keys and he thumped her because he was still a better driver. When they arrived at The Prairie, after intermittent blows, the beating intensified.

The litany of abuse is hard to track, however, because neither party was keen on drawing attention to the violence. Jules sometimes refused treatment.

Pete Bielecki said in a garda statement that Bailey once told him he exercised control over Jules Thomas and her daughters, and feared losing that mastery. Pete retorted that Bailey had no right to control anyone.

Our investigations in England were, however, revealing a pattern of behaviour that was not down to blameless Bailey being continuously provoked by a single individual in Ireland. No, history was instead repeating itself – just as the silent intimidatory phone calls would recur. As with Jules, with Sarah – and probably with others. Jim and I were the past-finders, and we had reason to believe we were in a target-rich environment.

CHAPTER 24

Gleanings in Gloucester

Before we flew over to Bristol, in the white heat of the post-arrest, I had commissioned a piece for *The Star* about Bailey from his former boss, John Hawkins, editor of the Gloucester and County News Service, which ran on 13 February 1997.

The Brash Ian Bailey That I Knew

Editor recalls young reporter

Even as a fresh young junior reporter, Ian Bailey (who now styles himself as Eoin) looked big and sounded big. The six foot, four inches ex-grammar school boy came to work for my news agency as a confident, almost brash, nineteen-year-old in 1975. He quickly learned his craft, but soon became bored with the humdrum day-to-day routine of local journalism. Ian, a butcher's son, seemed more interested in the social opportunities the job offered and never missed a chance for a party or lunch. A keen sportsman, he did his fair share of drinking and socialising too at Gloucester's Old Cryptians Rugby Club, where he played as a second-row forward.

He left my agency in 1978 after qualifying as a journalist and began freelancing in opposition to me from Cheltenham, ten miles away. During his time there he was one of the reporters involved in breaking the story of the Geoffrey Prime spy scandal at the top-secret GCHQ [Government Communication Headquarters] eavesdropping base. Prime, who had been sending secrets to the Soviet Union, was later jailed for 38 years. Journalist George Henderson, who worked closely with Bailey at the time, recalls: 'He was very sociable, he liked a pint or two, and he liked the ladies as well. He talked big, he was always bursting with ideas for making his fame and fortune. He was very ambitious.'

Jim and I were working hard; trying to cover all bases of Bailey's personal and professional life. After our visit to Sarah's family home, we then we went to the *Gloucester Express*, to meet another of Bailey's employers, Dennis Apperly. He wanted a full account of the case for the inevitable story – 'Local News Man in Ireland Murder Probe' – and summoned over a journalist to take notes. Dennis also delivered on his side of the bargain, and I was able to transmit a story that would be headlined 'Won and Lost Job in Just 10 Days':

Ian Bailey got a staff job at a newspaper and lost it in ten days. He was threatened with the sack just four days after joining the *Gloucester Express* and was finally handed his cards six days later. Former employer Dennis Apperly told *The Star*: 'He just didn't do enough work. He thought he had made it by simply being there. He talked a lot about what he was going to do, but never, ever got around to it. But you need something to actually stick in the paper. And Ian would have his feet up on the desk talking on the phone.'

Dennis was scrupulously careful not to tell us the final straw that led to Bailey's sacking, just hinting at his epic laziness. Years later, an old Fleet Street hand named David Jones remembered 'something disquieting' about Bailey, with whom he occasionally worked. 'A Gloucestershire news agency sacked him for staging a drug-fuelled party in the office and bunking off a court case he was supposed to cover, so that he could attend Cheltenham races.'

It was a pity we didn't pick up those lines, but we had harvested plenty of others.

*

Bailey's old office colleagues shook their heads and rolled their eyes. So, Ian might be up for murder in Ireland? Blimey. He was a piece of work, alright. Larger than life, but also such a disruptive influence. They told me a story that led to one of my articles from Gloucester, even showing me the spot where the offending item had been affixed.

Nude Pic in Office

A full-frontal nude picture of Ian Bailey was once pinned up in a busy newsroom . . . by Ian Bailey himself. The wildly extrovert reporter boasted to colleagues that this was what they were up against – raw sex appeal that will always net him exclusive interviews.

At the time, Bailey cheerfully endured jibes that the picture 'must be an enlargement', and displayed no modesty or embarrassment whatever about the full-length snap. He even complained when the picture subsequently went missing, after co-workers took it down. Former colleague George Henderson remembered he was very proud of his prowess with women. 'He always hinted that he could pick them up at will. But he could also get into very strange states of mind. Once he was sat sobbing that nobody loved him, but he was just drunk and wallowing in self-pity.

'He aspired to be a Hooray Henry, a big shot. He would be drinking champagne from a bottle in an ice-bucket, saying, "Let the common people see us drinking champers. It will remind them that we are so much better than they."'

This was the only report from Gloucester that Bailey was furious about when it was published in *The Star*. Not the sacking, not the property wrangle or the insurance rows, not even the psychological cruelty being reported as one of his ex-wife's grounds for divorce. It was the nude picture in the newsroom. He railed against it to other journalists, usually female, jabbing his finger at the enlargement jibe, saying it wasn't true, and if it was true, then *he* certainly hadn't put it up, and had never even seen it.

He may have forgotten what Pete Bielecki and Ceri Williams distinctly remembered: that in 1994, Bailey had skinny-dipped in front of their kids at a beach. Pete thought Bailey did it to shock. He was about to complain, but then realised it would have brought more attention and Bailey would just have revelled in the fuss created.

*

Some of the material we gathered didn't go into the published pieces. There was one yarn about a chap who used to leave his jacket over his chair for hours, as if he had just popped out for five minutes. Ian Bailey, no great timekeeper himself, was suspected of cutting or ripping off one of the sleeves. There were also stories about him urinating in the porches of churches on nights out.

And then there was the 'you won't print this, but—' sort of scuttlebutt. It was claimed that Bailey had offered himself as a spook to MI6, the British foreign intelligence service, during the Geoffrey Prime affair. But how to check such a story? There wasn't time. He was also said to talk incessantly about the sexual details of that case, in which Prime sold out the United Kingdom's secrets to the Soviet Union for relatively little money. This was because Prime was impotent, Bailey claimed, and wanted to punish himself with a poor payoff. Prime's first marriage collapsed because he was obsessed with young girls. He was a paid-up member of the Paedophile Information Exchange, which was, incredibly, allowed to organise openly for a time.

Bailey 'couldn't get over' Prime's efficiency, whereby he amassed nearly 2,300 index cards on young girls and their addresses, jotting in school information, even photographs.

Bailey had his own fixation with young girls, as anyone who took a glimpse at his social media in later years could testify, yet it was long apparent. He had focused sexually on Ginny since first establishing himself with Jules, at a time when Ginny was only fourteen. In 1993, twenty-four-year-old Colette Gallagher was horrified to find Bailey climbing into her bed and touching her leg when she availed of Jules' offer of accommodation at the studio after a party. Bailey's excuse was that he drunkenly thought it was his own bed, and unoccupied.

As Sophie's murder investigation developed in mid-1997, the father of one girl turned over to the gardaí a letter his daughter had received from Bailey in 1995. It wasn't filthy, but it was clear grooming, and going on behind Jules' back. It was being written at 1 a.m., Bailey told the recipient, and it was filled with oily compliments. She was radiant, and 'it would be wonderful to meet you and hear your story although I dare say you will be very busy and have a pack of suitors vying for your time'. He drew a map to the studio, past Jules's house, on the reverse. 'Hoping to see you soon, with fond thoughts.'

On another occasion, not long before his death in 2024, Bailey was duped into turning up for a meeting with what he thought was a young teenage girl, only to be ambushed and badly beaten by some self-styled vigilantes.

*

Most unsettling on the Gloucester trip was for Jimmy and I to hear about Bailey's obsession with the murders committed by Fred and Rosemary West. In fact, he organised impromptu walking tours to the 'House of Horrors' at 25 Cromwell Street where most killings had been carried out, for anyone who would trudge the fifteen minutes from his house in Worcester Street. He liked to hold forth about those who had been murdered, how and when, until he was ordered by the police to leave on one occasion, which he did with bad grace, muttering about his rights and the Magna Carta. He was also said to have gone to a field at the village of Much Marcle, where Fred West is thought to have buried a missing girl.

Bailey had a particular view on Rosemary West, whom some detectives thought had been coercively controlled by her husband, given that one of her daughters was among the dead. On the contrary, Bailey asserted, it was Rosemary who had manipulated Fred into murder. In every such case *Cherchez la femme*, he maintained, with an air of secret knowledge. She was Lady Macbeth and worse, he insisted.

*

It was no secret Bailey thought he was God's gift to women. After his marriage break-up he had several girlfriends, among them Fiona Hanson, who was a local newspaper photographer. He also dated journalist Jane O'Brien, who left Cheltenham to work as a producer on BBC TV's *Wogan* programme. One of his exes, Ellie Carey, was glad to help our mission – once we had filled her in on what kind of trouble Ian was in this time.

We illustrated what ran in *The Star* with a nice picture

213

Ellie provided of herself clinking champagne glasses with Bailey on a glamorous night out at an awards ceremony. Bailey is resplendent in an evening suit with black bow tie. Under the headline 'A Dreamer, Not a Killer: Ex-girl tells of 'one off', the piece began: 'Ian Bailey "was a dreamer, a real one-off", a former lover told *The Star*. Ex-girlfriend Ellie Carey, a former journalist colleague of Bailey, added: "He's the last person you could imagine carrying out a murder."'

Yet Ellie also told us that Ian 'could go dark in a second', although she didn't want that in the paper. Sometimes he was so moody, smouldering with some suppressed resentment, that she just walked off on him, taking a taxi home alone.

> 'He liked to push situations to see what would happen,' she said. 'He enjoyed a wind-up. He could niggle and nark at people. But he would then back down very quickly if they got genuinely annoyed. He didn't like a real argument, only playful ones. Sometimes the drink might take him a bit far, but I honestly never saw him be overly aggressive to anyone. Far from it. He was one of those blokes who always seemed to upset the applecart, usually by trying to attract too much attention for himself.'
>
> Ellie now works in public relations, and is living in Tewkesbury, Gloucestershire. She said Ian became very distressed and depressed following the collapse of his marriage. 'I know there were a lot of rows. I knew his wife Sarah as well. I think they just got married too young and grew apart. She was from a wealthy family. And I think that Ian was just a little bit too madcap and unpredictable for her. She couldn't cope with living

with him. She wanted him to calm down and he couldn't. He was "go, go, go", just a rush of nervous energy all the time.'

Ellie posed for Jimmy with a great broad smile. We carried another few lines from her in a main newspaper piece about the ex-wife, which cited that psychological cruelty was one of the grounds for her divorce. 'Ian felt he had lost ten years of his life when that marriage ended,' said Ellie. 'He walked away with absolutely nothing to show for it. I really do believe that all the hurt and frustration of that episode changed Ian for later life. He stopped striving so hard and became less trusting.'

Bailey left Cheltenham in 1986–7 to try to break into Fleet Street journalism, and worked for several national newspapers on a freelance basis, never becoming staff. He moved to America for a short time in the late '80s, staying with a friend in New York, looking around for English-angle stories to freelance home, but there were established journalists assiduously working this seam already. He tried to write, but things did not work out and he began staying in bed all day, outlasting his welcome. Gardaí looked for any instances of offending in America, but drew a blank. Bailey meanwhile wrote in his diary that he would return to the UK: 'I will run . . . by the river Severn at Wainlode Hill, drive in fast cars, loving life, hating strife, dating, from earliest petting to copulations . . . and the cider, wicked cider, long live cider.'

In reality, he was crashing out of road and running out of drinking companions. Soon after his return to England, he would leave again, this time for Ireland.

CHAPTER 25

Connections 1: Did Bailey Know Sophie?

It was horrible that Sophie, newly arrived for a holiday in Ireland, had been murdered. But it couldn't have been him who did it. Bailey didn't know the woman, and he said as much to Pat Kenny and 300,000 listeners on the national airwaves on 14 February 1997, a mere four days after his arrest. Pat put it to Bailey: 'Had you any previous knowledge of this woman, had you met her before, were you acquainted with her, had you seen her before?'

Bailey responded portentously, 'I had never met her. I had never been introduced to her, and had never spoken to her. I had knowledge of her inasmuch as two years ago, in the spring, I was nearby with a neighbour of hers who pointed her out to me.'

This insistence became a mantra of Bailey's, and it worked a treat. Not knowing Sophie, never having met or spoken to her, arguably robbed him not only of motive, but of

Ian Bailey pictured with his partner Jules Thomas in the garden of
The Prairie and, right, the pair after release from custody in February 1997.

It is difficult for me to put down what occurred o due
to a bottle of whisky, two pints of porte, two pints of wine
a a number of tequila slammas I attacked o severly
beat Jules to such an extent she sought hospital treatment
and when on reedering the house I relieved my
attack o proceeded to cause further injury on top.
I feel a sense of sickness at seeing my own account
of that dreadful night. I actually tried to kill
her.
At present — two nights on she is badly hurt o walking
wounded with bruises on her face, lips, o body
that I could have perpetrated such violence on another

An entry from Bailey's diary in which he recounts details
of a violent attack on Jules, including the words 'I actually
tried to kill her'.

Evidence of the fire at the rear of The Studio, Lissacaha, where Ian Bailey lived. Neighbours Louise Kennedy and Brian and Ursula Jackson said it took place on St Stephen's Day, 1996.

During questioning, Bailey claimed to have seen Sophie through her kitchen window from Alfie Lyons' field – but this photo shows there is no view into her kitchen from there.

The infamous six-bar gate wrongly alleged to have been lost by Gardaí. It was stored for years by the national forensics lab, then disposed of when not wanted back by Sophie's family.

Chief Superintendent Noel Smith at Bandon, February 1997.
Bailey called journalist Dick Cross, middle with notebook,
claiming to have body pictures.

Ian Bailey pours tea for the author at The Prairie in a post-arrest
exclusive interview for *The Star* (February 1997).

Malachi Reed to whom
Bailey said 'I bashed
her fucking brains in'.

Bill Hogan,
local cheesemaker
and vital witness.

Richie & Rosie Shelley to
whom Bailey confessed
murder on New Year's
Eve 1998.

Ceri Williams, who
bumped into Sophie and
saw Bailey lurking across
the road on the Saturday
before the murder.

Pete Bielecki, a former
friend of Bailey's who
gave evidence about a
1996 assault by Bailey
against Jules Thomas.

Billy Fuller, Bailey's
gardening boss, who
heard lurid insinuations.

Garda Pat Joy, left, accompanies Prof. John Harbison to Sophie's inquest in April 1997, with Garda Michael McCarthy, right, who prosecuted Ian Bailey over the May 1996 assault on Jules Thomas. The inquest heard Sophie died from multiple injuries, including skull fracture and laceration of the brain. Proceedings were adjourned because of the criminal investigation, but the inquest could yet resume.

Caroline Mangez of *Paris Match*, with whom Bailey became obsessed, writing a screenplay in which a French journalist was murdered after investigating the death in Ireland of a French national, based on the killing of Sophie.

Brighid McLaughlin's profile of Bailey in the *Sunday Independent* in July 1997 described her feeling physically threatened by him. He continued to court publicity throughout his lifetime.

This page and opposite: Four self-penned sketches from Bailey's 'Black Diaries' which were discovered at The Prairie in 2000.

Self-portrait in garda custody.

Bailey initialled this sketch
of a woman's legs,
ending in boots.

A representation of his mind.

A scribbled image of a woman crying 'Help Help! Help!' alongside scrawled writing. Above the image are the words: 'I knew, 23rd December'. Below it, 'tired, let me sleep, womb like'. Top left: 'Broken pieces of a former self, apparently sound and whole to ordinary gaze, an illusion, a mirror reflecting a thousand shards, temporarily fragmented.' Bottom left: 'You tell me your (*sic*) in pain, I resent your pain, you complain.'

2004: Bailey loses a doomed libel action taken against eight newspapers. Judge Patrick Moran described him as a violent man, 'towards women plural', accepting Bailey had been introduced to Sophie and seen at Kealfadda bridge.

Sophie and her beloved boy Pierre-Louis in happy times.

Pierre-Louis Baudey-Vignaud fought tirelessly for justice for his mother over decades. Here he appears at a Paris courthouse for the murder trial, in absentia, of Ian Bailey. In 2019, French judges found Bailey guilty and sentenced him to 25 years.

opportunity. Yet he had admitted to Jules that he saw her in Brosnan's Spar. He was at least aware of who she was and where she lived.

Alfie Lyons told a different story, under oath, at the 2003 libel trial. He said he had hired Bailey for three days in June 1995 to clear his garden.

'Can you tell the court whether or not Mr Bailey ever met Ms du Plantier.'

'Well, I have thought about this quite often. I see Sophie du Plantier coming up to the house, as she invariably did when she arrived, just to say hello. As best my memory serves me, she came up to the house and Mr Bailey was working close by in the garden. And if somebody arrived into the house, up to the property, I would always introduce them to the person who was there with me. As far as I can recollect, I did introduce him to Sophie Toscan du Plantier.'

Bailey's counsel, Jim Duggan, pounced: 'You are a little uncertain, Mr Lyons? I know it's a long time ago. A little uncertain, would you agree?'

There is an old Law Library tenet that one should never ask a witness a question to which one does not know the answer. Mr Duggan cannot have expected the response in the light of Alfie's earlier tentativeness. This time Alfie Lyons was far more frank, devastatingly so: 'I would say that I am at least 90 per cent certain that I did.' *At least* 90 per cent.

Duggan, completely blindsided by such near-total conviction, said: 'He [Bailey] says, when he was on your property, she was below in her own house. I think there was a little boy there as well – was there a man? I am not certain – but you said to him that it was a French lady who had that house?'

If Alfie recognised a subtle reference to Bruno Carbonnet, Sophie's former lover, he chose to ignore it: 'She knew I was working on the property . . . she came up to say hello, and to see what was going on.'

Mr Duggan: 'Thank you very much, Mr Lyons.'

But Bailey claimed he never spoke to Sophie, and had only glimpsed her, perhaps, 'through the kitchen window', as he told gardaí in early 1997. Caroline Mangez of *Paris Match* found that hard to believe, considering instead that a person could be seen in the kitchen only if one stood physically in front of the window. Certainly, there is no direct view of the kitchen window from Alfie's upper field, where the angle is oblique. The window looks out towards the storehouse and is often in shadow. There is no view at all from a midfield or downfield position on the neighbouring property. Moreover, Sophie had a Belfast sink; anyone behind it was set back from the window. Bailey 'cannot possibly' have seen her, Mangez thought. Alfie's partner, Shirley Foster, agreed: 'I don't think you can identify anybody through that kitchen window. It's quite obscure. The sink is in front.'

At the libel trial, Bailey spoke of 'working for Alfie Lyons' in 1995, saying that yes, the next-door woman 'had been over', but it had happened without him. All he saw 'were sheep in the fields, the boys playing. There was a gentleman with glasses on, and, I assumed, the lady of the house in the kitchen'. Sophie's husband Daniel wore glasses but it was established that he had only been there once, in 1992, so it seems as if Bailey was trying to insinuate the presence of Bruno Carbonnet, with whom Sophie had had an affair. Bailey had made much in the early days after her murder of Sophie taking lovers, more than one, to her discreet 'nest'. However, in trying to place Carbonnet at the house in 1995, Bailey had made a mistake, with his counsel also briefed in error. Sophie's relationship with Carbonnet had finished at the end of 1993.

Ruling on these rival contentions, Judge Patrick Moran accepted Alfie Lyons' evidence, on the balance of probabilities, that he did make an introduction. It had happened. It may have been casual, however, and the judge also accepted 'Mr Bailey's evidence that he didn't know her to meet, to have casual conversation with or to go for a drink'. The court had heard a lot about Bailey's drinking, its occasional aftermath and effects. It was clear from this legal finding in Ireland that Bailey knew enough of Sophie to possibly want to know more.

It is separately commonplace that casual labourers and skilled workers often pick up new jobs from neighbours. It seems possible that not only had Bailey met Sophie when gardening for Alfie, but that Sophie might briefly herself have employed Bailey – although housekeeper Josie Hellen seemingly didn't think so: 'Ian Bailey never did any jobs in Sophie's house'. She held the keys when Sophie was away. But news photographer Billy McGill had a chat with Bailey when covering the murder. 'Bailey said to me, "I knew her, I did a bit of work for her. I was trying to survive, doing odd jobs, and I liked gardening."' McGill promptly told gardaí. McGill didn't know about Sophie's habit of hiring handymen at the drop of a hat, since money to her wasn't much of an issue. McGill said, 'My interpretation [from Bailey] was that he had worked for her.' But against this perfectly ordinary possibility must be set the Englishman's penchant for self-aggrandising.

This charitable explanation could also account for Bailey confidently telling neighbour Delia Jackson that he had met Sophie 'on a number of occasions'. To Helen Callanan, news editor of the *Sunday Tribune*, Bailey said 'that he had spoken to Sophie before she was murdered; that is, he had met her before'. She was a senior journalist, in charge of other people's contributions to the paper, and it was unquestionably her job to grasp detail.

Similarly with Paul Webster, the *Guardian*'s man in Paris. Ian Bailey rang him up to talk about Daniel. 'In the course of a conversation, in which I took brief and legible notes, he told me that he knew Sophie. Bailey had met and talked with her several times. I had no idea Bailey was a suspect and I did not press him for details. The substance of this conversation was reported by Arnold Kemp in *The Observer* [Sunday, 16 February 1997], and I confirm his account as an accurate summary of the conversation with the man purporting to be Bailey.'

Webster, a journalist for fifty years, wrote about French cinema and knew Daniel du Plantier professionally. He worked 'fairly regularly' for RTÉ radio, including on this story. But Bailey's call had come out of the blue. Bailey said that he 'knew Sophie well, but more as an acquaintance than a friend'. Webster imagined that Schull was a small community, and difficult for foreigners not to run across one other.

'He made it absolutely clear that he had talked to her. There is no doubt about that at all. And that he had seen her on the day she died. I can say, quite definitely, that's what I was given to understand over the telephone.' Bailey denied all this, of course, and Webster didn't have the overview to make the obvious point that Bailey, whose job was explicit communication, frequently seemed to leave a lot of people with an utterly wrongheaded idea of what he had just told them.

Besides Webster's notes, there was something else in writing. It was a garda questionnaire, distributed to all local households, which Bailey filled out. Question 9, 'Did you know the deceased? If so, how, and when did you last see her?,' has a line drawn through the area for response, followed by the word 'No'. But questioned on arrest, Bailey adjusted. He had seen Sophie once 'when gardening up at Alfie's last year, or the year before'. Superintendent Dermot Dwyer casually asked Bailey during his arrest what she looked like – and was taken aback at the response. 'He said that, to his recollection, she was plain.'

No one would describe Sophie as plain. Bailey was clearly attempting to underline his innocence, but in a despicable way. He could not have gone there that night hoping for sex, because he didn't find her attractive. Tearing down Sophie posthumously helped build his own defence, and there was no low to which he would not stoop. He could not allow what Ceri Williams had seen: that Sophie was classy, attractive, and stood out. Schull and Crookhaven people saw it, and so did Yvonne Ungerer, from whom Sophie detected jealousy when she was found sipping wine with her husband Tomi at Three Castles Head.

Billy Fuller, a gardener who employed Bailey occasionally for jobs in the locality, gives the lie to Bailey's dismissal of Sophie's looks. It seems Bailey retained a vision of Sophie seen simultaneously by Ceri Williams and himself, as he confirmed to Jules. But he transferred the experience to someone else – Billy. After Bailey had his stepdaughter Ginny as a 'tart' to Fuller at The Prairie, on Thursday, 6 February, Billy stated:

The conversation died again. And then he out of the blue said to me, 'You did it, didn't you?'

I said, 'Do not joke about it, because it's serious.'

But he carried on. 'Yes, you did, didn't you? You saw her in [the] Spar and she turned you on, walking up the aisle with her tight arse. So you went there to see what you could get. But she was not interested. So you attacked her. And she got away. So you chased her and stove something into the back of her head and went a lot further than you meant to.'

I said, 'That is like the sort of thing you would do.'

He laughed and shrugged it off. I got a bit afraid of him. Then he said, 'Actually, that is how I got to meet Jules. I saw her tight arse and wanted her.'

I finished my drink and left the house and I was shaking. I decided not to see him again for a good while.

Four days later Bailey was arrested.

*

Meanwhile, what did Yvonne Ungerer know? Bailey had called out to quiz her at Three Castles Head when he was researching Sophie's last days alive. Yvonne recounted that Bailey 'said that he knew Sophie, that he had met her while up at Alfie's one day'. In this same garda statement, made on 22 January, Yvonne said, 'Ian also told me that the back gate [at Sophie's house] was hard to open and this is why Sophie did not go up to Alfie for help, as I always wondered why she didn't.' Bailey not only had met Sophie, but he had told Yvonne what very few people knew: that Sophie's back gate was hard to open, and it required a knack. The gardener had now metaphorically moved from the middle of Alfie's field to the very edge of Sophie's neighbouring property.

In a crucial statement taken on 11 February 1997, Yvonne described a phone call she had received from Bailey earlier the same day – the morning after he had been released from custody:

'Ian [had] told me of going home that night [of the murder] at about 1.30 a.m. with Jules, but this morning he admitted to me that there was some time unaccounted for. He said that he had got up out of bed to do some work on an article, and went out. "That must have been the time they saw me."'

Bailey had earlier in the call told Yvonne that 'some witnesses had come forward who had seen him down by the water, or causeway'.

'I said, "What were you doing there?" and he said, "Oh, I suppose I was washing the blood off my clothes." He said that in a half-joking way.'

Bailey was beginning to establish a reputation for black humour, whether by accident or careful design.

CHAPTER 26

Connections 2: Fame and Fortune

Ian Bailey craved fame. His projected sense of self – however unconvincing – was of a beatnik, artistic type, an intellectual, and bon vivant. As poet John Montague and his wife Elizabeth Wassell knew, he was desperate to be viewed seriously as a poet, despite the clear evidence of his lack of ability. Bailey was irresistibly drawn to status and style.

Sophie had both. She was a successful television producer married to a leading figure in French cinema. They were a celebrated couple. Bailey was interested in both of these exciting fields of the visual arts..

His personal writings reveal however that he had difficulty separating fame from notoriety. Repeated entries in his diaries and notebooks establish his deluded hunt for glory and public esteem, as he noted in December 1993: 'It looks as though the drama group want me to take a lead role in the play. If offered, I should take it. I am under-employed

SOPHIE: THE FINAL VERDICT

and it is an ideal opportunity for me to concentrate on acting. I want to get into acting in films and theatre.'

Bailey boasted about 'working with' the prominent film producer David Puttnam, who lived in West Cork. He turned up at Puttnam's shoot in West Cork of *War of the Buttons* in 1993. One day he even managed to be hired as an extra, and noted proudly in his diary that he had collected IR£50. Bailey later 'worked with' him again. In reality, he was on a scheme for the unemployed, tinkering with a community video to which Puttnam was glad to lend his name. Bailey's role in the twelve-minute film was to co-write a script and co-ordinate a shoot. It took five months, from April to September 1995, and Bailey's storyline perhaps came from having worked in a fish factory. *Changing Tides* tells the story of a trawlerman who falls overboard and drowns, amid local lore of the corpse surfacing after nine days, and talk about which way it might be carried by currents.

It had its world première at Skibbereen Community Centre and was well received, although Puttnam was presumably prevented from joining the sixty-strong attendance by pressure of work. Bailey nonetheless met him once or twice, buttonholing the lauded producer about his own pet ideas. 'Puttnam didn't like him, even though he [Puttnam] is very down to earth,' said Bill Hogan. 'But that was Bailey all over, approaching celebrities and famous people whenever he got the chance, whereas people here leave them alone. Darina Allen, the renowned chef, had to evade him once at a market. That's putting it mildly. I saw that.'

By November 1996 – just over a month before Sophie's

murder – Bailey thought he might finally be getting places. He wangled an invitation to the Cork city première of Neil Jordan's movie *Michael Collins* and went with Jules to the Capitol cinema on Grand Parade. It was a swanky dress-up affair. Bailey loved the movie, though the British are cast as historical villains. Bailey wrote a gushing review in the *The Examiner*. He'd been at a pre-launch press conference in Cork headed by Hollywood star Liam Neeson, alter ego of the 'Big Fella', whom Bailey indulgently noted was the same height as himself, although the real Collins was five inches shorter. A media commentator who sat beside Bailey referred to his and Jules' 'bitching about Julia', with Ian down on women again because co-star Julia Roberts, who played Kitty Kiernan, had defied local rumour and was nowhere to be seen. In a personal notebook, Bailey wrote, 'Julia Roberts has the acting ability of a barrowful of turnips.'

Was fame the spur? Bailey was forever jotting film ideas into his notebooks – actor Jeremy Irons, who had a house in West Cork, is named with Puttnam on a post-arrest page. Bailey, styling himself 'suspect Numero Uno' on paper, invites the guards to come back to re-arrest him 'if you dare'. More prosaically, he once sought a job with movie rental company Xtra-vision, but they never got back to him.

Caroline Mangez of *Paris Match* was told to come alone to the studio on 15 January 1997 because Bailey had something extremely secret to discuss. When she got there, it turned out to be a book, based on the murder, that he was going to write, which would undoubtedly be turned into a film.

'He then said that he had an idea for the end. A French

journalist would arrive to cover the story and she will be very close to solving it, but will never actually do so. She will fall in love with the country, buy a house here and two years later be murdered in the same circumstances on a moonlit night. I asked him, "What does she look like, are you talking about me?" and he replied, "Guess!" It made me very uncomfortable.'

Especially when Bailey put on a Pink Floyd record, *The Dark Side of the Moon*, and reminded her that Sophie died on the night of a full moon.

'He wanted me to stay in the house, but I told him I had to go, and I left.'

Bailey later again spoke of making this book, or film, commenting on it in the company of Jules Thomas and Yvonne Ungerer. He had the callousness to write out an opening scene, exactly like Sophie attending Les Bains Douches, a superior Paris nightclub, as she did for a Unifrance Christmas party the evening before she flew to Ireland. In his turgid attempt, Bailey has husband Daniel Toscan du Plantier thinly disguised as a character named 'Del De Barro'. He is fat, twenty years older than the 'small pretty woman' in his shadow at the gala event. Drunk on his own importance, 'he pulls his wife towards him and makes her kiss [him]'.

*

Did Bailey ring Sophie at her production company in Paris, Les Champs Blancs? French witnesses afterwards thought so. Sophie's cousin Alexandra Lewy said she spoke to her a few days before she left for Ireland. They discussed a man who had telephoned her offices in Paris, someone who lived in Cork, 'in the area of Sophie's house', Alexandra said in a statement. The man was a writer, an independent journalist. He was looking for a meeting to discuss cultural matters. Sophie had not spoken to the man, but expressed surprise to her cousin that he had obtained her number. Yet such people have their ways and means. Sophie did not seem worried about it, and Alexandra did not press the matter, so didn't know whether Sophie left with such a meeting in mind.

Alexandra, who lived in Geneva, and to whom Sophie occasionally flew when irked by her husband, knew the holiday home well. She had even stayed in it herself one Christmas. 'I came to visit on Christmas Day 1994. I was alone and got the key from Josephine Hellen. I stayed four days with no problems but, during this visit, there was a violent storm that caused some slates to fall from the roof. A few neighbours came to help me put them back in place.'

Nothing was too trivial to be mentioned between them: Sophie once wrote to Alexandra and described a fox near the property. 'I don't think she intended to do something she was afraid of. Sophie was never afraid of anything in Ireland.'

Alexandra went on: 'Sophie would certainly have answered any knock at the door during the day. I'm not sure at night. I think she locked her doors at night. I think if she had a big issue we would have spoken.' Sophie faxed Alexandra her Irish travel plans that December, but her cousin was unable to come to West Cork. Their last conversation was her wishing Sophie *bon voyage*.

Sophie's best friend Agnès Thomas recalled: 'Sophie told me one evening – I don't remember when, because we spoke every day – that she had talked with a man who wrote poems, and was planning to meet him for her job. She told me she was suspicious of him. She didn't tell me his name, because I would have remembered that.' It was a man in Ireland.

Guy Girard was a friend of Sophie, a producer/director who lectured about violence on screen and its artistic place, versus whether showing it could normalise or even incite such behaviour. Sophie too, he told French investigators, had a strong interest in the theme of violence and how to reflect it as part of the human condition. A month before her murder they met face-to-face and talked about a man who had killed his wife with an iron in Besançon because of a 'bad pleat' in the completed laundry. Then there was the case of Jean-Claude Romand who killed his wife with a rolling pin, before killing his children, driving to his parents, killing them and shooting their dog. Could the evil in human nature ever be eliminated by civilisation, and how should cinema, as a cultural medium, treat it? In this discussion, Sophie mentioned the name 'Eoin Bailey'. Girard immediately and enthusiastically agreed with the reference, but he had misunderstood.

He thought that Sophie was citing Edwin Baily, a director who had established a reputation three years earlier with *Should We Love Mathilde?* a film about a woman whose brutal husband had left her and who now planned her own future, weighing up the remaining men in her life. 'No, no,' she interrupted Guy, who told gardaí: 'Sophie corrected me with a smile, saying I couldn't know who she was talking about because Bailey was a writer in Ireland.' Girard realised his mistake when Sophie pronounced the name more precisely. 'I got the impression that he [Bailey] was also working on the theme of human tragedy.'

Guy Girard was 'sure I heard Sophie mention the name Eoin Bailey in the office' on another occasion. He re-emphasised his statements personally to gardaí when he visited Bantry garda station in 1999. He said he had spoken again to Sophie on the day before she flew to Ireland. They were together in the production office and she again volunteered the name of Bailey. This time, however, he could not remember the context.

Sophie mentioned she had a book for him, this writer, said Girard. The gift suggested she was going to meet him, whoever he was. Guy might have expected to hear more when Sophie came home, or even before. He rang Sophie's house in the early afternoon of Monday, 23 December, but there was no answer. To French investigators, he said, 'You've asked if Sophie met this Mr Bailey. I cannot be certain. The way she talked about it can only make me think yes.'

Sophie had many books in her holiday home, including pulp crime novels, but investigators found no obvious present of a book for anyone. There was a new book, the pages held open by a jar of pure Irish honey, left lying on the kitchen table – but it was in French, about the star Sacha Guitry, entitled *Cinema and Me*.

There is the sense, meanwhile, that Bailey has always been the star of his own movie, his mode of dress deliberately designed to establish him as a man apart. He usually wore a wide-brimmed hat and an outsize neckerchief, frequently paired with boots, and these emblematic identifiers suggest he thought of himself as a modern cowboy: untethered, solitary but always in control. One of his dross poetry collections is called *A John Wayne State of Mind*, and Bailey regularly claimed to be in a mode of mental fortitude when vowing to take revenge on his enemies, as always achieved by his silver-screen hero. As it happened, the real John Wayne was also an alcoholic, hell to live with, and prone to tirades.

*

There is additional powerful evidence that Bailey knew Sophie and wanted to know her better. It lies in Cape Clear, the island close to Baltimore in County Cork, southwest of Skibbereen. There may have been an encounter there between Bailey and Sophie in 1995.

Yvonne Ungerer insisted to the author: 'I am sure he told me at the beginning that he had met her . . . He also said to me that he saw her on the ferry to Cape Clear Island.'

Ginny's friend Mark McCarthy saw Bailey on television saying he had 'never met the woman', meaning Sophie. He went to the guards. 'I thought this was strange because I had been in Cape Clear during 1995, at a storytelling festival. Ian Bailey was also there, and so was the Frenchwoman, Sophie du Plantier.' He had personally seen them together.

'I did not know Sophie but I recognised her afterwards when I saw her picture in the papers and on television,' said McCarthy when recalling the woman on Cape Clear.

'I have no doubt she was the same woman that was at the festival. I saw her talking to Ian Bailey.

'I did not hear their conversation but it was the sort of occasion in which everyone talked to everyone else. They would have only talked for a few minutes. At the time the thought crossed my mind that there was Ian Bailey talking to an attractive blonde. She was of average height and slim build, in her thirties, and her hair was tied up. I did not think any more of it.'

The festival took place on the first weekend of September 1995, and McCarthy had seen Sophie with Bailey 'outside the Club Bar, down at the pier on Cape Clear Island'. There is some corroboration from Sophie's housekeeper, Josie Hellen, and his boss, Billy Fuller.

Josie said, 'I have a record of Sophie being in Ireland at her holiday home in Dunmanus in the summer of 1995. She arrived on 16 August 1995 and would be here for approximately one week or more. I recall as well that she told me that she was going to Cape Clear Island on a visit, as her son Pierre was going fishing for the day with a friend.'

Billy Fuller said, 'During the summer of 1996 Ian was working with me. He told me he was going to Sherkin Island [sic] to some storytelling contest. He said he went the previous year with Jules and it was very boring. But this year he was going on his own as he could relax more and let his hair down.' [Only Cape Clear has the contest.]

The poet John Montague wrote in *The New Yorker* of Bailey attending the *Seanachaí* festival on the island – where he transformed into Eoin Ó Báille, the Irish-language translation of his name. 'As he described it in one poem, "The tall

Eoin Bailey, he chipped in his bit / with his poems on life he proved a big hit".' Montague would later, less poetically, compare Bailey to Raskolnikov, the tall, dark woman-killer in Dostoyevsky's *Crime and Punishment*.

And Ian Bailey himself confirmed he went to Cape Clear. He was asked in his failed libel case about Brighid McLaughlin's *Sunday Independent* story quoting a 'surly fisherman' who said Bailey had 'tortured the community, first with his poetry, then with his brutal bodhrán playing'. Bailey bristled at this slight. He could not help himself. He retorted: 'What she [Brighid] doesn't say is that my poetry has been broadcast on local RTÉ, on County Sound [radio], and that I have given poetry readings, and received payment occasionally.

'I had a crowd, at one point, of five hundred people on Cape Clear, who all applauded.'

Some may have been clapping in excessive irony, or in derision. Most were likely tolerant and well-disposed, appreciative at least of the effort made. Bailey did not say what year it was. But if this was the man that Alexandra Lewy and Guy Girard had heard Sophie speak about, then she had likely taken Bailey at face value.

He, however, was always chasing acclaim. And apparently he didn't see why talent should have anything to do with it.

CHAPTER 27

Confessions

Ian Bailey feared he could have had a blackout on the night Sophie died. It was what the gardaí had suggested to him, and. if they were right, then he 'must have blacked out and must have done it', he said. He made these remarks in Russell Barrett's boarding house in Skibbereen, where gardaí dropped him off on the night of 10 February.

The tale later emerged from one of Bailey's mates, Martin Graham. He told gardaí at Bandon four days later – 14 February – that Bailey had confessed to Sophie's murder within hours of being released from custody. Bailey then told Graham that maybe he hadn't done it after all. Events took a surreal turn, with gardaí recording that Graham had referred to an Irma Tulloch being asked to attend Barrett's house. Irma was a hypnotist, a former girlfriend of Barrett, and Bailey wanted her to put him in a trance, to try to recall events on the night of the murder. She agreed to come over, but Irma refused to hypnotise Bailey – saying she wouldn't do it because of what he had gone through at the station. Then she said her qualifications weren't recognised in Ireland. Bailey had previously attended Irma for counselling after beating up Jules in 1996. The gardaí recorded: 'As part of routine enquiries we called to this lady. She didn't want to get involved.'

Martin Graham was English, an ex-soldier who had served in Northern Ireland, now reliant on social welfare. Graham 'went on to describe [Bailey's] remarks, that . . . he must have blacked out and must have done it'. Bailey 'knew the exact time of death', and that a 'terrible screeching' – ascribed to foxes by a neighbour named Barry O'Meara – was 'the murder being committed and the French girl screaming'. O'Meara had been visiting the home of Dan Allen in Toormore, and left after 2 a.m. Bailey was now told to shut up, but Graham described an eerie feeling among fellow residents of the boarding house, as they listened, rapt. The former squaddie had no doubt as to the newcomer's guilt, and neither did Barrett 'after all that happened in the house'. They were 'thinking of asking Ian Bailey to give himself up'.

Russell Barrett, owner of the boarding house where Bailey stayed on the night of release, amply corroborated Graham. 'Ian said he had an ominous feeling coming from the pub on the night of the murder. The gardaí said he had a blackout, "and if that is the case, I must have done it", meaning the murder. He started to cry, and I sympathised with him. That [crying] was because he said the gardaí drove a wedge between him and Jules.'

Barrett felt Bailey was cracking up and told him to shut

up. 'In hindsight, if I had said nothing, he may have told me about the murder.'

That's if Bailey could remember actually committing the crime – ironically, any mental obliteration of events might have served to bolster his claims of innocence.

This wouldn't have been the first blackout that Bailey had apparently experienced. Jules had confided in poet John Montague, he claimed, that Bailey had suffered a blackout when he badly assaulted her in May 1996. It was 'caused by an abundance of poitín', Montague later wrote in *The New Yorker*. Ceri Williams had also recounted that Bailey 'said he saw red, or blacked out' when strangling Sarah Limbrick.

Billy Fuller also had a tale to tell. When they were gardening together in September 1996, Fuller spotted 'a nasty wound, two to three inches long, jagged appearance' on Bailey's leg. 'I said, "What the hell is that?"'

'And he said, "It's fine, I am treating it."'

'I said, "Where did you get it?"'

'And he said, "At the storytelling festival."'

'He had no knowledge how he did it. I said it looked very bad, that I would have noticed if I had done it to myself. He said the last he remembered was telling a story in a bar on the island and he must have blacked out, as he did not remember anything else until he woke up next morning in the mist, with his belongings and bodhrán beside him. He had no recollection of getting back from the island, or the ferry journey. He said that when he goes out on his own he is inclined to keep drinking and get drunk, to the point that he does not remember what he does. I said that was pretty dangerous, and he would be wise to sort it out.

236

'He said, "It is dangerous, because one day I could do something that I would not mean to do."'

*

The confessions would now come thick and fast. Bailey had given a 'black humour' admission to Helen Callanan, news editor of the *Sunday Tribune*, who did not take it that way. Rumours had started to circulate that Bailey might be a suspect, and she put it to him on the phone at the very end of January. He wanted to know their source, but Helen 'wasn't going to tell him'.

Then he said, 'Well, of course, yes, I did it. It was me. I killed her to resurrect my career as a journalist.' He asked again who had denounced him and suggested it 'would be worth IR£20,000' as a libel.

Helen finished the conversation. Disturbed, she wrestled with her thoughts over the weekend, and remembered editing out from Bailey's copy references to Sophie's alleged promiscuity. She phoned the gardaí on Monday, 3 February. Bailey's version was that he 'said to her as a joke that I had killed Sophie, that I was the murderer, and that I did it to further my career'. They agreed on the facts, but not on the tone, nor the intended meaning.

Yet Bailey seemed to have had a good grasp of what could have actually happened that fateful night, when taunting Billy Fuller three days later on February 6. Fuller gave it slightly differently in evidence in 2003, with the new elements here in italics. Bailey said to him, 'You did it . . . *You fancied her.* You went up there to see what you could get. *She ran off screaming. You chased her to calm her down.* You stove something in the back of her head. *You went too far. You had to finish her off.'*

Sophie had major wounds in the back of her head, photographed in postmortem pictures once the hair was shorn away. Bailey had reported as early as 29 December 1996 in *The Sunday Tribune* that 'she was pursued down[hill] . . . and killed by repeated blows to the back of the head'. And again in the following week's edition of 5 January, that 'Ms du Plantier was killed by a blow to the back of the head'. The blow might have knocked her down, before she got up again, but her attacker was catching up. Gardaí had not released such sensitive particulars, nor details of Sophie's flight path from the house, which he also reported on. A drop of blood on a small stone embedded in soil in the middle of Sophie's field would later prove the route.

But there was more. The base of the index finger on Sophie's left hand had been fractured, near severed, by what the pathologist thought a 'sharp weapon' that made a deep lateral cut. In the days after my post-release interview, when Bailey had decided to go on a mini media offensive, he mentioned to Deirdre O'Reilly, a reporter with Cork radio station 103FM, that Sophie had sustained a serious finger injury, obviously a facet of the case withheld from the public. Bailey then said he had heard it from a French journalist. First, he cited Caroline Mangez, who insisted that no, she had heard it from him. Then he ascribed the information to a photographer named Ian Vickery, who succinctly denied being the source: 'Nope.' Then it was a French journalist whose name he wasn't sure he ever got, but there were many. This led him into a further claim – that a French journalist had been present on the very day the body was discovered. Jules Thomas backed him up. She wrote an August 1997 aide-mémoire, which told of their being notified of the suspicious death: 'Ian is driving and we head off in the Dunmanus direction. He says the only French person who he knows of living in the area was the one living below Alfie, and so we take that road.

'Before the gap at the top [of the peninsula, the Bantry road] we see a non-local woman sitting in a car near the bend and Ian goes to talk with her as she looks lost, and we often help people. He says when he gets back in the car that it's a French journalist who is over to investigate a murder of a Frenchwoman, and wondered how she had been so quick to hear the news and get here too.' Indeed, and absolutely, it can only be wondered at, especially as journalist Eddie Cassidy said he had not mentioned a nationality and had not known it himself.

*

On Tuesday, 4 February 1997, schoolboy Malachi Reed, fourteen, had been staying around with friends after school. A second-year student at Schull Community College, who lived five kilometres outside town, he had hung around after school, and now needed to get home to his mother Irune and younger brother Levi. At 7.30 p.m., Malachi met a rough-looking Ian Bailey on Main Street and asked for a lift. Bailey agreed, but told him to give him an hour. Bailey needed to visit the East End Hotel, The Courtyard and The Galley first. When Malachi finally got into the passenger seat at 8.30 p.m., throwing his bag into the footwell, he knew he had to be polite.

'We started talking straightaway.'

He asked Bailey how his writing for the newspapers was going. Bailey was turning the car at Brosnan's car park.

The Englishman suddenly said in savage reply, 'A lot fucking better now, since I went up there with a rock and bashed her fucking brains in.'

Malachi told gardaí: 'Ian was quite serious when he said this, and he was drunk. He wasn't falling around the place or anything, but he was drunk. I got a shock and a cold shiver. I decided to keep quiet.' He noticed Bailey's driving was 'okay', but there were late heavy touches on the brake when going around corners.

'I didn't start talking to Ian again until about half a mile outside Schull. I created a false conversation about school, problems I was having with English, in order to relax the tension in the car. He gave me some advice. There was no more mention of the murder.'

Malachi was home at 9 p.m., his mind disturbed. He did not tell his mother, because he needed to 'think everything through in my own head. I was unsure what was going on. I strongly believed what he said to me. He was serious. There was a long silence after he said it – I was very nervous, until I got out of the car'.

The self-confessed killer then calmly drove off into the night, rattling away in the white Fiesta.

When Malachi came straight home from school the following day, his mother noticed he was agitated and questioned him. 'He told me Garda Kevin Kelleher had called to the school that day and was asking questions about Ian Bailey and his movements on the previous night.'

Kelleher told the author that a local resident, Marina Riley, had reported howling and rage outside her house in the early hours, and she believed it was Bailey. Kelleher had then made enquiries. In one of the Schull pubs where Bailey had been drinking on the evening just past, 'I was informed that when he left, he said he was giving Malachi a lift home.' Kelleher went to the school principal, Vince Ahern, and Malachi was called into the office. Fearful, the lad was evasive when asked about the lift. He didn't tell anything, wasn't pressed and mutely returned to class.

Irune Reed had to get to the bottom of it. 'Malachi then said he had not told the guard everything, and that Ian had been drinking on the night.' Kelleher already knew, of course. Irune told him to continue – and out tumbled the terrifying story. Bailey had said to him that he 'smashed her brains in with a rock or stone', Irune said. 'At this stage Malachi was upset. I think it was only then the impact of what Ian Bailey had said hit him.'

Malachi agreed: 'I was only now realising the seriousness of the situation.' It previously 'didn't really register'. He told his mother he was certain Bailey had not been joking.

Irune told her son the information was so serious she was contacting the gardaí. The next day Garda Kelleher called to the house. Malachi obediently made a statement, which was witnessed and signed by his mother. Irune later gave her own account, attesting to the facts above, and to her good relationship with her eldest boy. 'We are open with each other. There is no way Malachi would make up this story.'

The advice then was not to do anything to arouse suspicion, since Bailey might have forgotten what he had said. This resulted in Malachi thinking that he should avail of further lifts from Bailey, even though no one had gone that far in suggesting a continued appearance of normality.

'Since the murder I have been in Ian Bailey's car on a few occasions,' the poor lad added in a subsequent statement. 'At one stage he mentioned that the mafia was involved. On another he said he was the main suspect because there were scratches on his hand, and blood on his clothes. He explained the scratches were a result of cutting a Christmas tree, and the blood was because he had killed turkeys.'

The gardaí kept Malachi Reed's information quiet. Bailey was asked about the incident when arrested the following week, but denied saying anything to his young passenger. He later complained bitterly to Billy Fuller that it was now apparently a crime to give schoolboys a lift. All kinds of things were being said about him, he said; the worst rumours, every one of them invented. The gardaí were coming after anyone he met, to debrief them and suggest he had made admissions. Bailey claimed that even when folk rightfully resisted, the guards were saying things anyway about the innocent encounters. It really was utterly wicked – not to mention lazy and contemptible when there was a killer to be caught.

*

A man who always had to be a sober driver now took a wrong turn into the fray. Taxi man Jim McKenna lived in

Bangor, County Down, 600 kilometres from the crime scene. But he could have a social drink on holiday in Schull, where his mother-in-law resided on the Colla road, beside Malachi's school. On a Tuesday night in April 1997, Jim and his wife Diana went to the Waterside Inn for a meal and, afterwards, ventured to The Galley for a drink.

He later told the guards: 'I sat down near two people. I took it they were husband and wife. A conversation began with the female. She appeared well drunk. The male spoke with an accent I knew was not local. The lady was an artist and spoke about her paintings. This couple appeared happy that someone was talking with them. She pointed out a painting on the wall of The Galley and told us she had painted it. I thought it quite good. He told me that he worked for *The Examiner* and had worked all over the world. He got up and went out, and came back after about ten minutes, when he seemed to be fresher, much more relaxed. I recall asking the female where her partner was going, and she replied that he was away for a carry-out. I understood she meant alcohol.

'My wife was in conversation with the lady. I was on my second pint. I leaned over to the man and asked if he would write a poem for my wife.' Jim and Diana had a silver wedding anniversary coming up in July, and the uxorious McKenna wanted something special. Yet Bailey the poet was in an opposite frame of mind, with little time for tenderness. He changed the subject.

'At this point he said to me, "Do you know about the murder in the town?"

'I replied, "I saw about it on the television in the North."

'He turned around to me and said, "That is me." He smirked as he said it.

'I immediately took this as an admission that he had killed this lady. I looked at him for a few seconds. I was shocked. He was looking me straight in the eye. I could see he was smirking, and content that he was able to brag about his involvement in the murder. I could not believe what I was hearing. I turned my back on this man in disbelief. I was numb. After a few moments, my wife asked what was wrong with me. I gave him the cold shoulder, but he was asking if we would like to call to his home the next day with our dogs.

'Very shortly after this, they both left. At that stage, the girl behind the bar, Maura, came running around to say, "Do you know who you were with? He is the person that killed the girl." All the bar clapped. I think they were doing this because the couple had left. I was in despair. We left the bar shortly afterwards – I did not finish my pint. I can remember thinking to myself that I must speak with a guard, and I actually looked for one as we walked back to our accommodation.'

Diana backed up her husband. She had already heard of the murder from her mother, while Trish, the waitress in the Waterside Inn that evening, had mentioned that a local man was under suspicion. 'But at no time was I made aware of who he was.' She added: 'The next day, we went into The Galley once more, around 6 p.m. As we drank our first and only drink, the same couple entered the bar. We acknowledged each other's presence by nodding, but there was no conversation between us. We finished our drink and left.'

There was no doubt about whom the McKennas had

been talking. The Galley's owner, Dave Galvin, confirmed it was Jules' painting on the wall, a view of The Lobster Pot bar in Goleen, bought eighteen months previously. Barmaid Maura O'Callaghan told gardaí she had indeed walked over to Jim and Diana, whom she knew. 'Jim said to me that [Bailey] said, "I'm the man."'

*

It was New Year's Eve 1998, two years after Sophie had been killed, and young Schull couple Richie and Rose Shelley were out celebrating. Rose Shelley kept a diary, and this is her entry for that evening:

Anyway, New Year's Eve we spent in Hackett's, having been turned away from everywhere else because it was too late . . . At the stroke of midnight, we were sitting with Ian Bailey and Jules, and, perhaps consequently, nobody else.

R [Richie] was kissed by Jules, and Ian and I felt a bit left out . . . The Baileys claimed people were adjourning to theirs and so we went off with them, out into the middle of nowhere where they, in all senses, live.

Nobody else arrived or, we suspect, [were] ever intended to. We sat drinking vodka and smoking, and I had to go off and be womany with Jules when my period appeared. Ian went off to put on his native American loincloth, and, spiritual powers thus enhanced, proceeded to try and put Richie in a trance.

But matters were about to deteriorate, reflected in the diary and also in formal statements given to gardaí.

'He spoke about the murder,' said Richie in a statement. 'He showed us paper clippings and stuff. It went on most of the night. We were there until about 3 a.m.'

Rose thought Bailey 'quite obsessed; he wanted to talk about all the different angles. This conversation went on for so long. Normally you would talk about different things. It would have been two hours, all in all. I kept trying to steer the conversation in different ways, but he didn't want to [leave the topic]'.

Bailey brought out blankets, but the Shelleys had a quick consultation in the kitchen and decided to ring Richie's father, Johnny. 'My wife was uneasy with the way the night was going. She wasn't comfortable.'

Richie went looking for a phone and stumbled into Bailey's bedroom. 'He was in the bed. I woke him. I think he said the phone was in the kitchen. I called my father to collect me. He [Bailey] came back to the kitchen and said he was upset. He was crying, and put his arms around me, and said some words. He said to me, "I did it, I did it."

'I was saying, "You did what?" and he said, "I went too far."

'Then he let me go and just went back into his own room, just disappeared again. I assumed it was the murder.'

The Bailey phrase 'went too far' was also given in evidence by Billy Fuller, when he recounted being accused by him of carrying out the murder: 'You went too far. You had to finish her off.'

Rose Shelley had witnessed everything Bailey said to Richie, and was now 'very nervous' and wanting to leave. 'I felt very sober at that point because what Ian said shocked me,' she said. Ian had been 'despairing' when he had put his arms around Richie, crying and repeating that he did it, he did it, she said. 'It was very clear and succinct – that he had murdered Sophie Toscan du Plantier. It was an immediate recognition that he was doing some kind of confession. I was very frightened at that point.'

They walked half a mile from the house and Richie's father picked them up. Rose recorded it in her diary. He 'delivered us, safe as we ever may be, now that we are the murderer's best friends'.

The Shelleys met Bailey again hours later, 'the following morning' in Hackett's. It was before noon on New Year's Day. Richie said, 'He was there having a drink, and I was having a drink, and I approached him and said that last night I didn't think he was guilty, "Now I think you are." He didn't say anything.'

The Shelleys wrestled with their consciences, and came forward only after consulting a clergyman and respected family friend – who sent them straight to gardaí. Ironically, Bailey had made comments to Detective Superintendent Dermot Dwyer when the latter called up to The Prairie nearly two years earlier, on 31 January 1997. Dwyer had written a memo: 'He [Bailey] stated that he felt it was not a local person who committed the murder, as the person who did it would feel compelled to tell about having done it – and to date this had not happened.'

It is noteworthy that Jules did not take issue with the Shelleys' claims of Bailey saying 'I did it, I did it.' Instead she said in one of her statements, later repudiated, 'It looked like he was admitting to killing Sophie.' She confirmed the words used.

Billy Fuller met Jules' mother Beryl at The Prairie soon after Bailey's release from custody. 'I know her well,' he said. 'During conversation she said to me that, when back from her interrogation, Jules broke down to her and said, "I think Ian might have done it." She [Beryl] was upset when she was telling me this. The only thing she knew was that Ian knew the murdered lady, but he was a social leech and knew everybody.'

Fuller gave a statement to gardaí. He told the author: 'Bailey also confessed to my father. He said "I did that."' Two other people witnessed the admission, he said.

On a separate occasion, said Fuller, Bailey produced a picture of people at the Christmas Swim. 'He pointed to people in the photograph saying "It could be him, or it could be him".'

While continuously claiming a French connection, Bailey even stooped to naming his friend Alfie Lyons – from whom he regularly obtained cannabis – labelling him as a likely suspect to Caroline Mangez and in front of photographers Colman Doyle and Ian Vickery.

The guards already had plenty of circumstantial evidence that implicated Bailey – but the state prosecution service was continuing to sit on its hands.

CHAPTER 28

Twisting the Noose

By the summer of 1997, everyone, including Bailey apparently, was becoming fed up with the lack of development in the case, amid continuing community stress and strain. Biggs hardware store in Bantry had never been so busy, as people upgraded security with new locks or bought iron bars to keep by their beds. Yet Bailey continued to exhibit 'an absence of ordinary modesty', in the words of one resident. Journalists continued to make enquiries, to be met with standard garda replies that a file was with the Director of Public Prosecutions – even as it was quietly being added to, with gardaí then having to deal with further questions and further requests from the DPP's office.

When Jules was in detention, she had claimed Ian Bailey wore wellington boots on the night the murder took place, which was peculiar. Nobody that Sunday night at The Galley had apparently noticed, or thought it unusual, if he did.

None mentioned wellies in statements. There was mean-while no overall indication of senior garda thinking, but the uniforms were in a tizzy over internal questions about a bookie's pencil found at the murder scene. Had it been there before – or just dropped by some poor devil logging comings and goings? The incident room eventually decided on the latter.

There were no forensic revelations. It was all Sophie's blood. No other fingerprints or hairs, not even any results on footwear checked against the plaster casts taken of those footprints or bootprints. Sophie had washed those wine glasses, and there was no evidence that any guest had been in the house, investigators concluded. DNA analysis at that time was in its infancy; it needed a decent amount of fluid or tissue, lifted from a flat surface. Porous, uneven surfaces, such as rocks and stones, defied quick-swipe swabbing – while thin smears on metal were hard to fathom and could prove inexact by reason of being residues. At least the eventual full postmortem results, which came back in February, followed by an official report in March, showed that Sophie had not been sexually assaulted.

Thus, the case drifted, doomed now to be one of circum-stantial evidence. But, of course, tens of thousands of homicides have been solved in this way, from long ago to the relatively recent past. There was no DNA in the nine-teenth century, while fingerprints first solved a homicide in 1892. Scotland Yard only began to bank individual imprints in 1901. Before then, juries of twelve had been relied upon to punish the guilty 'beyond reasonable doubt', which in practice meant beyond any real uncertainty in their human assessment of the facts. Guilt or innocence was not wholly outsourced to science, and nor should it ever be, chiefly because traces can be found that connect utterly irrelevant individuals to locations and objects.

Yet Ian Bailey would rely on indicators and indistinct prints to suggest someone else must have been Sophie's killer. His industry in this matter went far beyond anyone else, and raises its own questions. There is reason behind a concept first coined by the Ancient Romans, which has lasted in codes of law for over two thousand years. In Latin, it is a question applicable to any set of circumstances: *Cui bono* – Who benefits?

*

Bailey may have started to play up to the whiff of sulphur about him, possibly thinking his very notoriety and eccentricity could act as a shield – he could not be a killer, because he was larger than life itself. It was this tightrope he attempted to walk in July 1997 when the *Sunday Independent* printed a dramatic first-person account by journalist Brighid McLaughlin. A slightly different version was carried months later in the *Independent on Sunday*, under the headline 'A Devil in the Hills'.

It was Bailey's first set-piece Irish interview since mine, five months earlier. He had been told by his solicitor to maintain silence, but a feature in Ireland's biggest-selling newspaper evidently attracted him. 'I had been bombarded from February onwards by the press and we had sent them away,' he said. But he missed the limelight, and – to adapt a business term – may have thought himself too big to fail.

McLaughlin unwittingly used the same verb as the actor Anne Cahalane: 'At 3.35 p.m., Bailey bounded into the hotel.' He was 'good-looking, big, with dishevelled, shoulder-length hair'. Bailey immediately offered some kooky wisdom: 'A Chinese lady read my fortune after the murder. This terrible thing was caused by jealousy.' He refused to expand.

Bailey was able to tell McLaughlin that he had met her before, in Kinvara, County Galway. She did not remember, but he provided details to verify the occasion. Then he said, 'You look like Sophie. It's your hairstyle.'

Brighid accompanied Bailey to the studio where she saw a disorganised writer's table, with a bottle standing on top. Bailey watched her, commenting, 'Vodka. Gives clarity of vision like no other drink.' There was a magazine cover, about the resurgence of interest in Michael Collins since the Neil Jordan movie. 'Hero or Villain?' ran the tagline. They chatted, he enlarged on his suffering and murder theories, and then Bailey offered to drive Brighid back to her hotel.

Instead of turning left down the narrow road that would bring me to Schull, he took a sharp right and belted up a mountainside. 'I haven't had much concentration since the murder,' he said, swerving past a large rock. 'I feel nervy, as if something has broken my spirit.' With flustered hands, he laboured with the gears. He seemed to be getting more excited as he spoke of the murder. There were beads of sweat on his chin.

After twenty minutes, he jammed on the brakes at the top of a hill overlooking a vast emptiness. 'This is where I stopped on the night of the murder,' he said, wiping his forehead. We sat there in silence. After five long minutes, he opened the door and bolted out towards the back of the car. My heart dropped when I saw him return with a roll of blue nylon baling twine.

He stretched it slowly out, fingered it for what seemed like an eternity, then twisted it into a noose with a knot on the end.

This is it, I thought. He's going to kill me, for sure. 'What's the baling twine for?' I asked with exquisite caution. He said nothing, just kept twisting. I have never felt terror like it. 'It's for my tomatoes,' said Bailey in a high, clear voice. And then, he slowly rolled the noose back into a ball, stuffed it into the side of his door, and drove me back [to The Prairie].

Bailey had bounded out to buy the paper on the Sunday morning. 'After I read it, I felt sick to the pit of my stomach,' he told the libel trial he would initiate in 2003. 'She betrayed me. She told me it would be a sympathetic piece. Yet she refers to me as prime suspect a number of times. I didn't describe myself as the prime suspect. I was a suspect, but I didn't consider myself a suspect.'

There had been no menacing of McLaughlin, he insisted. There were several ways to Schull. 'I brought her back over Hunt's Hill. Things in the car were fine. She didn't say she was nervous. There was a spectacular view.' He granted that he had 'a bead of sweat', but this was because it was a hot, sunny day. 'I can't remember whether I laboured with the gears. Before the Methodist chapel I saw a ball of twine and I stopped to collect that. I did not shoot open the door, didn't bolt to the boot. I got out of the car and got the twine and got back in. She was curious about it and asked what was that for, and I explained. I was shocked at the context that she put it in.' And the liquid in the vodka bottle 'was water, because the supply in the studio was tainted'. He protested: 'She seemed normal. After the trip to Hunt's Hill, I brought her back, and she spoke to Jules with no indication of fear, or paranoia, or anything.'

*

During the interview, Bailey gave Brighid the exact remark he had previously made to me: 'There was a claim that because it was a full moon that night, I became some sort of werewolf monster.' It was word for word, but while gardaí had asked him whether he was affected by the moon, the transcripts of his interviews show the 'werewolf' word was never put to him, let alone 'werewolf monster'.

Bailey had form for odd nocturnal wanderings. In the summer of 1994, he had called to Billy Fuller's mother, Mary, late at night. He had drink taken. 'When on a break from my father, she was staying in a caravan in Gleantáin. Bailey visited friends there. He left quite late – then knocked on my mother's caravan at 1 a.m. He was stood with a big staff. She asked what he wanted. He said a chat. She invited him in. They had tea and she asked him to leave, which he did, quite respectably.' It wasn't unusual for Bailey to roam around late at night, but his presence wasn't always appreciated.

On the night of a full moon two months after Sophie's

death, 22 February, Ceri Williams heard terrifying noises outside her home. 'I had the doors locked, and I put on my boots to go see, but decided not to go out. I heard a rage and shouting of words. It was a powerful voice and I recognised it as Ian Bailey, whom I know well. I got a knife and a poker. I was upstairs with Katie, my daughter.'

There was bellowing and roaring. 'I heard him shout the words, "No, No, No," and the last "Nooo" was long and sustained. The wind had also picked up and I was almost sick from fear. I thought I heard the word "Sorry" being shouted, but cannot be sure. It stopped about 1.20 a.m.'

Bailey continued toying with this werewolf concept, tempting journalists into his occult world. He had done the same with Superintendent Dermot Dwyer at The Prairie: 'He showed me a small bottle labelled 'Rescue Remedy' which he always took with him, and took a few drops at times of full moon. He mentioned that the full moon does have a real effect. He always felt unease, fear, edgy, something like pre-performance anxiety.'

Brighid also quoted one unnamed local: 'He plays surreal games with the gardaí. He eggs them on. After the murder he was the only person who seemed to be enjoying it. He was on a high with excitement.' This opinion was suggestive, and the whole article was the subject of that compendious legal writ, later dismissed at a hearing.

The newspaper's lawyer had removed a paragraph, never published, that started with someone calling Bailey an 'aggressive boyo', and ending with a friend referencing his violence towards women. 'He sees women purely as objects. A woman like Sophie du Plantier wouldn't have had any time for his artistic bent and probably rejected him. This would have made Bailey very angry'.

Brighid mentioned in print Bailey's sense of martyrdom: 'At least I have the freedom to be out selling lettuce. I can go to a music session, not like the Guildford Four or the Birmingham Six.' Except that there had not yet been any miscarriage of justice in his own case. No prosecution. Not even charges laid.

Another tone-deaf quote: 'Positive things are happening. Now I'm told it's not hair they found in her hand, but coat fibres. That is no use to the gardaí. But I know all the DNA tests have come back negative. That is what I've heard from my own sources. I didn't kill du Plantier. I have nothing on my conscience.'

Next, he claimed that the gardaí had tapped his phone – Bailey would go to the Jackson home to make calls – and had opened his mail. Then he made an entirely spurious claim about myself, which I read with arching eyebrows: 'They sent a journalist over to Gloucestershire where I lived and worked. My ex-wife is saying that I beat her up. But in my heart, I am not a violent man.'

I read this newspaper article carefully at home, thinking it over. Bailey said, 'My tracks would have been there if I had done it. The gardaí drove all along the lane. At one stage, two vehicles were driving past the body. Any tracks are gone. It's so frustrating not being able to write about this.' I saw in these words the usual suggestion of garda incompetence, but also Bailey strongly implying something else – that the killer had used a car.

Brighid McLaughlin offered another perspective on cars.

When Bailey gave her a lift, she had been brought back to The Prairie after the incident on Hunt's Hill, instead of into Schull as originally planned. '[Jules] Thomas needed to get some groceries in the village, so offered to bring me back into Schull. "I'll come, too," he said, squeezing into the passenger seat. As we entered the town, her car hit a kerb on Ballydehob road. Nothing could have prepared me for Bailey's reaction. He simply lost it. His whole personality changed as he called Thomas every name under the sun. She remained calm, but her hands were shaking on the steering wheel.'

McLaughlin was also unwilling to buy some of Bailey's earlier reporting, such as his contention that Sophie was promiscuous, something which the gardaí also refused to accept. 'She came to Ireland for peace and tranquillity, not sex,' said one. Bailey took his visiting journalist to The Galley, 'where I was last seen on the night of the murder'. It still seems a peculiar thing to say. Perhaps he enjoyed the hubbub of nervous gossip created when they entered.

The article finished with valedictory words from Bailey: 'He turned to me with a knowing, radiant smile: "Mind yourself, Brighid." I was petrified.' But Bailey was adamant that he certainly didn't use that phrase 'and I wouldn't use it'.

After Bailey's death in early 2024, Brighid wrote in the *Sunday Independent* that she suspected that he was indeed guilty of Sophie's murder, 'though I have no concrete evidence'. She wondered about the mentality needed to withstand 'the hot tongues of gossip, the pressure of twenty-seven years of suspicion'.

CHAPTER 29

Unravelling Marie Farrell

Marie Farrell rapidly became aware that everyone knew she was the star witness after her formal identification as 'Fiona' by gardaí. Perhaps there was nothing else for it – and so she went on national television, at Kealfadda bridge, confirming to *Prime Time* in summer 1997 that she had seen someone there on the night of the murder. It was either brave or foolhardy. Immediately after Bailey's release from arrest, she had assured gardaí: 'I am definite it was him.' Then, Bailey began intimidating Farrell.

She contacted detectives, saying she was concerned for her safety. 'I felt if he was capable of murder, maybe I was at risk.' She told them that she was receiving silent phone calls, and worse. Bailey was glaring, staring, making cut-throat gestures in the street or when passing – even pointing fingers and thumb to his head in mock gunshot, free of any irony from his own accusations against the guards. Kerrie

McKenzie, Billy Fuller's girlfriend, said Bailey had threatened her with the cut-throat gesture because he knew Fuller was talking to gardaí. Rose Shelley, after her own New Year's Eve experience, reported that Bailey intended to 'systematically intimidate' female witnesses. Marie asked the guards why he wasn't being arrested and charged with the murder. 'He could kill me in two minutes.'

Bailey brazenly walked into her shop one day in 1997 and asked her to cash a cheque. He produced it, held it up and moved closer. 'That is all her death was worth to me,' Bailey said. 'There is no money in bumping people off. I billed them for thirty pounds, but they only sent me this.' It was for twenty pounds. Nervously, she cashed it and Bailey walked out. *The Examiner* cheque was later passed to gardaí, even as Marie earnestly sought more protection.

Bailey came up behind her in a pub, hissing, 'We need to talk.' She received more phone calls, heavy breathing – and knew it would have come from a call box. She met Bailey on the street and he was agitated. 'He shouted at me, "You didn't see me washing any blood"' A woman telephoned her at home and said, 'Keep your bloody mouth shut.'

Marie said, 'My life was a living nightmare. I am afraid to let my children out, in case he does anything to them.' Then she got a message that Bailey was going to come in and see her at the shop one Saturday – 28 June 1997 – when her husband was out.

Bailey later claimed that it was at *her* request, because she was getting more calls from the police than he was, and 'didn't want an innocent man to suffer'. Marie denied ever extending such an invitation 'I don't think any woman in her right frame of mind would encourage Ian Bailey to come into her shop when she was on her own. It's a well-known fact that he is abusive towards women.'

Bailey arrived as promised, opened his coat to show a tape recorder, and said, 'I am all wired up.' He glanced around and asked if the place was clean, not bugged. He was in the coffee shop and ice cream parlour that Farrell also ran, adjoining Tara Fashions. Bailey did not know gardaí had supplied a tape recorder, which Farrell had ready, under the counter. She had expected a straight-up exchange. Instead Bailey, who had drink taken, wandered off to sit at a table, checking the location for listening devices, then beckoning her over. 'I followed him up there and he produced notebooks. He had a poem written about some of the detectives investigating the murder. He produced a sheet of paper, and on it was my husband's business address and our [previous] home address in London, even addresses where I lived in Longford, where I am from. He said that he knew things about me, and that if I scratched his back, he would scratch mine.

'He gave me a business card, told me to ring his solicitor, say that I made false statements about him. I told him I couldn't do that. I hadn't made false statements about anybody. He said at one point, "I didn't kill Sophie, but I know you saw me at the bridge." I was terrified.'

Marie Farrell made an excuse to check on the counter and told the girl working there to 'run out and make phone calls to detectives to tell them what was going on in the shop, and [to] get up here'. Two fifteen-year-old boys now wandered into the coffee shop and Marie was 'relieved to see them', according to one named Oisín Quinn. He and Noel McBrearty sat down nearby and eyeballed Ian Bailey, whom they claimed was drunk. It was the middle of the day.

Bailey had made his point, assuring Marie he was an investigative journalist and had been doing some digging into her background. He could easily inform the UK authorities of her whereabouts, after her family's midnight flit from London when their welfare fraud had been discovered, he threatened. There had been a false claim for income support and housing benefit on the basis of Farrell being a lone parent, which she wasn't, and she was ordered to repay £27,000. Marie Farrell later lied about it in court: 'It was investigated and found to be a false complaint.' Bailey had left by the time the guards made it to Marie's shop.

Marie Farrell went to her solicitor about the endless menaces. A letter was sent on her behalf by Rachel O'Toole of Patrick Buckley & Co., solicitors, to Ian Bailey's solicitor on 31 July 1997. It warned Bailey to cease and desist from 'continual harassment and intimidation' of Farrell, citing cut-throat gestures and incidents, including that Bailey 'continually parks his car outside our client's premises', saying his campaign had left her 'severely upset and frightened'. Ms O'Toole sought a series of undertakings.

Bailey's solicitor never responded. It would have been standard procedure, however, and professional courtesy, to seek instructions from his client in such circumstances.

Marie Farrell did not withdraw her statements. Attempts were made by Bailey to get her to The Prairie. He wanted

Marie to make a tape-recorded confession that the police had put her up to the Kealfadda sighting. Bailey would later insist it was instead the guards who were supposedly black-mailing Farrell, over the British benefits fraud, to force her to denounce him.

The weeks rolled into months, and District Court summonses against Marie's husband, Chris Farrell, on minor matters were struck out when gardaí failed to appear to give evidence. Warrants for the non-payment of fines up to IR£1,500 were returned as unable to be executed. Some gardaí protested against malfeasance, but there seemed a greater game in play: keeping Marie Farrell sweet.

In September 1997, a 327-page file on Bailey was submitted to the Director of Public Prosecutions, seeking permission to bring charges on foot of the evidence. But there would be no decision to formally charge anyone, even when the file was substantially augmented. So, Ian Bailey was still free to roam at will.

CHAPTER 30

Switching Sides

At some point Marie Farrell had had enough of everything – rumours, menaces, her own ongoing dread, and official inactivity. Years had gone by and the case had fallen fallow, becoming a prolonged legal argument between Ireland and France. Farrell made persistent complaints about intimidation, repeatedly seeking garda protection, saying she was in fear. The gardaí did their best to help her. And yet they had raided her house in 1998 and seized a revolver. 'The firearm was forwarded to the ballistics section at garda headquarters where it was found that the barrel was bored and it was no longer deemed to be a firearm.' An official report said that 'the gun was returned'.

By January 2004, Bailey was smarting after his libel action failure against a number of newspapers, which saddled him with a legal bill of at least IR£200,000 which he could not pay – nor a bill for his appeal to the High Court, which he was forced to abandon after he falsely alleged improper conduct by solicitors for the other side. Bailey's next move was to send Farrell a retaliatory legal letter threatening action if she did not withdraw her remarks about expecting garda action that she had made after his courtroom defeat. Her solicitor's response asserted truth and again demanded he cease his campaign of intimidation.

A year later, in early 2005, Bailey let it be known he would be launching a suit against the state for wrongful arrest. Within weeks he had secured the full backing of Marie Farrell. Just as she had switched Ian Bailey from one side of the road to the other at Kealfadda, now she herself simply switched sides entirely. Her defection to the camp of the murder suspect caused utter consternation in the ranks of An Garda Síochána. It also prompted a major internal investigation.

The woman, who had at first gone to great lengths to disguise her identity but later appeared on national television about her sighting at Kealfadda, would now say she had been browbeaten by the guards into placing Ian Bailey at the bridge. She had also given false evidence to the 2003 libel trial, she said, but now vowed that she would lie no more. Marie was going to unburden herself and tell the truth at last.

Her shop assistant, Geraldine O'Brien, had a point of view about this unexpected turn of events. 'Marie Farrell told me of her involvements with the investigation. From my recollection she had no complaints against garda. In fact, if there was ever a problem or if she was ever upset about anything, she could contact Schull garda station and there was always somebody to help her at the other end of the phone. I recall that everybody was scared of Ian Bailey at that time. I was scared of him, and Marie was shaking when he came into the shop, absolutely terrified. I was very friendly with Marie. We would have socialised in the same pub. We confided in each other.' Geraldine O'Brien was aged seventeen at the time.

Now, much later, the two women bumped into each other again in Cork city. They promptly went for a chinwag at a café. Marie said 'there was a case coming up that Mr Bailey was involved in, and that she was going to be a witness. She'd been told that he would receive substantial amounts of money'. Geraldine could not believe her ears at Marie's blithe turnaround. 'She said a couple of million. Then she said she would probably get something from that too.'

'I certainly did not say that. It never happened,' Marie would complain in response to Geraldine's assertions, although she could not explain why Ms O'Brien would make it up – nor then make false statements about her to gardaí.

*

Bailey was also eyeing a great achievement. He was looking at his superstar witness, as she entered the High Court witness box in his wrongful arrest suit on 2 December 2014 and took up the testament to swear to tell the truth. Marie Farrell wasted no time in making lurid allegations. She said a detective sergeant had followed her into the ladies' toilets at Schull golf club in 1998, where she worked. He exposed himself; she wasn't interested. He allegedly said to her, 'Isn't it a real turn-on, fitting up the long black bollocks [meaning to frame Bailey]'. The garda was intoxicated, but tried to get her up against the wall and to open her clothes, she said. As gardaí in court shook their heads and grimaced, Farrell insisted she had pushed the garda away and reminded him that his wife was outside. She also declared that she had been instructed by a detective to send cease-and-desist correspondence to Bailey through her solicitor. None of what was alleged in that letter was true. 'It was a mad time,' she said. 'It was like something surreal.'

It was about to get worse. Gardaí in the early days were actively trying to influence her against Bailey, she said. They told her he was a strange person, 'into all sorts of weird things'. When there was a full moon, they said, Bailey 'would go to Barleycove beach and sit in a rocking chair as ten lesbians danced around him reciting poetry'. It must stand as the single most bizarre line ever typed into an Irish court record by a stern stenographer. Farrell said she had gone along with the guards because they told her Bailey had killed Sophie and might kill again. They had at first assured her that, on being confronted with her account, Bailey would confess, plead guilty and be sentenced to life imprisonment. She would not even have to give evidence.

Farrell said she agreed to garda requests that she sign blank statement pages. She signed them over and over. 'To be honest, I didn't give it much thought.' A garda provided her with a mobile phone, she said, then took it back a year later because it was needed for 'a drugs bust'. The guards had ideas that were 'like something out of *Miami Vice*', the TV detective drama – and the meeting in the ice cream parlour had been a garda plan for him to 'confess everything'.

They wired up the shop but she couldn't activate the recording system 'because the plug was too big to reach the socket [*sic*]'.

Marie kept going: another detective had stripped naked and asked her for sex while she was minding a house in West Cork, she claimed. She told him where to go. But counsel for the state now had the chance to cross-examine her 'wholly incredible' evidence. She first agreed she had perjured herself about the sighting at Kealfadda throughout the earlier libel trial, when she gave evidence for the newspapers. But she maintained: 'I am not a liar', even though it had all started with a lie to her husband about a girls' night out. Now she could not remember what year it was when the naked detective, no longer undercover, demanded intercourse. She was further told that the detective sergeant was rejecting her ladies' toilet story as 'the height of fantasy'. Two women at the golf club were also disputing her claim that one of her tasks was to check the toilets. They maintained that she hadn't told anyone about the alleged sexual assault. Marie said she did not regard it as a big deal. After all, when she was younger, incidents like that happened 'every other weekend'.

Farrell said she had been misquoted in a *Daily Mirror* article two years earlier about blank garda statement forms she had supposedly pre-signed. She was shown her own quote: 'They weren't blank, they were already filled out, and I just signed them'. Farrell resisted an invitation to claim that the reporter had made it up. 'Maybe it was written down wrongly.'

Written down wrongly had been some of her own contradictory statements about the Kealfadda bridge incident, to which questioning now turned. It was shortly before midday when Paul O'Higgins, for the state, suddenly asked the witness on her oath to name her male companion, 'the man in the car'. Farrell said she would not do that.

Judge John Hedigan interrupted: 'This is one of the most serious cases heard for many years. You are obliged to say the name of the person.'

Farrell replied sharply: 'I'm not. I'm going. I'm having nothing further to do with it.'

With that, Marie, who was already wearing her white outdoor coat, took her handbag, descended the steps of the witness box, and exited the courtroom as the entire attendance watched open-mouthed. The judge told Bailey's legal team: 'It's your witness. She has walked out. She's been directed by the High Court to tell the whole truth to the jury. You cannot tell part of the truth.'

Bailey's senior counsel, Tom Creed, protested that she had not told a lie; 'she just hasn't told a name'. A sole solicitor had to pursue Farrell into the busy Dublin street to beg her to return to the witness box, warning that she could otherwise be jailed for contempt of court. A TV news crew caught it all on camera.

Farrell finally agreed, after forty minutes, on being warned that she would be arrested and brought before the court if she did not. At 3 p.m. she resumed her place in the box and was told by the judge that she had to publicly name the man. Mr Creed rose and wondered if it would be possible to write down the name on a piece of paper and hand it to His Lordship and the jury? The judge was having none of it. This was a free and open trial and Farrell had named others in a manner 'extremely embarrassing to them and their families'. She must state the name.

All eyes upon her, Farrell meekly said it was a childhood friend from her native Longford, John Reilly. 'I knew him when I was a teenager.'

He was dead, of course. So why all the secrecy?

'I just didn't want to make things difficult at home. I just wanted a quiet life.'

The woman who had made the most lurid allegations against gardaí added without a trace of irony: 'I stormed out of court because it feels to me as if it's turning into a personal assault on my private life.' She denied inventing Reilly, but had previously implicated others – telling some guards that the man she had been with was Oliver Croghan, a musician from Longford, who had died of Hodgkin's disease. A third Longford man was named under oath, Farrell claiming that the guards had put his name in her mouth. Her husband Chris suspected a Dutchman. Other purported lovers were interviewed by detectives in Schull, outraged by the false suggestions and desperate to stay unidentified. The guards kept confidence.

At this, the wearied judge now adjourned for the day, doing so with a grave warning to Farrell: 'Any further walk-outs will be your last. I would like you to give very clear consideration to the manner in which you are giving evidence. There are very serious penal sanctions for perjury.'

The next day the judge – exasperated by a video showing Marie Farrell confessing the truth of her UK benefit fraud to garda investigators when she had insisted in his courtroom that it had been a 'false complaint' – said he would be referring her testimony to the authorities for consideration of a criminal charge over deliberate lies in evidence. But no such prosecution would ever be brought, as destined with the wider murder. Much to the relief of maligned gardaí – one of whom had been inadvertently recorded calling Marie a pervert – the entirety of Farrell's testimony was branded from the bench as a tissue of untruths. It was a fatal blow to Bailey's case for damages.

Judge Hedigan went on to throw out the bulk of the plaintiff's claims against the state, saying they were statute-barred, the allegations not being raised within six years. Out went wrongful arrest, and much more besides. But Hedigan allowed two stark questions to go before the jury. The first was: 'Did the gardaí conspire to falsely implicate Mr Bailey in the murder of Sophie Toscan du Plantier by threats, inducements or intimidation, such that he became the man seen at Kealfadda bridge?' The second: 'Did gardaí similarly falsely conspire to obtain statements from Marie Farrell that Bailey had intimidated her?'

The foreman nodded that they understood what was being asked, and the jury duly retired. They were all back in a short while, filing into their seats with that 'couple of million' metaphorically hanging in mid-air. The clerk asked them had they reached verdicts on which all were agreed? They had. The foreman handed over the completed issue papers. The clerk read them aloud. To the first question – whether Bailey had been deliberately framed by gardaí – the jury had answered No. To the second – conspiracy to bribe Marie Farrell – they once more answered No. Gardaí were grinning all around the court, both standing and seated. Many others were smiling too.

The judge thanked the twelve for their service. The case was concluded. A gavel banged. All rise! The judge left the court and Ian Bailey blew out his cheeks, sagging in his seat. This would be another bill he couldn't pay.

Marie Farrell had money problems too, extensive debts. Some, she had testified, were from hiring staff for her shops so that she wouldn't have to face Bailey if he walked in. She eventually moved to Roscommon – where she initiated legal moves after claiming to have won a €13,000 local Lotto jackpot. Tarmonbarry village organisers, however, refused to pay out, saying they were unable to find the winning ticket.

Marie Farrell's number was up, but she had caused havoc with the case. Where the guards could have been working on other leads, they had been forced to protect and dance attendance on an erratic witness, whose Kealfadda bridge sighting was now utterly worthless. Despite the fact that a case might have been mounted without her, the lunacy of it all seemed fatal contamination. How would they find Sophie's killer now?

CHAPTER 31

Timing Is Everything

Back to basics. The murder scene itself. Marie Farrell's testimony could now never be used, with no more notion of anyone ever seeing anything at Kealfadda bridge. The guards had gone to great lengths to have her waste their own time, and that was an end to it. Sub-aqua unit searches in the estuary by the long stream, and even off nearby beaches, had found nothing. Yet irrepressible Ian Bailey was still very much going to put himself into the picture, and to a quite literal degree.

First principles remain. Who had means, motive and opportunity? There had been more than a thousand statements taken, yet no credible new suspects had ever emerged. To test their thinking, the gardaí had consulted international colleagues, including the FBI Academy at Quantico, Virginia. They had also secured a series of profiles of the killer from international psychoanalysts, each of them working independently. There was then a disclosure in the *Irish Daily*

Mail in February 2007, a revelation that the reports 'dove-tailed into a single type – a self-publicist who would not be able to stop talking about the murder'.

Such opinions were not hard evidence, but they reassured detectives that they were not on the wrong track. The patient piecing together of small items of detail – to make up a mosaic of hard fact – is essential in the tough slog of circumstantial cases. For instance, if the killer was right-handed, then the left hand that pinioned the victim was more likely to be scratched and bloodied. Fundamental to keep in mind was that someone – some man – had obliterated Sophie, and had to be brought to book for her sake, that of her family, and for all society. Naysayers and nitpickers of any candidate might also have a moral obligation to credibly establish the alternative case for another.

What did chief suspect Ian Bailey know and when did he know it?

*

Return to that fateful Monday, 23 December 1996. Eddie Cassidy of *The Examiner* had stumbled on the story. At 12.20 p.m. he had telephoned Bantry garda station about another matter. He was told that Superintendent J.P. Twomey had gone to Schull to investigate 'a serious incident'. Cassidy then telephoned Schull and reached Twomey. 'He revealed that a female body had been found, around Toormore. He gave no further details,' said Cassidy. Hence the journalist's whirlwind of calls to people who might know the lie of the land in Toormore, or who could recommend someone else to call who might have information.

'I was not aware the body was that of a French national, or a young or old person,' said Cassidy. It was a dead female, out in the open, and could be – probably was – the result of accident, misadventure or natural causes. 'I rang back the superintendent after about fifteen minutes and he told me the woman was in her late twenties. He did not give me specific details of where to go.' A woman dead in her late twenties was a story – Cassidy tried to get a paragraph or two into that day's *Evening Echo*, but the paper had 'gone early to bed', meaning it had gone to print. With all that Christmas advertising, it had to be on motorbikes and in vans to get onto shelves and streets for maximum sales availability.

Cassidy's net closed a little when he rang Fr Denis Cashman, who was based in Goleen, the largest settlement in Toormore district. He had been to the scene, but would also 'not give me any details'. Something about the timbre of the priest's voice told the experienced newsman it was very bad. It didn't sound like a fall from a horse, a heart attack or a hit-and-run. Further calls followed because Cassidy's antennae had become fully attuned. He discussed with other journalists any 'likely location, names of people'. An auctioneer, Dermot Sheehan, mentioned Kealfadda. By 1.38 p.m., Eddie had made hasty calls to compare notes on the suspicious death with Tom MacSweeney of RTÉ, Dick Hogan of *The Irish Times* and Dick Cross of the *Irish Independent*. All southern correspondents, they wanted to first of all establish the location. All they had was Toormore, a regional name for thirteen townlands.

Cassidy knew of a local freelancer – Ian Bailey – who

had been looking for work, and now he had a job for him: find out anything – who, what, where, when, how. Bailey gave various times for when he was called by Cassidy, who himself originally thought it was at 1.20 p.m. His phone records established the truth – he had called Bailey at 1.40 p.m. on the afternoon of the body's discovery. Eddie waived his privacy rights, while a court warrant produced phone records at the other end. Eddie's call was received at 1.40 p.m. at The Prairie.

This contact with a landline in the name of Catherine Jules Thomas is an anchoring point. The call lasted two minutes and thirty-three seconds. In other respects, Eddie Cassidy never varied. He told Bailey all he knew in the hope that he could help – Toormore, suspicious death, woman, young. Not much to go on, but the more people trying to find out, the better. In the meantime, there was a message left on his phone by *The Examiner* newsdesk, also about the incident. 'It instructed me to travel to Schull.' But Cassidy waited a little longer until he could link up with a photographer.

*

If Ian Bailey was not aware of a possible murder before 1.40 p.m., and could not respond in advance of that time, then it raises serious questions about his activities earlier that day. The records show Ian Bailey made two phone calls that morning, two hours before he was told anything by Cassidy.

The first, at 11.30 a.m., was to Pól Ó Colmáin, originally from Dundalk, now living in West Cork. He'd met Bailey at pub sessions and they had a mutual interest in poetry and music. 'I got a phone call in the late morning, the day of the murder, from Ian Bailey,' Ó Colmáin told gardaí. 'He rang me up, he was very excited. He had recently decided to go back to journalism and joined a back-to-work scheme.

'He told me there was a *murder* in the area. I took his excitement to mean that this was quite a break for him as a journalist, to have a big story almost immediately. I can't remember whether he said the name or nationality.' He did mention whereabouts, 'but the location meant nothing to me', and Pól could not recall it. 'I was in bed at the time. My son answered the phone downstairs. He came up and told me, and I went down and talked to Ian and got that news from him.'

Ó Colmáin couldn't really pin down the time, but science would see to that. 'My normal habit would be that I am not a late riser. I don't get up at the crack of dawn, but I'm not late.' On the other hand, it was the holidays, and he had been out late the night before. 'So I would say it was probably about 11.30 a.m., if I was still in bed. But I got up shortly after that. I have two young sons, so I had to feed them.'

Bailey thus knew of a murder over two hours before he was 'officially' told. His reaction, however, was to deny he had mentioned any murder to Pól Ó Colmáin, because he naturally did not know about it. He had rung him up to discuss various things. He could not remember precisely what. They were trivial and forgettable. He was keeping in touch with friends over Christmas. But then he said – if somehow there was mention of a murder, which he very much doubted

– it would have to have been in the afternoon, after he had been told by Cassidy. There was one other matter. Bailey dropped a satchel over to Ó Colmáin's house in January 1997. He asked him to look after the bag for a couple of days. 'He said he had some writings in it and he didn't want anyone to take it.' The satchel contained what would become known as Ian Bailey's Black Diaries.

Ten minutes after the excited call to Ó Colmáin, Bailey was ringing the Leftwicks. Richard and Caroline were local market gardeners, originally from Devon. Bailey admitted in one of his court cases that he had rung them 'sometime before midday', which did not much help his cause. Caroline Leftwick thought it was between 11.30 a.m. and 12.30 p.m. The guards, of course, knew precisely when it was – but have never said. Let Bailey's own evidence stand: 'sometime before midday'. Even if on the stroke of noon, this was over an hour and a half before contact from Cassidy. Only two people knew what was said in that call.

'I answered the phone,' said Caroline. 'He said he would not be able to keep his appointment that day.' It was 'to collect some garlic we were keeping for him'. Why unable? 'Because there had been a murder.'

'Garlic' was said in court later to be a code word for cannabis. Caroline maintained that Bailey reneged on their appointment because 'there had been a murder in the locality, and he had the story. He sounded kind of excited about it'. Stop here too – Ó Colmáin and Leftwick were both reporting that Bailey was 'excited' about the murder on that morning, whereas his position was that he only learned about it, professionally, in the afternoon.

Caroline Leftwick was not excited. 'I was shocked. I asked him who was the victim – I was concerned it might be someone known to me. He said no, it was a Frenchwoman, on holiday, not someone I would know.'

Bailey denied telling Caroline about the murder in that phone call. She was certain he did: 'It was how I heard about the murder, this major event in all our lives in West Cork. I didn't forget that.'

And Caroline instantly told her husband. Richard gave a statement to gardaí in May 1997, when authorising them 'to carry out a check of incoming calls to my home on 23 December 1996'. He said, 'On completion of the call my wife told me it was Ian Bailey on the phone and there had been a murder, that he had to cover it. My wife said Ian Bailey sounded excited.' He told her it was Bailey's job. They 'put on the radio to listen to the 1 p.m. news to find out more, but it wasn't on it'. Not yet – but this simple act showed that the call to them was made long before Cassidy's to Bailey. Richard thought it could have been as early as noon. But the guards soon knew precisely: that the call was placed even earlier.

*

Jules Thomas was seen out and about in her Fiesta early on Monday, 23 December. Where was her partner? There would later be strong indications that Bailey had also been roaming abroad that morning, but had left the car by the time Jules was spotted behind the wheel. Billy Fuller remembered that he 'left home around 10 a.m. . . . and [later] drove down towards Kealfadda bridge. I saw a white Fiesta

278

in front of me. I knew straightaway it was Jules' car, and knew it was Jules driving. It was about 11 a.m. I followed her, in my blue VW Transporter, all the way to the main Schull–Goleen road, where she turned left – and then immediately turned right across the causeway.

'I must say that, shortly after I saw her, she was going around a bend and she put her left arm across to the passenger side, as if it was to stop something falling over on her. When she pulled into the causeway I just carried on [towards Schull]. She was alone in the car. The first I heard about the murder was when I came home between 6 and 7 p.m. I had not been up around Sophie's house or Alfie Lyons that day.'

What was it nearly tumbled over onto Jules as she drove, if Billy's story is accurate? Why did she stop at the causeway? Nonetheless, after completing whatever she was doing in the vicinity of Kealfadda, Jules drove out again and turned left towards the village of Goleen, just over five kilometres away, or only a six-minute drive.

She then went to a market there and visited Jimmy Camier's vegetable stall, where Sophie had been less than two days earlier. 'Jules approached the stall. I know this lady well. Ian Bailey had worked casually, now and then, with me,' said Camier in early 1997. 'I was struck by the fact that she was very distressed. There was a distraught, strange complexion about her. She looked very worried. Ian's name came up in conversation in relation to vegetables and his work for me. Out of the blue she said, "Ian has gone to report on the murder."'

Gardaí would later surmise that she had dropped Bailey

off in Dunmanus West, carrying her camera, before she was spotted alone in the car by Fuller. But now Camier was shocked. 'Immediately I asked her, "What murder?"

'She replied, "A Frenchwoman." She hung her head. "It's sad. But that's his job, to report."

'I am absolutely positive that the first I heard of the murder was from Jules Thomas between 11 a.m. and 11.30 a.m. on 23 December. My wife Geraldine and I discussed what she said to us after she left, but we decided not to say it to anyone else until it became common knowledge. The next person who spoke about the murder was Nicky Regan, a fisherman. He came to the stall around 2.45 p.m. From then on, the news was widespread. I'm positive that Jules Thomas mentioned it was a Frenchwoman that had been killed. Nicky Regan didn't say it was a Frenchwoman dead. I'm certain of that.'

Years later, in 2002, Geraldine couldn't remember when the conversation had been, just 'at some stage during the day'. Her husband had given Jules a chrysanthemum as a sympathetic gesture. All she could recall was Jules saying something like, 'It was a terrible thing to happen, but it's good for us', meaning that Ian would have some work out of it.

Jules rejected both the Billy Fuller and Jimmy Camier accounts, but they are chronologically close to each other, almost intersecting.

*

Fenella Thomas, Jules' youngest daughter, was briefly arrested in 2000. She gave a statement, amid bouts of crying, which placed her mother and Ian out of the house on the morning of 23 December, whereas they claimed to have stayed home until *The Examiner* phoned. Farmer Donal O'Sullivan vitally saw both in the Fiesta, returning to Lisscaha before 12.30 p.m.

'They were in Goleen,' said Fenella, who had just turned eighteen when detained. 'I have a vague recollection of them going, it was about 9 or 10 a.m., I think.' They were away for 'a few hours, maybe an hour or two. She [Jules] would usually bring the camera. She is an artist and if the weather was okay she would take photographs'. It was Fenella who answered the 1.40 p.m. phone call after Jules and Ian got back. She noticed Bailey had 'definitely marks on his nose, that's the best I can remember'. She then handed him the phone. 'It's the Cassidy guy.' Asked what exactly Bailey had said after the call, Fenella answered, 'There's a woman dead nearby, I don't think her nationality was discussed, just woman dead, body found; that's all, somewhere nearby in Schull.' This ended her formal statement, which she signed.

Cassidy said he didn't know the victim was a non-national until he arrived at the scene. Superintendent Twomey had only relented and given him clear directions to Sophie's house in a call placed at 2.52 p.m. He was there within the hour.

CHAPTER 32

In the Frame

Ian Bailey knew Eddie Cassidy would soon arrive in the area and that his own role would then quickly diminish. He wanted to be a part of the action, and it was within his right as a freelancer to try to carve out his own slice. After his call with Cassidy, his next move was to call Dick Cross of the *Irish Independent*, speaking to him at 1.45 p.m., when he described himself as a photojournalist. Cross said, 'The man calling himself Ian Bailey told me there was a murder at Toormore.' This was the call when, remarkably, Bailey offered Cross crime-scene photos. Bailey claimed they were taken before any guards had arrived on the scene, although 'the body was a bit away'.

Bailey asked if Cross would like him to cover the story for the *Indo*. He informed the veteran newsman, who would retire the following year after decades in the field, that Cassidy had told him to ring. This was a lie. The call lasted less than two minutes. Cross couldn't commission Bailey to do his job for him – he was about to head to Toormore himself – but nor could he turn down the offer of photographs taken before the area was cordoned off.

Cross noted the time of the call as 1.45 p.m. in his meticulously kept log book. Detectives from Anglesea Street station in Cork city came about three weeks later, and heard his story. One of them smiled and said, 'It was sixteen minutes to two.'

'I told them there was another call from Bailey, further liaising, at about five minutes to two, also in my log. They said it was at three minutes to two.'

Cross had given Bailey the number for Pádraig Beirne, photo editor of the *Irish Independent*. Beirne was adept at making the quick decisions his job called for. He got a call from Bailey at about 1.55 p.m., offering not only a picture of the scene, but of the body – and something else, too, even more extraordinary, which Bailey had not mentioned to Cross: an image of the woman alive, head and shoulders, known as a 'pick-up'.

The caller 'knew the woman was French. He said he had a picture of her, and asked me was I interested for the morning *Independent*'. Beirne said that depended: what was it like, and how did he have it? He wanted to make sure some middleman wasn't flogging someone else's picture that would produce another invoice afterwards. It was then he heard assurances that it was Bailey's own picture of the woman, which he *personally* had taken, and that she was a 'very good-looking woman'.

Beirne immediately perked up at this prospect. Could

Bailey wire it? If so, it would be a coup for Beirne at the afternoon conference about content for the following morning's paper; Beirne could flaunt it. However, Bailey didn't have a wire machine. Beirne proposed to connect Bailey with Mike McSweeney of the Provision agency in Cork, who did. He'd get Mike to call him, arrange to meet. On that call to Beirne, Bailey offered a complete photo service – he repeated that he had pictures of the scene. Beirne couldn't care less about a picture of the scene once he had a head-and-shoulders of the victim – and McSweeney could snap the scene when he arrived to collect. This was why portraits of people are called 'pick-up' or 'collect' pictures: newspapers want the victims seen in life, and they generally have to come from relatives, via the 'death knock' on someone's door. Bodies are extremely tricky, and landscapes generally a disaster because it had better be *really interesting* to go across five columns.

Beirne knew his trade from long experience. He wasn't going to rely on a newcomer, but instead on trusted hand Mike McSweeney. He also had to get the exclusive pick-up before anyone else. It was going to sell papers by the shed-load. Beirne himself went to the trouble of ringing McSweeney, grunting out what Mike had to do. McSweeney, for his part, knew a pick-up was pure gold. Beirne had now put him on his mettle.

McSweeney rang photographer Mike Brown of Reuters on his mobile, knowing his colleague was already on the way to the vicinity. He told him not to muck about trying to find the scene, but to ring this guy – Bailey – and meet him first, because he had a pick-up of the victim that was bound for the *Indo*. Brown pulled in his BMW to jot down the number. He called Bailey to find out where he was, before taking off again. 'When I rang Bailey from my mobile I asked him had he got [victim] pictures as I'd been told by Mike McSweeney that he had.' Only now did Bailey confuse Brown by being unclear about the pick-up. 'He said his partner took two pictures with a long lens at the scene earlier. I said we would talk about them when we met.'

Beirne was confident when he 'went into our daily editor's conference at 2.30 p.m. The murder was discussed and I outlined that our freelance photographer was en route and we hoped to have a pick-up of the dead woman'.

When Brown arrived at The Prairie at around 3.45 p.m., Bailey didn't have what was promised. There was a problem – no pick-up, no picture of the victim at all – and it would have to be communicated all the way back up the chain. Beirne, when he heard, would likely have been furious.

What had happened between Bailey's bragging about a lively image of a 'very good-looking' woman and this frustrating letdown? It would be some years before an answer to the mystery seemed to arrive, and in a profoundly sinister twist.

For now, what was clear is that, after speaking to Beirne, Bailey had taken positive action. He had driven straight to a scene that had not yet been made public, accompanied by Jules who had a camera. Jules said they acted on a hunch, because a foreigner had somehow been mentioned and Bailey remembered the Frenchwoman, among all internationals, that he had seen from a distance at Alfie Lyons' property eighteen months earlier. But Sergeant Hogan's question in the squad car holds good: even if he divined that 'foreign' meant French, how did he know she would be holidaying there in dreary December?

Jules also said it was pure 'luck' that they got to Dunmanus West. Yet a journalist has to think logically – as Cassidy, Cross, Beirne, McSweeney and Brown were all systematically demonstrating. Playing the percentages is the name of the game, massaging them into one's favour by first making calls, not haring off on a hunch.

McSweeney was livid when he finally got Bailey's pictures from Brown, who reported that there never was any pick-up, that it was some misunderstanding. Brown had gone to *The Examiner* office and developed both his own prints and Bailey's. 'His were no good. There were just two pictures on Bailey's roll, the rest blank. Those pictures were of the house and scene, taken also from behind the tape,' Brown said. In other words, not captured before the scene was cordoned off. Bailey had been lying; but to what possible journalistic purpose if returning to the profession after a long lay-off? He didn't have what he promised; he was a time-waster. McSweeney angrily described the sum total of Bailey's frames as 'the back of a garda's hat'. He threw the prints and 'negs' straight into the wastepaper bin. What an idiot, that guy Bailey was. Some photojournalist!

*

Bailey had to live with this humiliation a long while, even if he instantly started to achieve success just as a journalist, without any 'comprehensive' service. Tackled by detectives about what he had said to Cross and then to Beirne, the suspect had the usual excuse – people who heard the words he said were misunderstanding them and he had actually said something else entirely. Yet journalists habitually take contemporaneous notes when they are being told things over the phone.

Now, I knew Beirne well. I also know he would have rammed down the phone within thirty seconds on anyone promising *proposed* pictures; they would be lucky to hear an emphatically worded growl to call back when they actually had the *blankety-blank*. If Bailey didn't yet have pictures when Cross – on foot of a promise – gave him Beirne's number, then he had an ace up his sleeve; he could call Beirne later, when the photos were in the bag. But incredibly, Ian Bailey straight away played that ace. He put down the phone to Cross, and he called Beirne.

To make this even more emphatically clear: Beirne would never have called Mike McSweeney if Bailey only *might* be able to get some pictures while finding out about the victim. Beirne would not have given a nano-second to such nonsense. He would have eaten Bailey alive. And he would not have mentioned a pick-up at afternoon conference, where many others heard his grounds for optimism about getting an exclusive picture for page one that would smash the opposition. Yet Beirne did, in fact, call McSweeney, and McSweeney then called Brown, and Brown called Bailey – who must have thought better of it in the meantime.

*

In 2000, Patrick Lowney came forward. He lived in Clonakilty, and had been visited by a man who wanted him to develop a roll of film. The stranger had first phoned, to ask the garage owner if he was still doing photography as a sideline. He mentioned something about Ginny, who later became a professional photographer. Lowney remembered her as Jules' daughter, both being into photography. He agreed to process the roll. A few days later, the customer made the handover. Lowney assumed he'd be left with the job and was about to ask for a name, but the man said, 'No, can you do it now?' He asked how long it would take. Lowney said seven minutes, or a bit longer to let the prints dry.

He went upstairs to the darkroom, put on the heater, and 'threw the roll' into a developer tank, having pulled out the black-and-white film from its canister. 'After about seven minutes I took it out, held it up and shook off the water [fixer fluid]. I was glancing through the negatives up at the bulb. Thirty-six frames. The first ten or twelve were only people around a table. The next twenty to twenty-five were of a woman lying on the ground.

'The area around the body was a laneway, stones and grass in the middle of the road, grass verge and briars. One thing I did notice was that there was a strange-shaped stone somewhere between the woman's left elbow and wrist.' There was a brightness; she definitely had clothes on. The lower item of clothing was 'hip-tight and then it went out', stretched away from the figure. Lowney said the photos were 'all taken at night, of a very good quality'. Whoever took them knew what they were doing. In some of the negatives, he could make out a farmyard gate. There was also 'something like a sign fixed onto the gate'. Sophie's sign read: 'Please close gate.' Beyond its steel bars, her body had its white elasticated leggings strained to the barbed wire.

The photos were from different angles, 'some taken straight over the body, standing over – you could definitely see the shoes of the photographer', Lowney said, without describing whether a man or woman's, nor giving further footwear detail.

The customer had also arrived up as the images were developed, and the atmosphere became tense as Lowney's scrutiny continued. Then the man became agitated. He came over and took the still-wet prints from Lowney's gloved hands. They would have to be pegged up to dry, Lowney protested. The man took them away to a clothesline he could see in the rear, not for clothes but for drying prints, and said he would do it himself, making sure to ask for his negatives back. He was soon presented with those strips, unpegged the prints himself, popped them in a paper bag, and paid in cash. He promptly left. Lowney wasn't happy at what he had been forced to view, although he no longer had any hard evidence of what that was. He called the gardaí.

Detective Sergeant Ger McCarthy could tell the worried Lowney did not wish to make a written statement at the time, but the Bandon officer immediately wrote a memo. 'I suspected the person who wished to have the roll of film developed was Ian Bailey.' Soon after, McCarthy produced a montage of twelve photographs, including one of Bailey, and showed them to Lowney. It was double the number of faces normally used in a live identity parade, in which individuals have to stand before a hidden witness.

'He immediately identified the man that had called to him. The photograph selected by him was that of Ian Bailey.'

Next McCarthy and Detective John Moore accompanied Lowney to the location where the body of Sophie Toscan du Plantier had been discovered three and a half years before. 'Having examined the scene, he was satisfied this was the location seen in the shots developed for Mr Bailey, and the only striking difference was that the briars were not now as high.' They had been slashed down in the course of a garda fingertip search, carried out by seven officers on their hands and knees.

Was this Bailey's roll of photos from the scene that he had tried to sell on the day of the murder? Conceivably it had been withheld by him because of the questions it would raise. On that Monday afternoon, a new roll had been loaded into the camera, and only two poor-quality photographs were taken at long range, when the scene had been sealed off. The guards had long since developed their own forensic films, but this canister was unopened. Had it been in the satchel, along with his writings, that Bailey deposited with Pól Ó Colmáin for safekeeping before his arrest and subsequent search of The Prairie? Or was this Lowney story just too good to be true, reliant on one man's word?

A son, Shane, told the author he had seen Bailey, whom he recognised, with his father. Lowney Snr said he'd developed negatives for Bailey, yet made no mention to his son of any corpse. Bailey's black-and-white prints, and any pick-up picture he purported to possess of Sophie Toscan du Plantier, have to this day never been discovered.

CHAPTER 33

Black Diaries 1: A Monster in Their Midst

Patrick Lowney's disclosures led to an application for a warrant, granted by a court, and a full-scale search of The Prairie for the images processed at Clonakilty. They didn't turn up, but the effort instead produced something unexpected and equally dark: Ian Bailey's 'Black Diaries', found and seized in September 2000.

Inside one was a sketch by Bailey, helpfully labelled 'I Knew, December 23'. Roughly diamond-shaped, it shows a figure saying, 'Help! Help Help!' Bailey appears to have used his pen to obliterate the head of another figure standing astride the first in the lower half of the drawing. 'Tired, let me sleep. Womb like,' says the caption. Rather than a womb, some saw the sketch as suggestive of female genitalia. To the left are lines of dark doggerel: 'You tell me you're in pain. I resent your pain, you complain.' A separate drawing seems to imitate Edvard Munch's *The*

Scream, with a similarly long open mouth that cries, 'Help Me!'

In the top left of the first sketch, boxed off from the rest, is more free verse: 'Broken pieces of a former self. Apparently sound and whole to ordinary gaze / An illusion; a mirror reflecting a thousand shards, temporarily fragmented.'

In 2003, extracts from the Black Diaries, as they became known, were read aloud to Cork Civil Court in the libel case brought by Bailey against several newspapers for their coverage of Sophie's murder. It turned into a disaster for the plaintiff, who claimed he was being portrayed as the killer and therefore defamed. This despite the fact that he had pronounced himself the chief suspect, saying, 'they are not looking for anyone else'. The case was bad for him in other ways. I had to attend because *The Star* was a joint defendant, although Bailey would withdraw his claim against the paper mid-case, acknowledging our coverage as accurate, even the Gloucester stuff. That was a big win, and person-ally satisfying – but I wasn't about to leave and go home. I was going to watch this fascinating case to the bitter end.

Bailey complained in evidence to the court about returning to The Prairie in early 1997 to find 'a garda forcibly yanking hair from Jules Thomas' head' for forensic analysis. It appalled him, he said, conveniently forgetting that he had yanked a giant tuft of hair from Jules' scalp in one vicious attack, and more hair in another. Pictures of Jules taken by a friend after Bailey's attack on her in 1993 would prove it, along with Bailey's own assault references read into the record from his diaries.

Jules defended him: 'There was one incident in which he

beat me up and I was taken to hospital. I wasn't detained, but stayed with some friends in Cork for a few days. This was a once-off incident and Ian has been very remorseful.' She was admitted to the A&E in Cork's South Infirmary on 21 August 1993 at 5.40 a.m., her medical notes indicating that she had been assaulted an hour earlier.

Jules said she had been kicked in the chest at home. She had pain to her ribcage on the right-hand side, but refused an X-ray. Instead, she accepted a supply of painkillers and signed herself out just twenty minutes later. 'Tell us about [another] assault on Jules in Cork city,' Bailey was asked, the pair having been on a trip to the Jazz Festival in October 1994, which some accounts suggest was 1993.

'We were sharing a small bed and it was very cramped, and I forced her out. I didn't strike her as such, but there was violence,' Bailey said, using the passive voice. 'Most of it was because of drink. We were both under a lot of pressure. It shouldn't have happened. It wasn't premeditated.' On further probing: 'We had a fight. I will accept that there was blood on the wall as a result.'

Garda Bart O'Leary had questioned Jules about it when she was arrested: 'Isn't it true that blood had to be washed off the wall after he assaulted you in Cork?'

Jules offered an interesting reply: 'That was his own blood, not mine.'

'Did Ian ever bite you?'

'He did.'

'You wouldn't do that to a dog in the street.'

To which Jules answered, 'I'd report it, if he did that to a dog in the street. Ian is a different man when he drinks

293

whiskey.' She described it as a 'tussle' and said the extent of her injuries had been exaggerated. 'We were staying in a small bed, we drank too much, a fight ensued. It was over in a minute. It was a moment of alcoholic madness.' Ian promised he wouldn't ever beat her again. 'I believed him.'

But the court heard of further violent assaults carried out by Bailey on Jules, including one on her forty-seventh birthday, 17 April 1996, after a jazz concert at The Courtyard. In May 1996, came another. Paul Gallagher SC, for the newspapers, having obtained the plaintiff's own writings on legal discovery, took Bailey painstakingly through the May battering. It had started in the Fiesta, Bailey driving, as they headed home:

'Following the assault, she had a swollen eye the size of a grapefruit, and had hair missing,' senior counsel put it to the claimant.

Bailey: 'I pushed her away. She had loose hair. She did try to bite me.'

'So you were pushing her away with an open palm and her hair fell out?'

'In the heat of the moment, I may have pulled the hair.'

'And her lip was severed from her gum?'

'I tried to push her away. She bit me. There was some injury to her face.'

'Her lip was severed from her gum?'

'If that's what is said.'

'You were there. She needed stitches, didn't she?'

'Yes.'

'There were bite marks on her hands and arms?'

'She put her hand to my face. I might have bitten her.

She was trying to scratch me. I honestly don't have a precise recollection.'

Gallagher asked if the reason he couldn't recall was because of the drink – or because it was not remarkable?

'It was quite remarkable. It wouldn't normally happen. It happened in a short space of time but I saw the aftermath.'

'And you'd know if you were biting someone? You'd see the marks?'

'Yes. I knew I hurt her.'

'Specifically?'

'I also bit her.'

'And she had scratch marks on her face?'

'Yes.'

Counsel asked if he remembered writing about it.

Bailey answered, 'Yes. In one of my books.'

This was the time Jules Thomas had to be taken to hospital, but Bailey had the keys of the car and refused to hand them over. Ginny had to fetch a doctor and then a neighbour, Pete Bielecki. Bailey admitted shrieking at Ginny as she demanded the keys, with Jules 'curled up like an animal screaming with pain', in the words of Gallagher. Bailey answered, 'On the ground, floor, yes. I knew I hurt her badly.'

Counsel asked him to look at photographs, to see hair that had been pulled out. 'It didn't just fall out,' he said.

Bailey's slow answer caused gasps: 'She has a hair condition.'

'How would you describe a person who did that to his partner?'

'If it was out of the blue and totally unprovoked, very bad. I was in the car . . .'

The judge, Patrick Moran, cut off the explanation and asked for an answer to Gallagher's question. What would he call it?

'Not very nice at all.'

Gallagher queried mildly: 'Not very nice?'

'Yes. It's appalling.'

Gallagher: 'Have I to ask two or three times for you to give a truthful answer?' He asked if it was animal-like.

'No,' retorted Bailey.

'What sort of person does this to a defenceless woman?'

'It wasn't planned or premeditated. It happened in the heat of the moment.'

Gallagher pounced: 'Does that mean you are a person who loses control?'

'No, I was in the car and . . .'

'Did you lose control on this night?'

'Yes.'

'So you are a person that on at least one occasion lost control?'

'On this occasion. I am ashamed of it.'

'Did you get treated for your injuries?'

'No. I only had scratches.'

Bailey had denied that it was animal-like. Gallagher read from the diaries. 'I am an animal on two feet . . .'

Bailey interjected to explain that he was 'writing in a style', not to be taken literally.

Mr Gallagher continued reading: 'One act of whiskey-induced madness . . . and in an act of awful violence I severely damaged you and made you feel death was near.'

Bailey protested from the witness box: 'That was written in an abstract form.'

The court audience groaned audibly.

Gallagher: 'You said you made her feel death was near?'

Bailey: 'Death is always near . . . it isn't to be taken literally.'

Gallagher read more: 'And as I write I know there is something badly wrong with me. I am afraid for myself, a cowardly fear, for although I have damaged and made grief your life, I have damaged my own destiny and future to the point I can see that in destroying you, I destroyed me . . . and time will tell that I am damned to hell.'

Bailey had also written the following in his diary:

It is difficult for me to put down what occurred due to a bottle of whiskey, two pints of porter, two pints of wine and a number of tequila slammers. I attacked and severely beat Jules to such an extent she sought hospital treatment and on re-entering the house I relived my attack, and proceeded to cause further injury on top. I feel a sense of sickness at seeing my own account of that dreadful night. I actually tried to kill her. At present, two nights on, she is badly hurt and walking wounded, with bruises on her face, lips and body. How could I have perpetrated such injury on somebody I both love and owe so much to? I cannot properly explain. I have never had a history of violence towards women but of late – since Easter – I have on a number of occasions struck and abused my lover, a thing I always believed to be the worst crime a man can commonly commit against one's mother's sex. I know each time has been worse. Drink has definitely played a major role. On all occasions I had taken drink.

I watched Bailey squirm repeatedly on the stand as he was confronted, over and over, with that sentence: 'I actually tried to kill her.' During the libel trial, there had been testimony of him trying to kill Sarah Limbrick, until he stopped. But now, in Bailey's maturely recollected world-view, it turned out he didn't actually attempt anything of the sort with Jules. 'I'm not disputing I fought with my girlfriend. I accept that I'd been violent.' What happened was to his 'eternal regret', but the relationship was quite stormy. He accepted 'full responsibility', but he had not 'actually tried to kill her'. It wasn't as if he wanted to *finish her off*. Nor that he *went too far*. His literary angst was not to be taken literally.

Gallagher asked, 'Tell us now of any other occasion when you lost control or hurt someone like this.'

Bailey replied, 'Two years ago my leg was in plaster.' It was 2001, he had ruptured his Achilles tendon, and had been sleeping on the sofa. Jules had come in, sat quietly on the floor, and had begun to go through the contents of her handbag. The clacking of a nail varnish and a lipstick woke up Bailey. So he whacked her hard on the head with a crutch.

And then whacked her repeatedly.

Gallagher went through the injuries sustained. 'A black eye?'

'Yes.'

'A swollen cheek?'

'I won't dispute that.'

'Bruised lips?'

'If that's . . .'

'A cut chin?'

'I didn't see a cut.'

'So this assault was to Ms Thomas's face?'

'Well, she pulled the crutch towards her . . . she started pulling the crutch. I was trying to get it back and she was pulling it, and I let go – it struck her.'

Bailey had let go of the crutch, but Gallagher pointed out that Jules had been repeatedly struck. 'Did you use a second crutch to hit her?'

'It may have come in contact with her.' Bailey then said he had tried to hobble past, out of the room. 'But she was in the way. I was immobile. She was hysterical – she had also taken drink.'

'So it was her fault?'

'On occasions in the past when we have drink, it has led to violence.' Passive voice: the drink did it.

Bailey seemed to have a moment of clarity under this withering cross-examination. He tried to pull things back, recover ground. The violence was 'just with Jules'. He added: 'I have a temper, which . . . as I said, alcohol does not suit me.'

Paul Gallagher: 'Just with Jules, you're *sure* of that? You said, "I'm here to prove my innocence", so think carefully about that, Mr Bailey.'

Bailey now feared Gallagher had something else, that he

was ready to produce it. And so he prevaricated for some time, trying to figure out what the senior counsel might be driving at. *Just with Jules?* He certainly didn't need any other broken rabbits to be produced from a hat. It seemed an age as he searched his mind for what other women – men, even – he might have been violent with or beaten up. He looked worried. The lawyer's chin was tilted up, frozen in the moment, expectant. Seconds ticked by. The whole court watched the witness twisting in the wind. Gradually, Bailey settled nervously on his answer: No, he had not been violent with anyone else. 'Just with Jules.'

'Was this latest attack another instance of you losing control?' Mr Gallagher asked.

'Yes.'

'When you lose control does it mean that you can't stop yourself?'

'In these instances, yes. I should have been far more responsible.'

'So it means you can't stop yourself doing injury to her on those occasions? May His Lordship take it as lucky her injuries were not worse? Isn't Jules Thomas lucky today, to be here, because you had lost control?'

'No.' Ian Bailey insisted again there had been no premeditation. 'I didn't intend to hurt her.'

'Hadn't you really lost control?'

'Possibly. Let's say yes.'

Bailey sought to retrieve the situation. Jules had started it in the car, and also on the other occasion when he was on crutches, he claimed.

Gallagher asked him, 'If we take it that Jules started it,

300

does that mean she deserved to end up like this? Why did you stop? Why didn't you go further?'

'I don't know what stopped me.' It seemed an admission that he was capable of going beyond. He revisited his not handing over the car keys so that Jules could be taken to hospital: 'There were always two pairs of keys – in the car, and a spare set in the kitchen.'

Gallagher brusquely reminded him that a barring order had been taken out against him. Why was that?

'Maybe she was under pressure too. She was advised by people to get an order against me.'

Pete Bielecki, the neighbour who had taken Jules to hospital in May 1996, was returning to Schull from Clonakilty by bus on Monday, 23 December when he heard on the radio of a savage murder in the locality. 'I immediately assumed that Ian Bailey had murdered Jules Thomas,' Pete told gardaí. 'Obviously, I was relieved when I found out it wasn't Jules.' He remembered the aftermath of the beating Bailey had given her: 'I have never seen anyone in so much pain.'

Gallagher asked Bailey why Ginny had to call the doctor. 'Did you take any steps to care for Ms Thomas? You regained control, saw your partner was hurt; did you do anything?'

Bailey admitted, 'I did not.'

'So her eighteen-year-old daughter had taken control?'

'Yes.'

'Why didn't you try to remedy what you had done?'

'Ginny was there and did that. I was very upset. I know I am not a violent person. I was responding to her [Jules].

301

The violence started with her. I am not violent, but when we both drank, violence occurred.'

*

The case continued into the new year. Judge Patrick Moran ruled on 19 January 2004: 'Violence once would be unusual. Violence twice very unusual. Three times is exceptional.' In 1996, the District Court had imposed a six-month suspended sentence for domestic violence, 'because his partner said she forgave him', Moran noted. 'Otherwise, the judge would have had no hesitation imposing a custodial sentence. I certainly have no hesitation in describing Mr Bailey as a violent man – and I think the defendants have no problem in describing him as violent towards women, plural.'

And indeed, he *was* violent towards women, plural, as the female household of The Prairie could confirm. Jules's mother Beryl had a run-in with Ian Bailey in the autumn of 1995, after he'd returned from a festival. As the owner of the studio, she was his landlady; yet there was little respect or gratitude. She kept a bucket at his house, of sheep and cattle droppings she had gathered, to use as plant fertiliser in Jules' garden.

'I asked him to hand me the bucket,' she said. 'Ian fetched the bucket and threw the contents on the lower half of my body. My clothes were messed up. I drove back home and I had to bathe and change. He does not control his immediate reactions. I did not speak to Ian for a year. I contacted Jules and said, "You'd better watch out there."'

CHAPTER 34

Black Diaries 2: Sex-Centred Bailey

Just as the Black Diaries revealed Baileys' violent inner landscape, they equally shone a light on his sadistic sexual obsessions. 'I'm totally, totally obsessed by sex, I love my drugs and adore alcohol,' he proudly penned. Another entry contained a detailed account of sex with someone who screamed with pain, and Bailey wrote that this did not matter because he was in control. As with his accounts of violence, he told the court these were sexual fantasies in writing, not necessarily reports of real events.

Bailey's Black Diaries show he focused on Jules' daughter Ginny from age fourteen. 'There are times when I get strong sexual feelings towards her. Yet I have no doubt I will fantasise about the taking of a young woman and her friends. I just find them so attractive. Any man would.'

Bailey's former friend Billy Fuller told the author: 'When waiting for him in the morning he'd . . . answer the door with a hard-on and say, "Come back and get me in an hour." He would say, "Why are we going to work when we could stay home and shag all the girls in the house?" Everything was very gross and sexual with him.'

In custody, Bailey had denied propositioning Ginny. She gave a statement to gardaí on 2 January 1997 at Schull garda station in the early aftermath of Sophie's murder, describing the domestic violence she witnessed in her home. She then said: 'Ian also made a pass at me on Christmas Day 1995. I was travelling in the car with him when this happened. He didn't physically touch me, but implied that he would like to have his way with me.' She told a friend of her mother's the following day, in order to avoid a scene. The arrested Bailey blithely denied the allegation: 'No, not at all. I know she said it, but there was no truth in it what-soever.' Jules said she was not taking sides on the claimed pass, and did not know where the truth lay. Nonetheless that Christmas had been spoiled, was being masked with alcohol. Bailey seethed at the hostility of the Thomas girls that he himself had engendered. Nor did he care for Ginny's Italian friend Arianna. 'He passed remarks about Ginny and her friend, calling them tarts and bimbos,' said Billy Fuller, while Caroline Mangez heard more disparagement of Ginny and her 'black bra'.

Bailey sets out his own repulsiveness in great detail in his diaries, naming a series of women and musing on his own depraved sexual obsessions, which include hardcore porn, teenage girls and much that is extremely explicit. There is also a lot of self-reproach and analysis of his various failures, and a considerable amount of hatred towards others, chiefly Jules, but also Ginny. Indeed there are often premeditated references to violence, including menacing reference to one of Jules' former lovers.

In July 1992, he tells his diary: 'If I could kill anybody now, I would. Imagine a powerful spirit manifest [*sic*] and said, although you know it is normally wrong to kill – there is so much evil in control . . . I will stub them out like cigarette ends.'

*

While he veered from the occult to derision of religion, Bailey frequently returned to his main topic. 'Sex has been the single most important energy in my life. Man and his todger.' He wrote that he had been addicted to pornography since age twelve, when another boy brought his parents' magazines to school. 'So began a life proper dominated by the male sexual reproductive organ.' He expressed the belief that he could give up drink before he could give up sex. 'I dwell on sex much of the time. My mind is often full of the most graphic acts of sex' – which he proceeds to catalogue. He claims to 'enjoy dozens of orgasms a week' in different and comprehensive ways. He talks of one woman now 'broken in to this form of intercourse'. And he fantasises widely, for example considering 'it would be good to do foursomes. I am keen to experience group sex'.

Bailey described his marriage bed and how 'we eventually parted to preserve both souls'. Eventually he explains, 'She started growing colder. The inevitable schism occurred. I had started taking occasional, unplanned lovers . . . she never had the courage or wickedness to go through with it.' He had wanted to watch.

After his divorce and various dabblings, he arrived in Ireland. He tried to turn over a new leaf in Dublin. But the man from Alcoholics Anonymous never turned up to a meeting in Bewley's on Grafton Street, being an 'unreliable gobshite, [his] life even more of a mess than mine'. So Bailey went back to St Stephen's Green to admire 'the beauty of the girls, almost all of them young' and worth a second glance. One of the days on the Green brought sexual success with a young girl. 'We both agreed that once was good, but more it should not be, for I was old enough to be her father.'

He turned to older women when he left for Wicklow: 'Arklow. I turned up at the home of a divorced lady with two children who said she could give me a bed for the night. She welcomed me in, and on my return last night invited me to join her in bed. I was in no position to refuse. Duly performed, although without my full heart in the matter. Being a prostitute is not as easy as the inexperienced male might think. In the morning, she cooked me breakfast, and walked me to the edge of town.' Next, he would try Kilmacthomas, County Waterford, which housed the headquarters of the fish factory he would later join in Schull.

He was also writing to keep depression at bay. 'I know the will to live is great. I have no desire to end it, but I fear I may be cursed or damned in some way.' Transferred to Schull, Jules befriended him when buying fish at the pier premises. They had a drink, then another meeting, followed by their first overnight stay together in Crookhaven, away from her children.

'I want a woman who will allow me to do it all,' wrote Bailey before a prodigiously explicit passage about 'every way' it could be accomplished. Then mention of 'a German lover who should be over later in the year. We are both keen to have sex with him. I am quite bisexual'.

Disillusion with his relationship set in: 'Oh that I would love her so. But I don't. I enjoy her body from time to time. I enjoy her whiskey and her wine. I enjoy her home and her fine food, but I cannot truly love this mother.' He was already looking around. On Saturday, 11 December 1993 he wrote: 'I loathe J. I cannot stand her. I just need a friend, not a lover. I find your conversation banal and unstimulating.'

In January 1994, he took an acting class in Skibbereen. 'What a treat it was. A whole load of ladies, only three men. A lovely blonde, maybe late twenties. A lot of sexuality too. Met another lovely called K—, a six-footer. I can't wait to explore some fresh female flesh.' Jules was giving him a 'headfuck', he wrote. 'I really have no desire to spend time with her. I don't want to go out with her. She loves the sound of her own voice, which is a dreadful monotone.' The diaries reveal that he had started assaulting Jules in the car because she had dared to enter into conversation with someone else in the pub – and to speak over him when he was spouting his poetry.

*

'Everybody asleep. Just watched a porno . . . I really enjoy watching hard-core pornographic erotica. I cannot get the acts out of my mind. I can quite clearly verify that exposure to erotica and porn does lead to the mind being taken over by lustful thoughts.'

Another revealing scribble explores his fascination with the idea of control: 'A lunatic walks on the face of the earth, a madman fool, who through night and day prowls. Then animal lust takes over and, out of control, I love and fuck in wild abandon.' And another: 'To be honest now, I am a whore. A sloth, an easy man who likes his drink and smoke. I am a lazy man, a sleaze, a foolish man who likes his cake to eat and cheat.'

Christmas 1995, the searing season of the Ginny allegation: 'In the kitchen. 6 a.m. approaches for the second morning. I am not asleep. Last night J woke me after I finally managed to slumber. This morning I woke her. Angry, I banged my head against the wall calling for Anadins. So I got up like a crazed beast and now I'm sitting with the cat and trusty old paraffin heater once again.'

He finally tumbled to something: 'I seem to have a sex problem. Not enough. It's a weird thing, dangerous though it is.' Jules reckoned it was the 'neurotic response of a person running away. I guess it's true in my case'. But the very next sentence showed he had no intention to restrain himself: 'There are perhaps a dozen or so ladies and girls, aged between seventeen up to around fifty, who I would delight in making love with, or [who] are accessible with the right approach . . .'

He wanted novelty. 'Arising to mind of late is L—, a bubbly beautiful blonde, 24, from Nottingham, and her close friend whose name escapes me . . . I may suggest they join me on holiday in Ireland.' He wrote of getting flash-backs of 'my first full-blooded ménage à trois'.

Over and over again, Bailey's own journals establish his extreme sexual obsessions and belief that women are *accessible with the right approach*. But they also lay bare his capacity to be cruel. He poured bile into his journals. There is one poem called 'Bitch', further denigration of Jules, and more about sex and his 'snake of temptation'.

The name 'Sophie' appears in his journals. Had he approached her? No definitive answer is revealed in those pages. But the message from his writings is predatory: 'I can't wait to explore some fresh female.'

CHAPTER 35

Covering His Tracks

It was not all sex. After Sophie was murdered, there appeared references that could be viewed as self-serving, as if future-proofing against the diaries falling into the wrong hands. In one entry, he wrote: 'In Loving Memory: Sophie, R.I.P. A bowel [*sic*] of carnations, roses, lilies.' His own name was in tiny writing in the top right corner. He also wrote a subversive snippet of a carol: 'Holy night, Christmas night. Drunk as drunk, and ready to fight. Seasonal style.' He also began a book about the murder: *The du Plantier File*. 'I will concentrate on the full story. It is too early to say how many chapters there will be, but I think it would be good to prelude the story with a quote from Patrick Galvin's 'The Prisoners of the Tower':

> If you are guilty,
> You know you are guilty

If you are innocent
You would not be here

You *are* here,
Therefore . . .

Bailey's prose was lifeless: 'As she dropped down the steep incline, Shirley Foster became aware of something on the trackway. Uncertain what it was, she put the handbrake on and left the vehicle to investigate. Unbelievingly at first, Foster, who had been living in West Cork for several years, realised the something was a body.

'News of the murder was like a bombshell when it hit the far-flung communities of the Mizen Peninsula. Not since the troubles of 1922 had there been a known killing in anger, and word of the tragedy spread like wildfire through the mountain gorse which grows so strong in West Cork.' But there was already an agenda at work: 'The first officers drove along the still-icy trackway towards the scene, and questioned Shirley Foster about her intended movements. At this point, the scene became contaminated.' She wanted to go to the dump. 'Foster, at the police behest, then drove along the track, a mistake which meant any forensic clues that could have been gained by a sharp-eyed single investigator were lost.' By the time Dermot Dwyer, senior detective for the county of Cork, had arrived, 'upwards of a dozen pairs of feet had trodden the ground and approaches to the scene'.

Bailey seemed to be literally driving at something – he appeared to be suggesting that the killer could have had a car.

Jules had been asked about it when arrested. Could Bailey have taken her white Fiesta? 'He has pushed it out in the past and could freewheel it down,' she said, starting the car by lifting the clutch into second gear, while rolling safely away from home. Where had he gone on these other occasions when he took her car? That question was not put. Certainly, the Shelleys needed a car to get away from The Prairie on that night of Bailey's New Year's Eve confession.

Rather than the gardaí, did Bailey himself contaminate the scene, and as soon as he got the chance? On Christmas Eve, the day after the murder, his neighbour Brian Jackson met Bailey in Arundel's pub in Schull and the latter said he was going to interview Alfie Lyons. In fact, Eddie Cassidy had mentioned to Bailey that Alfie was an obvious interviewee. He also offered proximity to the dead woman's property.

Sunday Tribune copytaker Rita Byrne told gardaí on 21 February 1997: 'He asked me did I wonder how he knew in such detail what was left on the table in Sophie Toscan du Plantier's house? He went on that a neighbour had keys and had let him into the house.' Housekeeper Josie said she was the only one with keys and hadn't facilitated Bailey. Alfie Lyons denied having keys, but said Bailey had rung him before he called up to his home on 27 December 1996. 'He asked me did I want anything brought. And I asked him to bring briquettes, and he did. I tried to be polite, but I didn't tell him anything. His girlfriend Jules Thomas was with him.'

The potential for contamination was a major garda concern. When Bailey and Thomas arrived that day at Alfie's house at 12.45 p.m., officers made sure to escort the pair away from Sophie's property, safely up to the Lyons' property 'through the field' from which Bailey claimed to have first spotted Sophie. Then, an hour later, they walked them back again the same way, to make sure there was no incursion. Yet, a week or two later, when the crime ribbons were gone and the scene no longer preserved, Bailey made sure to be photographed as he walked up to Sophie's house. No doubt he was tramping the driveway on another visit to Alfie, but it could have been an advance defence against any of his own genetic material being found on her land. In one of his diary entries, he mentions that the radio was on, 'discussing the proposal by police commissioner Sir Peter Imbert that all UK males be subject to DNA registration'.

A draft alibi was even drawn up by Bailey after his release from arrest, presumably in case the Kealfadda bridge sighting was proven. It was discovered within the pages of a book, set among others on a shelf, during a search at The Prairie in January 1998. Bailey had been told of 'witnesses' seeing him at Kealfadda, and needed a strategy since one might arguably be mistaken, but two or more would be a problem. The alibi memo, a closely guarded garda secret up to now, is believed to have been composed soon after he left Bandon garda station in February 1997.

Bailey had already written in the *Sunday Tribune* on 29 December 1996, 'Schull and Goleen have technology cottages allowing easy access to computers and the internet', in a murder sidebar story about West Cork with the headline 'The Europeans who Discovered the Best Kept Secret in Ireland', a place that was booming and now 'a second home for people such as the film producer David Puttnam and the actor Jeremy Irons'.

Now he was planning to say he was walking to Teletext Cottage, Goleen, a small business where he could transmit his cyberpubs story to the *Tribune*, even if he had to wait around until the sun came up on Monday – 'Have to get there early.' A complete nonsense, given that he could and did phone a copytaker when he finally submitted it late that afternoon. Yet he had established a reputation for nocturnal 'walkabouts', as Jules put it, and he defensively maintained it for a few years. His track record of tramping around at night with his moonstick, suspicious as it was, might just be turned to advantage.

There is also a drawing in the diaries in his own hand, initialled by Bailey. It shows the lower limbs of a female, with boots on the feet. To their immediate right is a V-shape, like a jutting right elbow, at the angle displayed by Sophie's corpse. If this is the case, then the right-hand side of the drawing shows the curvature of Sophie's driveway, and indicates where the body lay. The fact that Bailey would record such material is itself perplexing, even if he was by then familiar with the general layout of the murder. However, he claimed never to have seen the remains and arguably shouldn't have known about the jutting elbow.

CHAPTER 36

Lost and Found

The original copies of Bailey's diaries went missing in the libel trial, suspected to have been stolen. They had been on the table in court along with legal books and files in front of Paul Gallagher, counsel for the newspapers. Bailey, under oath, denied taking them. It didn't matter, their contents had been extensively copied. But other items went missing as the long case continued – from witness statements, including one of mine, to physical exhibits.

Some items and papers have occasionally turned up over the years, but scores of pieces remain missing. Vast amounts were shuffled back and forth between various internal inquiries and reviews brought about directly or indirectly by Bailey, including his action against the state for unlawful arrest. The most notorious piece of 'missing' evidence led to a controversy that could be called Gate-gate.

On New Year's Day 1997, the driveway gate to Sophie's

house was wrapped and put on an escorted low-loader to Bantry, where it was stored in a locked outhouse, with every use of the key thereto being logged. The gate was then transferred to the Forensic Science Laboratory in Dublin, again under escort. The lab would receive 134 exhibits in all, and tests on the gate revealed that 'the only blood group detected, AK1, was present in Toscan du Plantier's blood sample and Ian Bailey's blood sample, but occurs in approximately ninety-three people in one hundred of the population'. The gate was also tested for fingerprints, using a substance called Amido Black, fingerprints having been lifted from Sophie's corpse during the postmortem. Other sets were received, but 'no identifiable fingermarks were developed'.

Nonetheless, the gate – official exhibit EG12 – was kept for twelve years in all, then offered back to the du Plantier family, who didn't want it, because it had been replaced at Dunmanus West. The gate was then disposed of, since it had never held any evidential value. But it was Ian Bailey who claimed the gardaí had managed to lose the gate – a lie that ran around Ireland a million times before the truth had got its boots on. He was adept at starting rumours, and the gardaí have plenty of pages attesting to the fact, with sworn statements in support. One he tried to get going was that a prominent detective was sleeping with Marie Farrell. What can never be forgotten is that in his published articles as 'Eoin Bailey', he repeatedly demonstrated an assiduous campaign of disinformation.

But it would seem my surrendered reporter's notebook from the original encounter with Bailey, which also contained notes of his release interview, is missing too. Of course, it

too had been copied and its Gregg shorthand translated –
just as the gardaí commissioned laborious translations of
Bailey's Teeline shorthand found in his journals, which show
he could even bend mere squiggles into lewd language. The
meaning of his rare form of shorthand was initially lost on
officers, being practically unknown in Ireland where journalists are trained in Gregg, and was only identified through
an exacting process of eliminating other styles. An expert
translator was finally found in Ulster.

The translations show admissions – 'today I met MF [Marie
Farrell], made a cut-throat gesture' and 'need to pressure Marie'.

On Alfie Lyons: 'Sophie had been over from France . . .
I recall him telling me he thought she worked in TV.
Introduced.' This contradicts his claim that he never met
her. Garda Liam Leahy made a private appointment, some
little time after the turn of the century, to read over this
shorthand translation to ageing Alfie, 'and as a result he
could vividly recall the meeting where Sophie, Ian Bailey
and himself had a discussion in his front garden'.

The truth is that an awful lot was done, and thousands
of lines of enquiry exhausted – even if some evidence bags
were opened, papers deliberately pulled out or accidentally
lost, misfiled or left in a photocopier. Sadly, bad things
happen from time to time, or else there would be no police
force. At one stage, the garda file consisted of 16,000 pages.
The monumental process of feeding in facts, many wholly
irrelevant, means that some go astray, especially when a
decade goes by, then two, then a quarter of a century . . .

*

One story by Bailey had especially irked me all those years ago: 'Champagne Clue Probed'. It appeared in my paper, *The Star*, on Monday, 3 February 1997, exactly a week before his arrest. Bailey was reporting on an unopened bottle of champagne in the house: 'Sophie may have known the killer, who could have brought the bottle on his midnight call,' he wrote. Frustrated as a crime correspondent with no such 'killer detail' for my stories, I immediately rang Bailey, partly because I hoped he might let slip his source. He insisted it was true – moreover, he said, a very nice bottle of wine that Sophie had brought over from the Paris duty-free was *missing*.

How the hell did he know that? He was enjoying my envy. I asked for details, but he chuckled – said he'd probably write that missing bottle story himself for a Sunday paper, rationing his exclusives. I then rang local gardaí. They suggested Bailey was making things up. Forget it, they said. 'What about a bottle missing from the house?' I asked, because there was no Christmas present for the housekeeper, when Sophie always brought a gift for Josie. There were indeed exchanges, said Josie, but her son John put it best: 'Every Christmas when Sophie would come to stay she would always bring presents to us. I got a few presents from her over the years, but it was mainly the younger ones who received presents. I never gave presents. But my mother would always give something.'

The guards were adamant. 'Nothing missing from the house,' they said, not mentioning a little red hatchet, value IR£6, that had disappeared, its absence specified after a guided walk-through by Josie. Sophie had bought it at Biggs of Bantry, and kept it by the back door.

I was unaware for years that, amazingly, an unopened bottle of red wine had been discovered near the scene, and it had turned up two months after Bailey's 'Champagne Clue' had run in *The Star*. The guards kept it secret. John Hellen unearthed the bottle, which had been lying a couple of hundred metres from Sophie's house. Did it occur to him that it could be a missing present? He said in a statement, 'On Tuesday, 8 April 1997, I was working on our lands, spreading bag manure by hand. I noticed a bottle partially covered by withered rough grass. I picked up the bottle and saw that it was a full bottle of wine. I left it where I found it, and told my parents when I got home.'

The next day he guided his father to the spot. 'I collected the bottle and showed it to my father. He examined it, and decided to take it home. My mother, Josie, rang the gardaí at Bandon. This is the same bottle of wine that I now hand over. My fingerprints, and that of my father, may be on the bottle, my mother's also.'

The place where it was found, which is difficult to describe but is arguably on a 'driving home' route from Kealfadda bridge, suggests to my mind that it was lobbed over a fence from the road. If it was in a car, the driver would have to get out, and go around to the passenger side to chuck it where it was found. There is belief it was a Bordeaux, a Pauillac, an expensive bottle of wine valued at almost €100 by 2024 prices.

I gave a detailed statement to gardaí when I finally realised this staggering connection. There is proof I was not deluded: photographer Ian Vickery, who kept a diary, told gardaí of a discussion held at The Prairie on Sunday,

12 January 1997 when he was working for *Paris Match* with Caroline Mangez. Bailey 'asked if we had heard about the bottle of wine that was missing from the house, belonging to Sophie'. He was thus the sole person in Ireland to know about any missing bottle. I believe his boast to me was quasi-confessional, echoing his wine-glasses fixation, while the bottle found was a French vintage not ordinarily stocked in West Cork. The guards checked, and visited wine importers in Cork city, who were found not to stock the particular brand. The label was, however, marketed in Charles de Gaulle airport duty-free. The weathering meant that there were no forensics. Officers have since been extremely guarded about this bottle. It seems the exhibit, once stored at Bantry, has disappeared. But, at one stage, it formed a significant line of enquiry.

In April 1998, a typical Bailey rant was printed in the *Independent on Sunday*: 'I have lots of questions for the gardaí: Was the murder weapon found? Was the wine found? Where is her laptop computer?' Once more, he seemed to know more than they did – except the guards still aren't telling.

CHAPTER 37

Dirty Laundry

Despite the passage of time, information has still filtered through and, in recent years, new testimony was brought to light. Cheesemonger Bill Hogan gave a fresh statement to gardaí on 6 August 2021. I had been telling him his duty of care to the injured party was at an end, and he recognised it himself. It led to my *Irish Independent* exclusive, where Bill was not named:

> New evidence about the murder of Sophie Toscan du Plantier – and the alleged disposal of bloodstained clothes – has been supplied to An Garda Síochána. It involves a claimed confession by a woman that she aided a man in dealing with bloodied clothes in the immediate aftermath of the brutal murder, which shocked Ireland and France in 1996, and which has been the subject of two recent TV documentaries, seen

in nearly 200 countries worldwide. The woman is said to have confessed that she had been 'forced' to clean up after Sophie's murder and to deal with the blood-stained clothes worn by the perpetrator. She is said to have complied in fear.

It is claimed that the woman used bleach to purge spatter from the items – understood to be linked to a male suspect in the murder who was investigated at the time by gardaí. Nothing was said as to what then occurred with the clothes themselves.

A senior source said last night that the fresh claims, reported to Bantry garda station nearly a quarter of a century after the notorious killing, 'could be dynamite'. Another well-placed person said: 'This is being taken extremely seriously and will be pursued.' The original murder investigation was headquartered in Bandon.

The *Irish Independent* has learned that a local pensioner, who knew Sophie before her death, contacted a solicitor in the wake of the documentaries to make a new sworn statement in which he discloses the claimed confession about bloodstained items, made by a female four and a half years after the savage taking of Sophie's life. It is understood he gave a three-hour interview to gardaí yesterday in which a consolidated statement was taken, in addition to the formal deposition he supplied himself. The witness has grappled with his conscience after claiming to have been told the story by the woman in complete confidence some years ago. He was unnerved at the time, he asserts, and told her to go to gardaí – and even supplied her with the number of the Bandon station – but she did not do so.

[Hogan] says he had known the woman for several years when she suddenly told him that she needed to talk to somebody. The pair subsequently had a face-to-face conversation, which took place at a named premises in August 2001.

The premises was Manning's Emporium in Ballylickey, County Cork.

The woman appeared to be in fear and "looked awful". She began to cry and told how terrible her life had become, and that she was in a 'living hell'. She was 'forced . . . to clean up after the murder', and had to use chlorine bleach "to get rid of the blood stains", a sworn statement asserts. It has long been felt by investigators that the perpetrator would have been heavily bloodstained after smashing Sophie's skull with a rock and cavity block, raining down some fifty blows, the majority inflicted after death.

[Hogan] made a statement to another person in Ireland in the last four or five years.

This person was a retired garda.

Nothing came of that conversation – when he had expected that he would be formally interviewed by gardaí. He claims he was told then that it was 'your

word against hers', and did not take any further action
– until recent times.

He has now made a sworn statement through his
solicitor, which alleges for the first time that there was
a confession by an adult female who was an unwilling
accessory to the murder and who was then in fear of
her own life.

Bill Hogan told me that the woman got out of her car at
the rendezvous, 'wearing a big scarf and sunglasses, like an
Italian B-movie star'. She took off the dark glasses in the
Emporium, 'her face all black and blue, with a cut chin and
swollen lip. She was well battered, and had tried to put on
make-up, but it didn't work. She started blurting about
bloodstained clothes and how she had to help him clean
up. This time she was ending it. She mentioned bleach, and
Ian saying it got rid of the red blood cells. It was getting
very graphic, and I had a gagging sensation. I told her not
to tell me, to tell the guards, and gave her the number of
someone in Bantry'.

Bill spotted the owner, Val Manning, clocking the conversation. His phone records establish the outreach. But when
another newspaper contacted the woman after the story
ran, she said it was all rubbish. It was claimed she didn't
know Hogan. The woman was not named.

*

In Sophie's native France, Alain Spilliaert, lawyer for the
Justice for Sophie campaign, welcomed this 'major new
development', while Sophie's uncle, Jean-Pierre Gazeau,

said it was 'of the highest interest', and he would like to see official progress 'as soon as possible'. The French had already taken their own decisive action, with a murder charge brought *in absentia* against Bailey in 2019 by an investigating magistrate, who happened to be named Nathalie Turquey.

Bailey's advisers branded those proceedings 'a farce', as if impervious to any outcome. Yet the truth was that they had launched repeated legal attempts to block them from ever getting underway. The three-judge court of the Cour d'Assises in Paris heard the case on both Irish and French assembled evidence, and consulted its own experts, who concluded that Ian Bailey had a narcissistic personality and was 'psycho-rigid, violent and impulsive, egocentric, and intolerant to frustration, with an immense need for recognition', as well as prone to 'committing acts of violence under the disinhibiting effect of alcohol'.

French TV reporter Daniel Caron of RTL, who taped calls, testified that he once asked Ian Bailey by phone when he had got to the crime scene. The reply was 'immediately after the body was found, and [he] saw the first police vehicle arrive'. The judges found the invisible defendant guilty, and sentenced him to twenty-five years in jail.

It was all notional, because the devil looks after his own. Ever since the age of thirteen, Ian Bailey had never been brought properly to book – despite being strongly suspected of a fire at The Crypt School in Gloucester in 1970 that did considerable damage – and accountability was not going to happen now. Extradition attempts were mounted, and exhaustively failed. His drink-driving and drug-driving cases were endlessly appealed. European arrest warrants seemed valid anywhere but Ireland.

He had never renewed his British passport after it expired on 4 February 1998 – he wasn't going anywhere. Bailey turned the whole thing into a stand-and-fight story. He was determined to remain free.

CHAPTER 38

The Leopard in Winter

Ian Bailey was a violent, vain and sex-obsessed misogynist. Among the Black Diaries was a letter to Jules following his 2001 assault of her, in which Bailey reproached her: 'What has happened has happened. Even a powerful witch like you cannot change the past, but we have control over the future and the present. You know I am absolutely despicably sorry for the sadness I have brought into your life. You know I am moving. You know we will meet in court on May 23. You know I have lost you. I've also lost my home and the future I had worked so hard to establish here. You know I will never be able to return to West Cork. It seems as though I'm losing everything. What more do you want me to suffer?'

Bailey enlisted his neighbours, Brian and Ursula Jackson, to deliver this letter, and others in similar self-pitying style. In them, he pleaded for forgiveness and asked her to let him back into her life. When Bailey assaulted Jules in 1993, he had immediately gone to Ursula Jackson to ask what he should do, adding that it was 'the drink that produced the violence'. Ursula had told him to find a hospital for Jules and to go see a doctor and seek help with his drink problem. Bailey would eventually see a doctor, but only in order to deliberately express suicidal ideation – which saved him from a custodial sentence once the court heard about it.

Bizarrely, the successful ploy had been Jules's idea. And the put-upon partner only told Brian and Ursula about other incidents over the years when she was assaulted on a third major occasion, which resulted in Bailey being charged with domestic violence.

The night Jules was assaulted in 2001, she called her friend Sue Hill in Goleen. According to the Jacksons, Hill then bought Bailey an airline ticket to go to the UK. Brian Jackson thought it a cheap price to pay to save Jules' life, having seen the aftermath of one assault in 1996 'when he bashed her head and broke her jaw', confirming what poet John Montague reported in *The New Yorker*.

Brian Jackson told lawyers that he took Bailey to the bank and the supermarket, 'where he bought wine and whiskey to celebrate his last night in Ireland before he attempted to leave'. He helped Bailey to pack up his stuff that night in 2001. Brian and Ursula even said that they felt the gardaí were 'unfair' insofar as they knew he was planning to leave, yet arrested him only at Cork airport. Bailey subsequently received a three-month suspended sentence for the violence he had inflicted on Jules.

Even if he managed to evade sanction for his third hospitalisation of his partner, it appears he would have been arrested on arrival in Britain, if only for the insurance forgery, which was still under live investigation when Jimmy and I visited Gloucester in 1997. By 2010, France had obtained a European arrest warrant that applied across the EU but turned out not to be applicable in Ireland in this case, due to arcane domestic legal rules. It meant, however, that Bailey was trapped. He did not even dare travel to Britain for the funeral of his mother Brenda – whom he had once assaulted – when she died in 2013.

*

Ian Bailey did not change over the years. His fixation on controlling the narrative remained.

He studied law at University College Cork, and graduated with a master of laws degree in 2013. His thesis focused on an old question, asked since Roman times: who guards the guards? He compared complaints bodies and oversight internationally, but it was all in furtherance of his own schtick. Fellow students remember toe-curling moments when he asked about murder-related matters and protections for an accused. He sat alone in the cafeteria, a sore thumb among a gaggle of the young and vibrant.

And there were also the unsolicited phone calls and letters, including overly familiar missives, to French journalist Caroline Mangez. He had been calling her 'every other day' in the early stages, as she reported in *Paris Match*, and in later years 'called me a few times, notably for my birthday on 15 March, and also on full moon nights'. She was soon screening the calls. 'I would check afterwards, and it was on nights of a full moon,' she told French police.

Bailey spread rumours, no doubt buoyed by his Gate-gate success when the tale came back to his ears. Over the years, he wrote anonymous sneering messages in cards sent to investigating guards when they retired. In some, he promised to take their pensions.

Some journalists and broadcasters indulged Bailey, the more so as years slipped away and the savagery of the killing somehow became mere background detail to the Englishman's travails, along with tales of being targeted for the crime of being an eccentric bohemian. He repeatedly claimed to have given up alcohol, which was always a lie. He also skilfully used reverse psychology to make Irish people doubt themselves, to feel they had inherited historical baggage that clouded their judgement – gaslighting on a national scale. He never mentioned Sophie, but he was always the decent-sounding David against the garda Goliath.

In this remoulding he was no longer the bellowing terror of his neighbours, 'out late at night with nothing on but jocks and a hat in the rain', as seen by local Betty Johnson, nor the madman 'jumping on the road in the middle of the night' described by Aidan Coughlan, nor Steven Farthing's flabbergasting sight: a man covering himself in excrement under some intoxicant, saying it was good for the skin. He was at once all and none of these things but, above all, reasonable on the radio. He walked a fine line – shown when he boasted of a threesome in a letter to his sister, comparing himself to the 'many . . . great artists, poets and writers, who've walked the same sexual tightrope'.

The gardaí could not phone up radio shows to argue the case on the airwaves, and nor could Bailey's neighbours, now potential courtroom witnesses, who were advised by gardaí to hold their peace. The tide of fake information inevitably rose, as accurate memory of events withered. There had been no Christmas bonfire, Bailey insisted to anyone who'd listen. He didn't even know the woman. He still had an alibi for that night and was back to sleeping soundly at home. It was other people who were deceiving themselves, unmoored from the actual truth by a stream of garda lies and provocations.

In interview after interview, with original detail lost over time, he convincingly sounded more sinned against than sinning. Few laid a glove on him, let alone scratched the surface . . . Bailey the victim was a grotesque creation indeed, but a relatively successful one in the court of public opinion.

*

Abuse tended to follow when Bailey drank, sometimes ending in a crescendo of violent battery, something Jules Thomas knew about all too well. Now, she avoided him when he was on the spree, becoming maudlin and messy, and she carefully watched her words.

In spring 2021, Jules Thomas somehow succeeded in getting him out of the house. 'He drank every penny he got his hands on. It was awful,' she said. 'That's why we split up . . . he couldn't control it.' Her daughters would not visit the property, nor bring grandchildren there, while he was in residence. Bailey was told not to attend the wedding at The Prairie that July of Ginny to her long-term partner, Killian. He had written a bitter poem about the bride, years before, found in his diaries: 'Hip, Hip, Hurray! Ginny's Got Her Way'. It was about a previous banishment for domestic abuse: 'She's willed it and schemed it, pushed it and dreamed it . . . to see her mother's lover ousted from her home. To quote her very words: "The Worst Man in the World."'

Alcohol was Bailey's curse. Despite his persistent assertions of giving up, he could not stop consuming, and he turned into a monster the more he consumed.

The singer Sinéad O'Connor interviewed Bailey for the *Sunday Independent* in July 2021, nearly a quarter of a century after Sophie's murder. She noted that he drank profusely over lunch, and that 'with each drink and each question, the sweet old gentleman vanishes some more to be replaced by a brooding, angry giant'.

She asked Bailey three times what he thought should happen to Sophie's killer, until he became angry. 'He doesn't want to answer. Finally, he says nothing should happen to the real murderer, "because I have forgiven them". I ask what he would say to the real killer if they were sitting in front of him. He has no need to say anything to them, because he has forgiven them. "They are absolved." He keeps repeating that Sophie's murderer "is probably dead", and says there is "no point" looking for any killer now.' At this juncture, O'Connor wrote: 'He rises from his seat and his large frame towers over me. Hands on hips, he announces loudly: "You'd better stand down, lady." He utters the word "lady" as if a term of abuse.'

Sinéad asked if he would like to make an appeal in the interview for the real killer to come forward. 'He throws his eyes up to heaven. He doesn't want to do it. I tell him it could help him. He flicks his wrist again, and reluctantly makes the appeal in that "OK, fine, are you happy now?" tone that misogynists use when they want to shut a woman up. What would he say to Sophie, I ask, if he could say anything? "Nothing," he answers, again contemptuous of the question. Nothing at all? "Nothing." Then he looks at me and says, with sad eyes: "But I do pray for her."' Sinéad left it like that – just more empty pretence from the old atheist. Bailey, self-styled 'post-Christian pagan' in his diaries, the father only of lies.

*

Twenty-seven Christmases would go by, since Sophie's murder, before the curtain came down on a boring, repetitive actor. The lapse in time was a longer sentence for the suffering family than the judicial gesture made in Paris. Shirley Foster, now the widow of Alfie, was about to close the sale of their old house in Dunmanus West. On a grey early afternoon, fifty kilometres away in Bantry, a shambling wreck of a man left his bottle-clogged flat and walked between the Cosy Cabin and the Schooner bars, which face each other, heading towards the Carry Out off-licence on the town corner. He never got there.

'Shortly after 1 p.m. on Sunday, 21st January 2024, a man in his sixties collapsed on Barrack Street in Bantry, County Cork,' said a last garda statement. The local fire chief performed CPR for forty-five minutes. Pumping was Ian Vickery, the ex-photographer who had heard Bailey brag about Sophie's missing bottle of wine. Vickery sent someone running for a nearby defibrillator. A total of eleven shocks were administered, the jolts producing no response. There was no religious attendance; no-one whispered any Act of Contrition in his ear. The casualty was dead on arrival at Bantry Hospital. Some vulture chose to video the Bailey resuscitation attempts and then uploaded their mawkish creation to TikTok. A man who had avidly courted publicity and embraced social media – often in a disgusting, degraded away – could have few complaints.

'The investigation into the murder of Sophie Toscan du Plantier remains active and ongoing. An Garda Síochána has no further comment.' But a torrent indeed followed the death of this particular pensioner, six days before his sixty-seventh birthday. Not a long life. But certainly longer than some.

CHAPTER 39

Final Verdict

Ireland did not do right by Sophie Toscan du Plantier. On Christmas Day in 1996, her lonely brown coffin was mechanically elevated and loaded into the belly of a plane, to be flown home as air cargo. That fundamental wrong was compounded over the decades that followed. Taoiseach Micheál Martin was right to call it 'a terrible stain on our country . . . what happened to a person of great substance, who loved her visits to West Cork'. He made that remark when standing beside French President Emmanuel Macron at Government Buildings in 2021, and repeated it in the Dáil a year later – 'a stain on our society'. It will never go away. Mr Martin added: 'One could not but be struck by the nobility and the dignity of Sophie's family.'

This has been the most compelling story of my career, but also the saddest, when all is said and done. Nothing can comfort Pierre-Louis, Sophie's son, who still seeks the closure that would come from a criminal conviction – which will now not come at all. Bailey suggested to Sinéad O'Connor, with whom I had discussed the case, that the killer 'is probably dead', and for me there is now no doubt about it.

Bailey also claimed there was no point looking for any killer, yet there is, emphatically. There is no statute of limitations on the truth, and nothing that can wipe away what actually happened. Murder will out, and a garda investigation grinds on. For all those original members, now retired or passed on, who preserved the scene and solemnly stood vigil by the body on a freezing night, a finding is warranted.

Repeatedly written in the regulation log that Christmas were the words 'No unauthorised persons entered during the course of my duty.' But the 'unauthorised person' who turned up at Dunmanus West before the log was opened must still be unmasked.

I believe he has been unmasked, by the evidence presented in this book, which is backed by the family of Sophie Toscan du Plantier, to whom the Irish justice system owes a full accounting.

I looked into the eyes of Ian Bailey many times, after those early moments when I was mostly looking at the back of his head from the rear of Martin Maher's van. What I saw behind those eyes changed over the years. First, there was vanity and superciliousness, then a curdled contempt, and finally, at the Criminal Courts of Justice, a dull and listless defiance as he arrived in shambling bulk, his bloated head below a ludicrous trapper hat.

I watched with writer Michael Sheridan, who has also monitored this monstrous story through the years, as Bailey

SOPHIE: THE FINAL VERDICT

saw off yet another extradition attempt, then promptly repaired to the bar of the Ashling Hotel, drinking for hours before taking the nearby train home. In the end, he broke his own health, callous even in self-destruction, his eyes merely glassy.

Bailey sued all the papers, which meant I had to interrupt a family holiday to meet with lawyers at the Commodore Hotel in Cobh in 2002. I didn't know they would obtain the Black Diaries shortly before the action went to trial in 2003. Their content was akin to the plaintiff being atom-bombed by his own hand. He stood in the witness box, pathetically stumbling over words, grappling with his ongoing vicious battery of Jules Thomas and his written admission that he 'actually tried to kill her' – echoes of the near-strangling of ex-wife Sarah Limbrick.

He slunk away from those proceedings, forever branded by what he was: someone who carried out extreme violence against women in the plural. Judge Patrick Moran made another significant finding in the libel action: 'On the balance of probabilities, I accept what Mrs Farrell told me, that the man she saw at Kealfadda bridge was, in her view, Ian Bailey.'

This identification was ultimately contaminated, just one example of Bailey having the devil's own luck. In public, he availed of his every chance and could affect a superficial style.

But the hidden truth from behind the scenes was that he was truly vile. And there is no more cloaked scene than what happened at Sophie's house on that night of the full moon. Only two people were there.

*

Here's what I believe happened the hour of the murder: Firstly, Bailey drove there. It seemed that Sophie was still up, from the light glimpsed at Hunt's Hill, so he had to make haste. He freewheeled the Fiesta from The Prairie in neutral gear. Starting it some distance away, he drove to Dunmanus West, possibly freewheeling again down Sophie's lane. Then, he left the car by her gate, much as Shirley Foster would do with her Peugeot when morning came. Bailey got out, opened the six-bar gate and slipped it closed behind him. Disappointed that the house was now in darkness, he stalked up to where the back light outside the kitchen may still have been burning. He opened the gate that linked to Alfie's properly, then closed it carefully.

His last few footsteps crunched. He thumped on the door until Sophie woke. 'Who is it?' she cried, and heard his name. 'What do you want?' It was Christmas, he could make any excuse. Warily, she rose and went downstairs where she put on her boots. She crossed the kitchen to the back porch. Next, in a fatal moment beyond any recall, she opened the back door, and there he was, leering, lurching, looking to make his brazen way inside, wine bottle in hand – the lifted gift for Josie. So great was the sudden threat that Sophie grabbed the small hatchet nearby and swiped at the pushing figure. He was nicked on the hairline. He stood back, stunned, the bottle dropping on the gravel, before a tsunami of anger crashed in. The hatchet was wrested away. Sophie turned and fled with a piercing scream. She swept left, to vault into the field, because Bailey was blocking the way to Alfie's. He was after her. He closed in, grunting, threatening to overwhelm, as her blood pounded. Then she fell.

Bailey would later report that Sophie tripped in her flight. How did he know? A speck of her blood appeared on a pebble halfway down the field. She rose, wriggled free, was pursued again. The rest is frenetic, neanderthal barbarism. And afterwards, panting, he returned. He cupped his cuff to open the link gate to Alfie's, using its fabric to erase any earlier trace. He left it open, coming back to the house to collect his trophy, the bottle of wine, having pocketed the little hatchet. He elbowed the lights off, if they had indeed been on, then hooked his shirtsleeve into the handle to pull the door closed. In doing so he left a grisly sign at the house that was not passed over: a smear of Sophie's blood.

Next, he loped down again past his crumpled handiwork, arranging the concrete block atop her dressing gown. He opened the main gate with care to avoid prints, and left it jutting towards the body, exhibiting his kill. He climbed into the Fiesta, entered Sophie's driveway, reversed out again, and drove directly to the sea at Kealfadda. Here he parked out of sight on the causeway, to dispose of the hatchet and perhaps to wash. I believe this journey took place, not because of any eyewitness account, but because of an *ear* witness. A local in Lissacaha, suffering from insomnia in the early hours, heard the noise of a passing car on the night the Frenchwoman died. The listener was blind – and identified the vehicle from its sound; there was a particular engine signature and clunkiness. In other words, she thought she knew *whose* car it was, because the nine-year-old car had passed her by many times. And Jules also confirmed in a garda statement that there was sand in the driver's footwell.

No acoustic testimony could ever prove legally sound,

however, buried as it was by barking dogs. But when all the evidence is pieced together, there is an abundance of material implicating Bailey and pointing to his prosecution. The case should have run.

It seems to me extraordinary that a single lawyer in the DPP's office could effectively be a jury of one, deciding that each piece of evidence is not beyond all doubt, over and over again. What is instead reasonable is for the hundreds of individual hurdles to be lined up against Bailey in a case based on circumstantial evidence. Let him try to surmount them all if he could – let him even knock down a few – until a panel of twelve from the Irish public is fully satisfied where justice lies.

Bailey, of course, changed his story time and again, relying on people's lack of recollection, but it is the granular data that's damning, even in the matter of phone calls made and received on the day Sophie's body was discovered. The DPP, as an office, stood behind its single assessor and kept doing so, but the collective failure is sheer scandal.

Meanwhile, much became the stuff of turf wars, personal jealousies, vexatious claims and bureaucratic wrangling between the Irish and French legal systems. The suffering of Sophie's family was forgotten along the way. Yet all the while Ian Bailey himself was constantly waggling his finger ostentatiously in the wounds. He carved wooden penises for sale at market. His lust for attention and constant self-projection into the murder controversy shows just how off-puttingly insistent he could be, even when expressly not wanted. Just as he tried to force his way in on Sophie that dreadful Sunday night.

I was working the day he died, Sunday, 21 January 2024. Ironically, I had a Sophie story lined up for Monday's paper, about an offer to gardaí by the owner of a system that sucks DNA from rocks and which has successfully nailed offenders, one for a murder more than fifty years earlier. The piece evaporated with one stunning tip-off call. Bailey was dead. I didn't want to accept it. Then came a surge of intense disappointment. I thought of Sophie's family, people I'd met who were now friends, much-maligned guards. Bailey had successfully cheated the system, winning the race against retribution in a cold-case review that might have cast him into outer darkness. The last reel in his movie, the courtroom conviction, would now never come – even though some other twist might still be in store. I immediately spoke to the newsdesk, then started to hammer out a two-page spread, headlined: 'I Was Never in any Doubt that Bailey Killed Sophie'. A requiem postscript for her, definitely not for him. A chapter closed.

This book started with a working title, *Owed to Sophie*, and the debt remains unpaid by any formal verdict from society, although all can still play a part in coming to conclusions. For me, 'Eoin' Bailey was always owing, even if continuously out on bail in the court of public opinion.

And I too have owed him, through the old-fashioned journalistic duty of serving the truth. I hereby settle my account. For Sophie – may she rest in peace.

Timeline

1957: Ian Bailey and Sophie Bouniol are born; he on 27 January in Manchester, she on 28 July in Paris.

1991: Bailey, who had been working as a journalist in Gloucester, moves to West Cork and initially takes odd jobs before availing of home and board with Jules Thomas.

1993: Daniel Toscan du Plantier buys a holiday home in Ireland for his wife Sophie, née Bouniol. It is in the neighbouring townland to where Bailey, now unemployed, lives.

23 December 1996: Sophie Toscan du Plantier's remains are discovered in the laneway of her holiday home.

11 January 1997: A woman calling herself as 'Fiona' makes a call to Bandon Garda Station stating that she saw a lone male on Kealfadda Bridge on the night of the murder. She is later identified as Marie Farrell.

20 January 1997: *Crimeline* TV reconstruction is shown on RTÉ.

10 February 1997: Ian Bailey is arrested, followed by Jules Thomas. Both are released without charge.

17 April 1997: Sophie's inquest opens and adjourns sine die.

29 September 1997: File submitted to the DPP but no charges are brought.

27 January 1998: Ian Bailey is arrested a second time. Again released.

18 August 2001: Bailey assaults Jules Thomas and is arrested at Cork Airport.

17 September 2001: Bailey receives a three-month suspended sentence for the assault.

7 November 2001: Solicitor at the DPP's office Robert Sheehan writes 44-page assessment of the evidence. DPP decides not to prosecute.

8 December 2003: Bailey's libel action against eight newspapers opens in Cork.

19 January 2004: Bailey loses the substantive action. Two minor awards are made over unproven reports by *The Sun* and *Irish Daily Mirror.*

13 October 2005: Marie Farrell retracts her sighting of Ian Bailey at Kealfadda bridge on the night of Sophie's murder.

16 February 2007: Bailey's High Court appeal over his defeated libel action fails.

1 May 2007: Bailey initiates proceedings against the State for alleged wrongful arrest.

19 February 2010: European Arrest Warrant is issued for Ian Bailey. Irish courts will refuse it on foot of the DPP's stance.

November 4 2014: Bailey v. Ireland opens.

30 March 2015: Bailey loses his case against the State. His total liability for costs reaches €5 million. Dependent on State handouts for decades, he cannot pay.

27 May 2019: Trial of Ian Bailey (in absentia) opens in Paris.

May 31 2019: Three French judges convict Bailey of murdering Sophie Toscan du Plantier. He is sentenced to 25 years in prison.

June 28 2022: Garda Commissioner Drew Harris commissions a cold case review of the murder. The original investigation continues in parallel.

21 January 2024: Ian Bailey dies in Bantry, West Cork.

23 December 2024: 28th anniversary of the unsolved murder of Sophie Toscan du Plantier. There has never been any State apology to her surviving family for the dereliction in dispensing justice.

PHOTO CREDITS

Insert section p. 1: J. P. Gazeau x 2; STdP Family, VSD; 2. *Paris Match*, Colman Doyle donation National Photographic Archive (CD: NPA), AGS French legal file. 3. AGS Flf, Anon; courtesy Irish *Examiner*; 4. AGS Flf x 3, VSD. 5. Agnès Thomas, VSD, courtesy Yvonne Ungerer, VSD, CD: NPA; 6. VSD, Provision, Anon, Provision, RTE Archives, *Southern Star*. 7. CD: NPA, courtesy Roger Brooke, CD: NPA, AGS Flf; 8. RTE Archives, courtesy News Group Newspapers Ltd, Author, Anon. 9. CD: NPA x 2, AGS Flf. 10. All AGS Flf. 11. Provision, Jim Walpole: courtesy of *The Star*; 12. Courtesy Irune Reed, Author, Provision x 2, courtesy Ceri Williams x 2. 13. Provision, courtesy Mediahuis, *Paris Match*; 14. AGS Flf x 3; 15. AGS Flf, Haydn West: PA images via Alamy Stock Photo; 16. Family, Alain Jocard: AFP via Getty Images; Rear cover: Author/NUJ, STdP Family.

Map: Gerardcrowley.com.

Populations 1996

Bandon 5,000; Bantry 3,300; Skibbereen 2,300; Ballydehob 800; Schull 700; Goleen 250; Crookhaven 220; Toormore dist. 180; Leap 165.